*BE GOOD*

# BE G

**RANDY COHEN**

original writer of "The Ethicist" for *The New York Times*

## HOW TO NAVIGATE THE ETHICS OF EVERYTHING

# OOD

CHRONICLE BOOKS

SAN FRANCISCO

Be good and you will be lonesome.
—*Mark Twain*

*Text copyright © 2012 by Randy Cohen.*
*Illustrations copyright © 2012 by Dave Hopkins.*
*All rights reserved. No part of this book may be reproduced in any form without*
*written permission from the publisher.*

*Library of Congress Cataloging-in-Publication Data:*
*Cohen, Randy.*
  *Be good : how to navigate the ethics of everything / Randy Cohen.*
    *p. cm.*
  *ISBN 978-1-4521-0790-5*
  *1. Ethical problems—Miscellanea. 2. Applied ethics—Miscellanea. I. Title.*
  *BJ1031.C568 2012*
  *170—dc23*
              *2011040405*

*Manufactured in China*

*Designed by Benjamin Shaykin*
*Typeset in Williams Caslon and Brandon Grotesque*

*Frappuccino is a registered trademark of Starbucks U.S. Brands, LLC.*
*Rollerblade is a registered trademark of Rollerblade, Inc.*

*10 9 8 7 6 5 4 3 2 1*

*Chronicle Books LLC*
*680 Second Street*
*San Francisco, California 94107*
*www.chroniclebooks.com*

# CONTENTS

# Introduction

I WROTE "THE ETHICIST" FOR THE *NEW YORK TIMES MAGAZINE* FOR TWELVE years: 614 columns. I loved my job, especially the interaction with the readers. I admired the moral seriousness of their questions and the astuteness of their criticism—often fierce, occasionally discourteous, never sufficiently threatening to report to the police. But close. And that's fine. Ethics is a subject about which honorable people may differ. I was less sanguine about readers who disparaged not my argument but my character or my shoes or my nose, attacks that generally concluded, "You should be ashamed." I blame the anonymity of e-mail. And underprescribed medication.

From time to time the readers persuaded me that I was—what's that ugly word?—wrong. Then I would revisit a column and recant my folly. I first did so when readers powerfully asserted that yes, you could honorably bring your own food to the movies, despite a theater's prohibition. Another mea culpa ran close to Yom Kippur, Judaism's day of atonement, leading some readers to infer that I was fulfilling a religious obligation. Not so. Sheer coincidence. I've taken a resolutely secular approach to ethics in the column and in my life.

Neither on nor off duty did I seek moral guidance from a spiritual leader of any faith. I did consult members of the clergy for their technical expertise when a question impinged on religious doctrine. For instance, must you warn an observant Jewish in-law that, contrary to what he supposes, the soup he's about to eat is not kosher? I am grateful for their erudition and generosity and that of others who advised me—nurses and doctors, lawyers and librarians, scholars in dozens of disciplines, and the odd interior decorator (a profession that is indeed governed by a formal code of conduct). Apparently it is possible to do wicked things with fabric swatches. We should not.

At first, I was disconcerted when asked about religious law or medical ethics, being trained in neither. But I came to see that what the readers often sought was not a ruling on what to do—they seemed to know— but an argument for why to do it. They sensed that they shouldn't shoot the dog—even if it is a horrible dog: it barks incessantly; it befouls the couch. I was to provide a reasoned case for treating it with kindness. We should.

I received many questions about animals and even more duty-to-report questions: Must you blow the whistle on a friend's adulterous spouse, a tax-dodging repairman, an undocumented employee? The column did not focus on lofty public policy but everyday ethics: May you move to high-priced unoccupied seats at a ball game? May you pocket lots of motel soap and donate it to the homeless? Modest problems, perhaps, but when dissected they revealed much about power, money, race, class, gender, the mutual obligations and unspoken assumptions that connect us—the very things that public policy so often must deal with.

These twelve years brought no radical shift in the sort of queries I received, unsurprisingly; real social change and its attendant moral uncertainty occur slowly. There have been sudden flurries of questions responding to newsworthy events. Immediately after 9/11, many people sent disheartening variations on an e-mail that began, "My neighbor might be Pakistani . . . " and ended, "Should I call the FBI?" Happily, such paranoia (with its maladroit crime-fighting tips) was ephemeral, in the column if not entirely in the larger world.

A more gradual and persistent change has been the emergence of queries sparked by the Internet. Some involved intellectual property: illegal music downloads, students' failure to cite online sources. Others concerned evolving ideas of privacy, derived from experiences with Facebook and Google.

I say, with some shame, that there has been no such gradual change in my own behavior. Writing the column has not made me even slightly more virtuous. And I didn't have to be: it was in my contract. Okay, it wasn't. But it should have been. I wasn't hired to personify virtue, to be a role model for the kids, but to write about virtue in a way readers might find engaging. Consider sportswriters: not two in twenty can hit a curveball, and why should they? They're meant to report on athletes, not be athletes. And that's the self-serving rationalization I'd have clung to had the cops hauled me off in handcuffs.

What spending my workday thinking about ethics did do was make me acutely conscious of my own transgressions, of the times I fell short. It is deeply demoralizing. I presume it qualifies me for some sort of workers' comp. This was a particular hazard of my job, but it is also something every adult endures—every self-aware adult—as was noted by my great hero, Samuel Johnson, the person I most quoted in the column: "He that in the latter part of his life too strictly enquires what he has done, can very seldom receive from his own heart such an account as will give him satisfaction."

J. M. Barrie, best known as the author of *Peter Pan*, made a similar observation: "The life of every man is a diary in which he means to write one story, and writes another; and his humblest hour is when he compares the volume as it is with what he vowed to make it."

Dickens put it this way in *Martin Chuzzlewit*: "'Regrets,' said Martin, 'are the natural property of gray hairs; and I enjoy, in common with all other men, at least my share of such inheritance.'"

To grow old is to grow remorseful. And although writing the column did not require me to be a paragon, I hoped not to be a hypocrite. As the column gained readers, I grew mindful of how unpleasant it would be to face the public embarrassment of some variation on this headline: Ethicist Caught Being Unethical.

Eventually it happened. I was buying bagels at the Gourmet Garage when my regular checkout woman said, "Your picture is in the *New York Post*." I said, "No, it's not." She said, "Yes, it is." We could have continued cycling through that exchange for hours, but the customers in line behind me were growing restive, so she reached under the counter and pulled out that day's paper. My picture *was* in the *New York Post*, illustrating a full-page article denouncing me along with many other journalists for donating money to political organizations. I was astonished; I'd never been called a journalist.

The piece in the *Post* rehashed an article from www.msnbc.com— not the liberal television network, but what was then a conservative Web site—under the headline "143 Despicable Journalists Who Took Sides And Should Be Fired And Imprisoned." I may be misremembering. Slightly. My alleged moral failing: some years earlier, I donated $585 to the liberal activist organization MoveOn.org. The article forced me to confront a personal failing—I was a penny-pincher. Many of my coprofessionals had been far more generous than I.

My donation violated a *Times* work rule, but it was a bad rule and, in my view, flouting it was not unethical. It has long been a near universal stricture of journalism that a reporter may not participate in an event that he or she is covering. If your beat is, say, the auto industry, you can't join in a rally of autoworkers or donate money to a carmaker's lobbying organization. To involve yourself or your cash so directly could erode your ability to be objective. Abe Rosenthal, a former executive editor of the *Times*, crystallized this precept: "You can fuck an elephant for all we care, as long as you don't cover the circus."

That's the position many news organizations took when their reporters were named by MSNBC. David Remnick, editor of the *New Yorker*, saw nothing amiss in his writers—George Packer, for example—donating to candidates they did not cover. To become a journalist is not to forswear ordinary civic engagement. Reporters may vote (although Len Downie, former executive editor of the *Washington Post*, was curiously uneasy about even that). What's more, to refrain from participating in an election need not mean you are indifferent to its outcome. To decline to express an opinion does not mean you lack one.

In any case, I did not cover the circus. I did not cover anything. I wrote a column of opinion, and my job was to make my views utterly apparent. Nor did I see my forbidden donations as any more "political" than those the *Times* allows. MSNBC ran my comment: "We admire those colleagues who participate in their communities—help out at the local school, work with Little League, donate to charity. But no such activity is or can be nonideological. Few papers would object to a journalist donating to the Boy Scouts or joining the Catholic Church. But the former has an official policy of discriminating against gay children; the latter has views on reproductive rights far more restrictive than those of most Americans. Should reporters be forbidden to support either organization? I'd say not."

There were serious consequences to the MSNBC piece. Several reporters lost their jobs. But for me the upshot was milder. A Spokane paper that was about to carry my column in syndication reversed its decision. I was mocked by the right-wing press, more a badge of honor than infamy. And I got a phone call from the *Times'* in-house watchdog chiding me (courteously, without rancor or raised voices) for violating the paper's policy, as indeed I had. But, I insisted, it is a poor policy and certainly should not be applied unthinkingly. Rather than rebuke me (politely), I said, the paper should defend me against this unwarranted accusation of ethical failing. He did not agree.

I asked how donating to MoveOn impaired my ability to do my job. He acknowledged that it did not, but the paper might some day assign me to a different beat, might ask me to cover politics, in which such donations could be problematic. I volunteered to sign a document pledging never to accept such a reassignment. Would the paper now defend me? No, it would not.

He asserted that readers might complain about my transgression. I replied that reader complaints should be taken seriously, but not all have merit. When, as here, there was none, the paper should stand up for its writer and explain to the reader why it was doing so.

He disagreed (civilly, respectfully, unpersuasively). I said that while I thought the rule was misguided, I loved my job and would henceforth obey it. And I did.

While I persist in thinking I did no wrong in that case, there were ways I could have done my job better. For instance, even when a question turned on a *he said/she said* conflict, I worked with only one side of the story. I lacked the resources (or the resourcefulness) to contact both parties to a dispute and establish whose version of events was more plausible. I simply accepted the facts as given by the person who posed the question, albeit with some skepticism, and I sometimes reminded the readers that the other person involved might see the situation differently. It was a reasonable solution to this problem, but it was less than ideal.

Another shortcoming of the column—okay, of its author—I failed to answer the questions put to me swiftly enough to be of much practical value to the reader. By the time my response ran, the reader had already knocked down the fence or knocked down his neighbor or knocked back a drink in lieu of doing either.

When I received a query I thought I would use in the column, I dashed off a quick response, just a rough draft, and set it aside, unsent. When I accumulated a dozen or so, I e-mailed them to my editor for his comments. This was his chance to challenge my moral reasoning. (And I gratefully acknowledge what an astute critic and amiable coworker Dean Robinson, the editor for most of my tenure, could be.) His notes and comments equipped me with a file of a dozen questions from which I could assemble each week's column, generally trying to construct a pleasing pair—often one weightier, one lighter topic.

Once I was ready to put that week's column into production, I phoned the person whose question I was working on, to make sure I understood his or her situation and to learn if their circumstances had altered or if they'd resolved their problem in the weeks—sometimes months—since they sent it to me. If the sender had made a decision, it seemed perverse to withhold it from the readers, and so I began including "updates" as a way to announce these developments, even when—particularly when—the sender solved the problem differently from what I was about to prescribe. I never altered my basic approach to the answer after these conversations; that wouldn't be playing the game. When I wrote my response, I had the same information the reader had.

I became fond of the updates. They gave the column a narrative arc, a sense of conclusion. I liked knowing how the story turned out.

And they were stories, those questions. At their best, each was an eighty-word drama with a tough moral decision at its core. They were, it should be needless to say, true stories. And yet I was often asked if those questions were "real." Well, yes. The *Times* is quite starchy about what it deems "facts." I could have built a column around fanciful scenarios, hypothetical questions devised for the readers, as long as the readers knew that this was what they were getting, as long as I was transparent. The advantage of presenting actual questions from actual readers was the sociology of the thing. The column gave me a perch from which to survey the moral landscape and see what people were getting up to. Sometimes with another person's car or cash or spouse.

Having chosen a question, what method of analysis did I then apply to answer it? None. I didn't apply any method, and I suspect neither does anybody else, at least not initially. When deciding on correct conduct, it is first the verdict then the trial. I had what some readers deprecated as "just a gut reaction," an immediate feeling about right and wrong. But I didn't stop there. I subjected that intestinal tremor to various forms of moral scrutiny: how does it stand up to the Golden Rule, or to a greatest-good argument, or to the categorical imperative? These analytical tools helped me see the question from various angles and, sometimes, revise my initial response.

In his book *The Happiness Hypothesis*, Jonathan Haidt, a professor of psychology at the University of Virginia, makes an elegant analogy to explain this thought process:

"Moral judgment is like aesthetic judgment. When you see a painting, you usually know instantly and automatically whether you like it. If someone asks you to explain your judgment, you confabulate. You don't really know why you think something is beautiful. . . . You search for a plausible reason for liking the painting, and you latch on to the first reason that makes sense (maybe something vague about color, or light, or the reflection of the painter in the clown's shiny nose). Moral arguments are much the same: Two people feel strongly about an issue, their feelings come first, and their reasons are invented on the fly, to throw at each other. When you refute a person's argument, does she generally change her mind and agree with you? Of course not, because the argument you defeated was not the cause of her position; it was made up after the judgment was already made."

I would dispute some of what Haidt writes here. There's a difference between invention and analysis. While the arguments often follow the judgment, they can offer insight into that judgment or even overturn it. I've changed my mind about a painting—or a movie or a piece of music—on further reflection. Similarly, my first response to a tense encounter might be: I'd like to punch that guy in the nose. But a bit of analysis can lead me to reject my initial impulse.

Contrary to Haidt, argument does sometimes change people's ideas and future conduct. Just because it seldom happens in the first two minutes, during a dispute, does not mean that it fails to happen at all. Such transformations occur more slowly. Moral—and aesthetic—ideas alter over time, and argument is one way to effect that change.

Haidt draws on the work of evolutionary biologists who see a genetic component to our moral responses. Philosopher Michael Ruse, for example, is a proponent of this line of thought. And it is undoubtedly true. But we are heirs to those responses, not their prisoners. If we were bound by what evolution handed us as our initial impulse, there'd be a lot more hitting with big rocks, by people gorging on sugars and fats.

And we can get better at this process of confronting a moral dilemma, noting our initial response, and then subjecting it to ethical analysis. Practice can improve moral reasoning. Or speed at sudoku. The game metaphor is not a bad one. Over the years, many people told me that they treated "The Ethicist" as a family game played at breakfast each Sunday morning. One family member read the question aloud, then they went around the table and each person answered it. Only after did they read my reply and go on to discuss it. And pay off any side bets.

I've organized this book with that in mind. Think of it as akin to a set of practice problems for the SATs or a book of chess puzzles. Read a question, work out your own answer, compare it to mine, and discuss it with other people. And remember that there is seldom only one right answer; these are questions about which honorable people can differ. When you've worked your way through these ethical games, tell the Parker Brothers what a great time you had. And give them my phone number.

In the column, I responded to questions about everyday ethics, the situations ordinary civilians like me encounter in our daily lives. In the book, each chapter addresses one general area: family, school, work, for example. The reasoning we apply to those personal quandaries can also be applied to larger matters of public life. To illustrate that idea, to demonstrate a sort of moral analysis, I've introduced each chapter by taking a look at a related policy matter from an ethical perspective: international adoption, the mortgage bailout, ticket scalping, for instance.

The columns from which I assembled this material were written between 2001 and 2011. In organizing this book, I've revised a few, now and then reversing my original conclusion. I've also included some reader comments to columns that sparked a particularly vigorous response. Rather than update any topical references, for the most part I've left them unchanged to provide a feel for the time when they were written and a sense of how the sort of ethical questions that bedevil us have—and have not—changed with the times.

# *Family*

THERE ARE MANY KINDS OF FAMILIES. THOSE 1950S PARADIGMS, NUCLEAR families—a disengaged husband, a stay-at-home wife, and two eerily beaming children—that once roamed America in mighty herds have nearly gone the way of the buffalo. And there are many approaches to establishing a family, from the technically and morally complicated frontiers of high-tech fertility treatment to high-toned international adoptions engaged in by Brangelina and Madonna and their ilk. If such luminous creatures have ilks.

There is a creepy evocation of colonialism when a rich American or European swoops into a poor African nation and grabs a child, as if the country were a baby plantation. Critics charge that the adoptive parents benefit from the persistence of poverty. They do, but in much the same way that Lenny Bruce described the modus operandi of Jonas Salk, J. Edgar Hoover, and himself: "These men thrive upon the continuance of disease, segregation, and violence." That is, they respond to but do not promote human misery. (Okay, except for Hoover.)

What's more, poverty is not the sole reason children are abandoned. It was China's one-child policy that made so many girls available for adoption. Genocide orphaned thousands of Rwandan children. AIDS still reduces children to wretchedness in many parts of Africa. Adoptive parents do not seek to protract anyone's torment but to build a family and help a child, actions we esteem.

Adoptive parents might help children more effectively simply by donating money. A fraction of the typical $20,000 spent on an adoption or the $250,000 it takes to raise a middle-class American child could assist a great many African kids. But the ethical obligation to help suffering children does not apply only to those who wish to adopt; it is a general duty we all share.

We are morally required to aid a child who lies bleeding on our doorstep. Or a child across the street. Or across town. Or across the Atlantic Ocean. Rather than urge adopting families to redirect their expenditures, we should reallocate the money we ourselves spend on a ski weekend in Aspen, a flat-screen TV for the dog's room, a $3 billion stealth destroyer for our navy ($4 billion if equipped with optional—and fictional—leather upholstery).

Some groups, notably the London-based Save the Children, assert that the prospect of a foreign adoption encourages desperate parents to abandon their children in the hope of securing a better life for them. This claim is unconvincing. Families are demolished not by the possibility of adoption but the reality of poverty or disease or war, according to Dr. Jane Aronson, a pediatrician specializing in adoption medicine. It is vital to address these harrowing conditions, but that does not preclude adoption, she says: "To help one child is a worthy thing to do."

Save the Children is more convincing when it argues that children should be raised by their families in their own cultures. This is a laudable goal, but to achieve it, Aronson says, much needs to be done to "help rebuild communities around the world so families can receive proper social services and needn't give up their children."

As long as there are orphans, the ethical question is not whether it is okay to adopt but how to do it. Jacqueline Novogratz, the head of the Acumen Fund, a nonprofit that promotes antipoverty efforts throughout the world, says: "Reputable adoption agencies know where children come from. Some children are abandoned and some are placed in orphanages when their families can't afford to raise them. Finding those children good, stable, healthy homes could change their lives immeasurably. Going through the right agencies is key."

Sadly, such scrupulousness, while necessary, may not matter much in the end. If Malawi (or Russia or Ethiopia or Guatemala) threw open its doors to everyone on Earth who wished to adopt—no rules, no red tape, no embarrassing Madonna-indulgences—it would barely diminish the heartrending parade of homeless or orphaned children stretching to the horizon. Most estimates put their number above 100 million worldwide. And who will adopt those who are not adorable infants— a traumatized eleven-year-old Pakistani street kid or a five-year-old Nigerian with AIDS or, for that matter, a teenager shunted around New York's foster care system?

One other consideration: would endorsing foreign adoption compel us to stop teasing Madonna? Happily, no. While she seems to have at least attempted to act creditably in Malawi, as long as she dons a T-shirt emblazoned with the unconvincing slogan Kabbalists Do It Better, let the mockery be unconfined. She's rich, she's glamorous—a self-made success, still a pop star in her fifties. Of course we make fun of her; we need to.

After a version of this argument ran in the *Times*, some readers asserted that rather than undertake foreign adoption with its attendant problems, ethical and otherwise, Madonna and others should adopt locally. Sadly, as many families who have attempted this can confirm, it's seldom easy, and sometimes it's all but impossible. I know a couple of families who turned to foreign adoptions only after being thwarted in their other efforts to adopt here in the United States.

Which raised this question for some readers: isn't there a greater moral obligation to help those nearby? It was once commonly thought so. Samuel Johnson said as much to James Boswell, as recorded in the latter's *The Journal of a Tour to the Hebrides*: "A man should first relieve those who are nearly connected with him, by whatever tie; and then, if he has anything to spare, may extend his bounty to a wider circle."

Particular relationships do entail particular obligations. Parents have duties to their children that they do not have to strangers. But national borders do not define such relationships; they are not moral borders. And "nearly connected" has a different meaning today than it did in the eighteenth century. Our ease of travel (if *ease* can be said to apply to anything involving commercial aviation), as well as the flow of images and ideas, encourage and make increasingly apparent the connectedness of humanity. Philosopher Peter Singer is a notable proponent of the worldwide reach of our moral obligations, a subject he takes up in his book *One World: The Ethics of Globalization*.

Another concern for many readers: Madonna's motives. Is she publicity crazed? Is it all egomania? Johnson had something to say about Madonna, too, if not by name. (He was prescient but not *that* prescient.) "To act from pure benevolence is not possible for finite beings. Human benevolence is mingled with vanity, interest, or some other motive." I believe Freud reached a similar conclusion about our tangled motives, albeit from a different angle. Or to put it another way, failing to achieve sainthood ought not disqualify anyone from parenthood.

## ORPHAN NIECE

*I am half of a childless (by choice) couple. Recently, my wife's ten-year-old niece was orphaned by an automobile accident. No one else in my wife's extended family can offer her a home. The little girl lives in Eastern Europe, and unless we take her in, as my wife wishes, the alternative might be an orphanage. Is it our duty to adopt her?*

*—Name withheld, Pennsylvania*

You needn't adopt your niece, but you may not abandon her to a bleak orphanage. You must in some way ensure that she is provided for.

Philosophers have long debated this question: does family entail particular ethical obligations? That is, do you and your wife, as aunt and uncle, have a deeper responsibility for this child than does any other well-meaning person? I believe you do. Even putting aside any duty you have to the child herself, it is your wife's bond with her late sister, and your love for your wife, that compel you to honor the desires of both of these women by caring for your niece. A loving connection between people forges obligations between them: we all rely on those we love and who love us.

You may not have bargained on fatherhood, but consigning a niece to a desolate orphanage, over the wishes of your wife, will leave you feeling far worse. However, your duty to your niece does not mean that you must become her stepfather. It takes more than a sense of obligation to be a good parent. If paternity is beyond you, then you might better serve your niece, if immigration law permits and your wife acquiesces, by finding another loving home for her and remaining her devoted uncle.

But don't give up on fatherhood too quickly. Unanticipated adoption is the basis of many a wacky and heartwarming movie in which the serendipitous arrival of a child humanizes and improves the life of a previously disengaged person. It happened to Diane Keaton, and she ended up with Sam Shepard in *Baby Boom*. If Sam Shepard does start hanging around your house, don't let him curse as much around your young niece as he does in those plays of his. That's no way to teach a child English.

## iMAC AUTHORITY

*Three years ago, my parents insisted on paying for my new video-game system so they could determine how I used it. Yet when I recently bought a new iMac with money I earned as a busboy, my parents retained the privilege of taking it away when I misbehave. Since I paid for it myself, shouldn't I have total control over its use?*

*—Ivan Cash (age sixteen), Marlboro, NY*

Parental authority does not derive from the ownership of property. Your parents exercise certain kinds of control because they *are* your parents and thus responsible for your well-being, not because they paid for your stuff.

If they declared that their buying your video-game system gave them the right to govern its use, your parents erred. And if, by implication, they led you to believe that your buying your iMac would make you the autocrat of your bedroom, then that, too, was ill-advised. Similarly, if you found an after-school job bagging groceries, saved your money, and paid for your own Hellfire antitank missile, your parents could still restrict your blowing up minivans around the neighborhood (as could federal law). If your parents injudiciously suggested that your purchasing power gave you utter iMac autonomy, they should consider reimbursing you for your computer purchase.

## DEBTS OF THE DEAD

*My older sister died unexpectedly; my other sister and I had been named as beneficiaries. We used about two-thirds of her liquid assets to meet burial and other expenses. Do we have an ethical obligation to pay any outstanding bills like credit card balances or medical expenses not covered by insurance?*
—*Sheila Ramerman, Eugene, OR*

The law requires your late sister's estate to meet her business obligations; ethics urges you as an individual to respond to her personal obligations.

Herbert Nass, a lawyer specializing in trusts and estates, says: "The debt doesn't die with the decedent." While laws vary from state to state, in New York as in most places, Nass explains, an estate must cover credit card and medical bills, the sort of debts you mention, but if the estate is depleted, these debts are not transferred to family members. This is something businesses understand and for which they plan. If from time to time death robs them of repayment, so be it. Nineteenth-century novels notwithstanding, relatives need not spend years digging out from beneath a pile of bills left by a profligate uncle. Although that is a notion of family honor no doubt beloved by creditors. And casinos.

Personal debts are different. A friend's generosity should be esteemed. If that friend has limited resources, lacks bad-debt insurance, and would be hit hard by a default, you would do well to shoulder such a debt. The implicit moral obligations of friendship and family differ from the explicit legal duties of commerce. Where the law is silent, ethics should speak.

In striving to pay any personal debts of your late sister, you need not impoverish yourself. Talk to those she owes, consider their financial circumstances and your own, and work out an accommodation.

## CABIN FEVER

*Twelve years ago, my brother and I inherited a vacation cabin. Its value has escalated, and he wants us either to sell it or for me to buy out his half at current market value. He refuses to negotiate, because he "wants to give his children an inheritance." Back then, I could have afforded to buy his half, but he refused. Now we're both retired and living on fixed incomes. Must I be forced either to pay him or to sell a property that has been in our family for almost 100 years?*

*—L.T., Texas*

I'm afraid your brother has a point. If you mutually own property, he's entitled to his half. That's often where money comes in: it's so divisible, so easily shared, so much more convenient than using a chain saw to divide the cabin itself.

Thus, you could sell the place and split the proceeds, but there are alternatives. Your brother could seek a third party to buy him out, someone with whom you'd be content to share the cabin. Or, if he is anxious to guarantee the financial security of his kids, you might agree to accommodate them in the future, when they actually need the money, rather than sell the cabin today, or compensate them in your will. Simpler still, as several savvy readers suggested in response to this column: take out a mortgage or home equity loan and pay off your brother.

One thing he should not do is bully you into precipitate action. He must allow you time to come up with so large a sum or be open to finding alternatives, perhaps accepting a series of partial payments over the next few years. Mutual respect for one another's concerns should guide this decision. Your brother shouldn't be a prisoner of real estate, but you shouldn't be a victim of his impulsiveness.

## SPOUSAL EXEMPTION

*Recently a friend told me that he and his wife were expecting a baby, cautioning me that this news was confidential. Once they went public, I told my wife, who is very upset that I didn't tell her the news the minute I heard. She says that on nonprofessional matters like this, there is an expectation that a husband would tell his wife and that the confidentiality would not be violated. I say confidential is confidential. What do you say?*

—*P.J.M., New Jersey*

I'm with your wife. Her distinction between professional and personal confidentiality is a good one. The patient-privacy obligations of a physician or the trade secrets of a chemist allow for no marital exception. But when it comes to personal matters, your friend's injunction, "don't tell anyone," implicitly means "except, of course, your discreet and reliable spouse."

Nonetheless, belief in the spousal exemption, while widely held, is not universal. And so to avoid misunderstandings, when offered a secret, you should clarify the matter by saying something like, "I won't tell anyone except my wife." If that's okay with your friend, problem solved. If not, counter in this way: "My wife and I share everything, so if you don't want me to tell her, I'd rather you not confide in me."

On the rare occasion when you fail to issue the proper disclaimer and find yourself burdened with unwanted information, you should make marital openness your default position and share that secret with your wife. When it comes to casual confidences like the one you describe, the intimacy of marriage takes precedence over the small arcana of friendship.

Your present concern should be restoring domestic tranquility. Having kept your wife outside the cone of silence, all you can do now is apologize, bestowing on her a line as beautiful and euphonious as any in the English language: you were right and I was wrong.

## FULL MEDICAL DISCLOSURE

*During a checkup, I discovered that some time ago I'd had a "silent" mild-to-moderate heart attack. I'm in my sixties and otherwise in good health, but my wife excessively worries about health problems, particularly mine. I didn't tell her about this discovery, both to spare her the worry and to shield myself from the stress of her "hovering," which might increase the likelihood of another heart attack. I think this is the right decision, but I have occasional guilty feelings. Is it ethical?*

*—Name withheld, California*

Different couples allow one another different amounts of privacy. Some tell all; some keep things to themselves. None of these relationships are unethical, as long as both members of the couple understand and truly accept the family policy on medical disclosure.

In your case, I gather that your wife assumes that you are giving her all pertinent information about your health. If that's so, to withhold these facts is dishonest, violating your implicit agreement, and that may be why you feel a little guilty. What's more, keeping so important a secret can be as stressful as any hypothetical uxorial hovering. And so not only as a matter of ethics but also for your own peace of mind, you should fill her in.

If your marital policy is vague, often the case with implicit agreements, then you and she must come to a clearer understanding about how you'll deal with these things. When having such a discussion, bear in mind that if your heart problems in the past indicate a predisposition to similar problems in the future—something that could seriously affect your wife—then she has a personal stake in being kept informed, even beyond her love for you.

**UPDATE:** This fellow described his secret-keeping to his longtime GP and family friend. The physician's reply: "You jerk, you'll never get away with it." The GP suggested a less alarming way to present this information to the wife, using precise technical language—"they uncovered some scar tissue"—while avoiding emotionally charged words like "heart attack." The patient then spoke to his wife and is glad he did.

## PARENT TRAP

*Our fifteen-year-old daughter has a "boyfriend" a year older whose parents forbid their children to have such relationships or even attend mixed-gender parties. So this boy does so on the sly; that is, he'll call home from our house and say he is elsewhere. We see his parents at school events, exchange pleasantries, but do not let on that our children are more than "just friends." Are we guilty of an ethical lapse?*

*—Name withheld, Maryland*

Providing this boy a refuge from parental strictures you find excessive—no boy-girl parties?—is a reasonable thing; you are not an agent of his parents and do not have to enforce their rules in your home. But whatever your opinion of his parents' ideas—and I suspect most Americans would agree that forbidding socializing between boys and girls is weirdly extreme—the boy's lying is wrong, and you ought not abet it.

Beyond the boy's dishonesty, you should consider the effect of your own behavior on your daughter. By tolerating her boyfriend's deceit, you suggest to her that it is okay to lie when you disagree with the regulations made by others. At one time or another, every teenager finds every parent's reign draconian. Be wary of sending your daughter on a race to the bottom, sneaking off to the home of the most permissive, or indifferent, parents—those who let young teenagers not only drink, but also drink and drive, blindfolded, on their way to the gun shop.

There are circumstances when you would be ethically obliged to support a child's lie—if his parents were not merely unreasonable but inhumane. You'd certainly conspire to save a young person from regular beatings. But this is not such a case. And while you need not inform on the boy to his parents, you should talk to the kids. Let them know that you respect their feelings for one another, but unless the boy can be honest with his family, the kids will have to see each other at school or elsewhere in public, but can no longer use your home as a hipster haven.

## EGG DONOR

*My husband and I are planning to have a child through an egg donor. Are we obligated to tell our child that he or she is not genetically related to me? My husband thinks we must: the truth is always best. But I think that unless there is important medical information to be conveyed, it is unnecessary to tell a child something likely to be painful and confusing. Should we tell?*
*—Name withheld, Los Angeles*

The question is not whether to give your child a full account of his or her origins, but when and how. I believe you should start talking about this as soon as possible, albeit in general terms comprehensible to a very young child and, as your child is better able to grasp the nuts and bolts of reproduction, to provide increasingly more details. There's nothing shameful (or these days even all that unusual) about what you and your husband are planning. Indeed, it testifies to your determination to start a family and presages the love you'll have for your child. To keep this information from your child would suggest that there's some family crime that must be covered up, like a deranged murderous relative stashed in the attic.

It would be far riskier to withhold this. Real pain is likelier to result not from any particular way of establishing a family but from a child feeling deprived of significant information about his or her own life. It is the undermining of trust that is the danger here, not genetics. Stories that are innocuous if conveyed early and casually can grow ominous if concealed.

---

### SIBLING SCHOOLING

*We could enroll our older child in a school for gifted children or in a very good school for children who are bright but not gifted. The attraction of the latter is that it has a strong sibling admissions policy, all but ensuring her younger sister's acceptance. Should we consider our younger child's interests in deciding where to send our older?*

— *David Quinto, Los Angeles*

Your older daughter earned a place in the gifted school on her merits. You should not take that from her in the hope of giving her sister a leg up.

I am not asserting that you treat each child strictly as an individual, selecting the best school for the older and ignoring the effects of that decision on the younger. Parental duties extend to both children and require a more nuanced calculus. At mealtime, you would not let the older child eat her fill before permitting the younger to approach the table and consume only what scraps, if any, remained. Neither for lunch nor for learning do I advocate primogeniture.

In some cases parents must indeed make a greatest-good decision. That might mean sending one child to a less expensive college rather than to her first choice, in order to preserve some of the family's resources for her siblings. In such a situation, you would rightly weigh the quality of the schools. If choosing the more expensive meant paying full freight at Swarthmore and the less expensive were McGill, you might reasonably ask your daughter to bundle up and head north, confident that she could receive a fine education. If the alternatives were

Princeton or cosmetology school, you would make a different choice. (Assuming you and your daughter have conventional feelings about mascara.)

But your actual decision does not involve the equitable distribution of family resources. Rather, you contemplate sending your older child to a slightly worse school to game the system on behalf of her sister. This is too discouraging a lesson about merit, about fairness, to teach either child.

**UPDATE:** Deciding that "each boat floats on its own bottom," the Quintos enrolled their child in the gifted school.

---

### SMOKING AGE

*Our family is planning a trip to Amsterdam, and our son is pleased to be going where marijuana can be consumed legally. We've always discouraged this activity, mainly because it is illegal here. He's over eighteen, so I suppose it is his decision. But is there a double standard in allowing your children to engage in an activity in one place that you prohibit in another?*
*—Name withheld, Connecticut*

You can unhypocritically urge your children to heed a single standard: obey the law. You could argue that citizens in a democracy generally have not just a legal but also an ethical obligation to do so—and the absence of a legal barrier to pot-smoking, as in Amsterdam, means the absence of an ethical one. While there may still be good reasons for your son not to smoke marijuana there—concerns about pot's long-term effects, belief that time spent not looking at Vermeers is time wasted, the risk of tumbling into a canal—fealty to U.S. law is not one. When a Saudi visits the United States, she has no ethical obligation to forswear driving simply because it is illegal for a woman to do so in Riyadh.

Whether or not this single standard is a wise one is debatable. Making ethical judgments requires more than consulting local statute books. A twenty-year-old who buys a beer in Windsor, Ontario, does nothing illegal. If the same twenty-year-old buys a beer just across the border, in Detroit, he breaks the law. But it would be tough to argue that, the law aside, he acts unethically in one case but not the other, or that moral reasoning requires us to carry a map, or that "legal" is tantamount to "ethical."

# *Home*

MOST OF US WOULD RECOGNIZE A DUTY, AT LEAST IN THEORY, TO HELP someone in need, including someone overwhelmed by a mighty economic tsunami. And yet, to a person who is cautious in his finances, it can be galling to see his taxes used to bail out a neighbor who took on a great whopping mortgage he clearly couldn't afford. This seems to penalize the prudent and reward the profligate.

But such aid is indeed ethical. Assisting the financially afflicted does not unreasonably damage the prudent any more than hiring life-guards penalizes strong swimmers. A decent society responds to people in need, even if that means temporarily suspending moral judgment. ER doctors treat the wounded. Firefighters douse the blaze. Neither response is contingent on the cause of the catastrophe or the putative moral worth of the victim.

We should, of course, be cautious with our money, moderate at table, temperate with liquor, and see the dentist twice a year. But when a wastrel's life of boozing and gluttony (and failure to floss) drives him to collapse, we do not let him die on the street. We send an ambulance.

There is a case for letting him lie there. The moral-hazard argument holds that insulating people from the consequences of their actions encourages risky behavior. For example, some studies suggest that because seat belts make drivers feel safer, they drive more recklessly. But few who endorse this analysis actually remove the seat belts from their car or pack the trunk with explosives as an incentive for safe driving. This is not to suggest inaction. Rather, we augment safety as a community, seeking to improve road design, driver training, traffic laws, and automobiles themselves.

One particularly two-fisted manifestation of the moral-hazard argument, debtors' prison, was not abolished in New York until 1831. The idea was to make economic failure so terrifying that discretion would prevail. But despite squalid cells, disease, rats, and public humiliation, people continued to fall into debt. Some observers denounced this as mere obstinacy and called for danker cells, rattier rats. Others countered that debt can result from forces over which the debtor has no control.

Even where this is the case, it can still rankle to see a fool saved from his folly at public expense. Such feelings may be nearly universal, originating not in our reason or our culture but our genes. Some evolutionary biologists claim that we are hardwired to resent perceived injustice. Research by Sarah F. Brosnan and Frans B. M. de Waal demonstrates this tendency in monkeys. It is unclear whether the monkeys had fixed or floating-rate mortgages.

But while evolution goads us to resent a prodigal neighbor, it also impels us to crave fats and sugars. In an environment where cheap doughnuts and no-money-down mortgages are easily available, such urges are not a reliable guide to right conduct or wise social policy. We must think further. (And it's worth acknowledging that there are more altruistic evolutionary impulses, like rendering aid.)

I do not allude here to folks who lied on mortgage applications. Some acts are clearly unethical. I refer rather to people who seemingly should have known better. But a foolish financial decision need not be a moral failure or even unusual. A housing bubble only becomes a bubble because many people are similarly deluded; it can be inflated only by an army of exuberant nincompoops. And it is noteworthy that many people took on hefty mortgages as a result of razzle-dazzle salesmanship or even deliberate fraud. Here in New York, prosecution of such crimes was lackluster.

Some people do take extravagant chances with other people's money. We call them hedge-fund managers and we reward them lavishly. Ours is an age that glorifies ostensibly risk-taking entrepreneurs. It seems inconsistent to condemn that trait in a home buyer, particularly when rapidly rising housing prices promised big profits to all. Home ownership itself has been exalted as a national virtue, an essential element of the American Dream. It would be odd to suddenly scorn those who chased that dream, albeit a bit too energetically, and assisted by those financial steroids, the subprime mortgage.

There are actors in this drama who did behave unethically. A banker has a professional obligation to issue sound mortgages and the training and experience to make such judgments. To knowingly lend money to a family unlikely to repay it violates that obligation. Federal regulators are similarly blameworthy. They have an explicit duty to define and enforce banking standards. To forsake those professional responsibilities is an ethical transgression.

The essential task now is to set the financial system in order. We rightly begin by throwing a lifeline to those in peril, even those whom

Victorians might classify as the undeserving poor. (What's more, helping a neighbor avoid foreclosure can sustain the values of all homes in the neighborhood, including our own.) Then we must devise and enforce regulations to forestall such disasters. When tempted by the exhilarating prospect of an improvident neighbor receiving the sound financial thrashing it feels like he so richly deserves, consider this from Montaigne: "There is no man so good, who, were he to submit all his thoughts and actions to the laws, would not deserve hanging ten times in his life."

After these thoughts first ran, I was surprised that so many of those *Times* readers who most fervently rejected my position referred to their "greedy" neighbor. Apparently nobody facing foreclosure is an "unlucky" neighbor or a "swindled" neighbor or a "foolish but incredibly good-looking" neighbor. Must be a rough neighborhood.

Many readers asserted or simply assumed that these borrowers should have known better. I'm skeptical. It is no longer an article of faith, universally held by economists, that people can be relied on to make rational decisions in their own interest. Back in 1957, the Nobel Prize–winning economist Herbert Simon coined the term "bounded rationality" to describe economic decision making, a neologism that seems delightfully optimistic in light of recent events (or, for that matter, in light of the Dutch tulip mania of 1637).

This evolution in thinking underpins the lively field of behavioral economics, whose practitioners draw on work in psychology and sociology. The ideas emerging from this field and the experience of the past few years suggest that relying on individual reason and rectitude is unlikely to prevent another mortgage crisis. Left to themselves, millions of people will borrow imprudently (and drive SUVs while smoking and talking on their cell phones on their way to take out that ARM on their ludicrously overpriced deep-fried sugarcoated McMansion).

But there is much we can do as a community to create the conditions where discretion is more apt to prevail. People tend to obey the law—at least those laws that are enforced with more than a nudge and a wink—hence my emphasis on creating wise standards for mortgages, demanding that bankers adhere to them, and that federal regulators see that they do. Policy, devised with care, expressed as law, and administered by professionals with explicit ethical duties, can succeed where individual giddiness—and, yes, from time to time, greed—have led to disaster.

## SHRUBBERY ROBBERY

*Since my neighbor walked away from his mortgage and abandoned the property, I have been watering some of his trees but not his oleander bushes—my hose can't reach that far. Coincidentally, my own backyard is bordered by oleanders, with spaces where some have died out. I say this is the universe speaking, and I should move my neighbor's oleanders to my yard where they will thrive and my border will be complete. OK?*

*—Jim McCloud, Avondale, AZ*

I'm sorry, but if I understand Arizona law—and believe me I don't—before I can reply, you'll have to show me your papers.

Oh all right, I'll take a chance. Abandoned property is often up for grabs, but you've not yet established that these shrubs are truly abandoned. Your next step is to contact your neighbor or the bank that now owns the place (and the plants), if you're able to do either, and seek approval of your shrub saving. If you are unable to do so, let the transplanting begin. But drop a note in the mail slot so that if a rightful owner emerges, he can reclaim his wandering bushes.

While mine is an imperfect approach, if you do nothing, the plants die of a lack of water and an excess of legalism. But perhaps the most virtuous solution: get a longer hose.

Incidentally, when you hear the universe speaking, a bit of skepticism is appropriate: it may well be a crank call from your self-interest.

UPDATE: Local nurseries advised people not to transplant during the then current heat wave—temperatures were over 114 degrees—but to wait for cooler days, and so McCloud postponed his decision.

## GREEN HEAT

*I'm the proud owner of a new, highly efficient, green condominium. However, this winter I noticed something strange. If I turn off my furnace, my apartment stays warm even in subzero temperatures because of ambient heat coming through the walls and ceiling of my neighbors. Is it ethical to keep the furnace off? It seems a little like stealing to me.*

*—T. Hollister, Chicago*

You do gain heat from your neighbors, and they gain heat from you: that's efficiency not theft, an ecological, economical, and ethical advantage urban apartment dwellers have over suburbanites in single-family homes, leaking heat through every outside wall and window and driving around the streets on their riding mowers in a vain search for a decent loaf of bread, a good French film, and a bookstore open after nine o'clock. Or a bookstore.

You and your neighbors virtuously insulate one another's apartments. In an era of global warming, such prudent use of energy is praiseworthy. You would be wrong to surreptitiously cut vents through your walls or drill holes through your floor to siphon off your neighbors' heat. (And they would be wise to install better insulation.) But if you forswear illicit ductwork, you may honorably set your thermostat to whatever setting you find comfortable, much like everybody else.

To turn off your furnace entirely might make you feel like a free rider, forcing neighbors to pay for your apartment's warmth, but what can you do? Because each apartment has its own furnace, there is no simple way for all tenants to equitably share the cost of heating the building. That's where we New Yorkers have an edge. Here most apartment buildings have a single furnace for the entire structure, its cost borne by all tenants. There is a downside to this system: the tenant who keeps her windows open in February adds to everyone else's cost; she has no incentive to use energy more providently. On the upside, unlike you, we have no icy wind off Lake Michigan. And no Lake Michigan.

## ANTISOCIAL SECURITY

*Hypothetically, would it be unethical to place a security firm's lawn signs around my front yard even though I have not installed its security system? These fake "caveats" would discourage intruders, and the security firm would get free advertising for its product. So who's hurt?*
—*James Morgan, New Brunswick, NJ*

The same dubious justification can be trotted out by anyone who, for example, vaults the subway turnstile or hooks into cable TV without paying. You are shifting your share of the cost of the service—or, in this case, of its crime-deterring reputation—to paying customers. If everyone followed your free-ride example and refrained from paying, there'd be no money to finance subway service—plus my imaginary Aunt Minna would injure herself severely trying to hurdle the turnstile in heels and a demure suit in a nice cotton-poly blend.

Here's the particular damage inflicted by your insouciant freeloading: every counterfeit dilutes the legitimacy of the authentic. Those security service signs deter crime only to the extent that they convincingly signal imminent intervention. The more fakes on display, the less risk a burglar has of encountering actual security guards, and the likelier he is to go ahead and rob a house with a genuine security sign. (Assuming he's a rational burglar. Who calculates probabilities. And who, despite his acumen, hasn't gone straight.)

Now, installing signs of an imaginary security service—James Morgan Alert, perhaps?—might not mar the reputation of any particular company, but it would undermine confidence in the industry as a whole, which some might regard as a good thing. One criticism of these services is that they don't diminish crime, as genuine police work is meant to; they merely shift it to the house next door, the one without private guards, the one owned by your less well-off neighbor.

While you may take reasonable measures to keep your home burglar-free, your safety should not come at someone else's expense or by sullying someone else's reputation. To illustrate: you may not pepper your front yard with signs reading "Guarded by the Ghost of Charlton Heston" (if he is not actually in your house bearing arms and rattling chains), but if you are awakened in the night by a crowbar prying open your back door and fear yourself in imminent danger, you may bark like Charlton Heston to frighten off the intruder. When faced with immediate peril, trickery is permissible; just ask the cop who is *standing right behind you*!

---

**GOING DOWN**

*Our condo includes a small building with an elevator. The first-floor occupant does not need the elevator and has consistently refused to pay a portion of her maintenance fee that she attributes to elevator upkeep. Is she justified?*
*—Marilyn Sachs, New York*

Legally, yes; ethically, no. Does she refuse to pay the share of her taxes that goes to the National Park Service because she never visits Yosemite? When we are part of a community, there are times when we simply share the cost and do not parse the details of actual usage too closely. If narrow self-interest is to be the guiding principle here, the parsimonious tenant might comfort herself by considering that even if she never rides the elevator, the more amenities the building has, the more her own property is worth.

If you truly embrace her tightfisted fee-for-service model, then hang a clipboard in the elevator where tenants record every floor they ride to. Elevator expenses would be assigned proportionally. Certainly, those who live on higher floors should pay more than those on floor two or three: the former use the elevator much more than do the latter. You might install a scale, too, and calculate elevator fees by the pound. After all, a heavier load causes more wear and tear on the machinery. And I suppose your fellow tenant could also refuse to pay the share of the electric bill that goes to light the third floor hallway. That should make the building a delightful place.

But even in the face of irrefutable ethical argument, by which I mean my opinion, the law sees this differently. As several readers informed me, in Paris and in some cities in Italy, ground-floor tenants do not share elevator expenses, a custom that arose, I suspect, when elevators were introduced to older buildings. One savvy lawyer clued me in to the fact that the Common Interest Ownership Act, in effect in most U.S. jurisdictions, provides that any common expense that benefits fewer than all units shall be assessed exclusively against the units that benefit from such service.

---

**SUICIDE**

*Our mother committed suicide at home, and now we're selling her house. Potential buyers know that the owner died, but do not know how. Under the law, we're not required to tell them about a death on the property. If asked directly, we would let them know, but do we have an ethical duty to volunteer this information?*

*—Name withheld, New York*

In many states there is a legal (and in my view, an ethical) obligation to disclose pertinent information about the house as a physical entity—an unseen construction flaw, for example, or unusually high heating costs—not to recount all that occurred within its walls or to delve into the spirit realm.

Your ethical obligation is more nuanced and is affected by your motives. You need not sacrifice your privacy or your own emotional well-being by raising this intimate and painful matter with a stranger. If, however, your real concern is neither privacy nor grief but the selling price of the house, then you might volunteer this unsettling story.

A potential buyer could be put off by the suicide. The desire to have your home life unclouded by associations with grim death is not unreasonable; the fear of ghostly manifestations is goofy but not unknown. Your coping with your mother's loss supersedes a buyer's claim to this information; your pursuit of profit does not. In this latter case, you should strive for the transparency that sustains honest transactions.

**UPDATE**: Without seeking the family's consent, their real estate agent disclosed the suicide to a bidder who, undeterred, bought the house.

---

### DRILL BABY DRILL

*Natural gas companies in our area can drill in one spot and extract gas more than a mile away by using "horizontal" drilling. These companies offered to lease homeowners' mineral rights—about $4,000 for my partner and me. For environmental reasons, we strongly oppose this drilling, but most of our neighbors are enthusiastic about the profits, so drilling will be done under our house whether or not we agree to the lease. What should we do?*

*—Jessica May, Fort Worth, TX*

It is understandable that you feel powerless in the face of community-wide sentiment—Gold rush!—but you should not sign the lease. To fail to resist what you see as injustice simply because you fear that you cannot win this fight assures the very defeat you dread. If nothing else, this is a short-term view. Political struggle is long. Even if you lose the first battle, you fight on, and by resisting from the outset, you shape the conditions of that struggle.

I reject your premise that drilling is inevitable no matter what you—and by extension, your neighbors—do. (Local environmental groups might suggest effective actions that you've not considered.) If the gas company believed that, it wouldn't continue to offer the money to all and sundry. What's more, the example of local resistance to such schemes can affect the actions of this and other gas companies in their future dealings in other neighborhoods.

But the most potent argument for your declining to sign what you regard as a devil's bargain is this: it violates your own principles. Even if all your neighbors are doing it. (Shooting a guy in an orgy of rioting: same deal. You shouldn't play along even if everyone else in the roiling mob is firing furiously.) In what sense do you oppose drilling if you sell your mineral rights to the first person who puts cash on the table? Ethics concerns our actions, not just our arguments.

---

**CO-OP CLEANING CREW**

*The board of our 273-unit co-op wants to replace our union cleaning service with a nonunion service to save $35,000 a year, although the board acknowledges that our present service performs admirably. Facing rising costs, the board stresses its duty to stay within its budget and hold down monthly fees. Is the board acting ethically? What can residents do if they disagree with it?*

*—Joan Greenfield, Boston*

The board's proposal is a dubious first step. It should instead begin by negotiating with the current service, seeking to preserve good union jobs without busting your building's budget. In tough times like today's, some unions have agreed to renegotiate their contracts. Dissenting tenants should express their willingness to pay a bit more rather than squeeze the cleaning crew. It would cost each unit only $10.68 a month to make up that $35,000—about 36 cents a day—less than the cost of a daily candy bar (and it can't be healthful to eat all that candy).

Here's another way to phrase the issue: should sacrifices be made only by the poorest-paid employees or should they be shared by their (presumably) wealthier employers? I'm going to go with . . . shared. To dump union workers often means saving money by denying their replacements health insurance, vacation, and pension benefits, not to mention decent pay. New employees are not more productive; they can just be induced to work for less—economic desperation has a way of doing that. While the board has financial obligations to the co-op owners, it also should treat its employees fairly rather than force them into a race to the bottom.

**UPDATE:** The board replaced its unionized service with nonunion workers. The union company found jobs in other buildings for the original crew, but not full-time work.

---

### CARPET

*My wife, two-year-old daughter, and I live in a small second-floor condo. The single woman living below us objects to the noise our daughter makes, particularly when she runs down our hallway. That downstairs neighbor asked us to install carpeting, at least a runner in the hall. Our lease calls for carpets on a fixed percentage of the floors, but we prefer hardwood floors.*

*We installed some carpets, but adding more would not look right. Besides, virtually all of our neighbors ignore that lease provision. Must we install the hallway runner?*

*—Name withheld, San Francisco*

You must. Your duties to your neighbor, both legal and ethical, trump your right to enjoy even the most magnificent hardwood. Even oak. Even teak. You signed your lease in good faith. That some people ignore some of its dictates doesn't erase your obligations. Such lapses can be tolerated when no harm results. But in your case, harm has occurred, and your neighbor has asked you to do no more than what you've formally agreed to. Unless you can come up with a mutually acceptable compromise—Get your daughter some soft-soled slippers? Swaddle her in Bubble Wrap?—you must carpet your hallway.

**UPDATE:** The family installed the hallway runner, bringing its carpet coverage to what their lease specified. The neighbor remains discontent and has asked for yet more carpets and "quiet hours," when the two-year-old would be kept from running, perhaps with a powerful sedative, if I understand this last demand, and I do not.

---

**BUGGED**

*We had our co-op apartment treated for bedbugs. When we informed the co-op board, they said it was up to us whether or not to alert our neighbors. The management company advised us not to for fear of spreading panic. I want to give our neighbors a chance to be on the lookout, but I don't want to scare them unnecessarily or alienate them with bad news. Should I tell?*

*—Name withheld, New York*

Here's one way to avoid spreading panic: shun the phrases "atomic bed-bugs" and "giant zombie bedbugs" and "mutant vampire bedbugs from outer space." People can be so nervous. But if you speak in a normal tone of voice and avoid sudden movements, I'm confident that your neighbors will stay calm and take appropriate precautions.

But they can't take precautions unless they're aware of the risks of infestation, and that's information they've a right to. If you know that people face a genuine, albeit insect-size, peril, you have a duty to let them know so they can protect themselves.

Better still, the building's management company should warn all tenants about this infestation, so that you will not be embarrassed or become the target of neighborly animosity. The management company should also provide folks in the building with specific measures they can take, including the names of local pest-control companies skilled at detecting and eradicating bedbugs. That is the management's obligation, and the co-op board should order its enforcement. If the building were on fire, I hope the management would not be similarly silent for fear of spreading panic. You should first urge them to act, and if they do not, then you should warn your neighbors both about the vexatious bedbugs and about the head-in-the-sand management. One should be eradicated, the other replaced.

**UPDATE:** This person did not warn the neighbors.

## TREED

*Without warning or consultation, our new neighbor cut down the trees that separated our properties, destroying our privacy and views. He had the legal*

*right to do this—I checked with the county—but does he have an ethical obligation to mitigate or repair the damage or compensate us in some way?*
—*J.T., Greenbrae, CA*

Ethics concerns the effect of our actions on others, and, property rights notwithstanding, your neighbor's Mr. T act (Sly Stallone act? Bette Midler act? All three have been implicated in messy arboreal incidents) had a truly baleful effect. The law may have permitted it, but your neighbor should set a higher standard than mere legality.

The law itself can be subject to ethical scrutiny. If it fails to weigh the ecological implications of this ax wielding on the wider community, it is dubious indeed. By removing those trees, your neighbor wrecked more than your view and privacy. Among other things, he diminished the air quality and perhaps worsened water-runoff problems for the entire area, destroyed something of beauty, and most likely lowered the value of his own property. (This last, affecting only himself, makes him a knucklehead but does not make him unethical.)

I'm skeptical about restitution. His building a fence would restore your privacy but not the lost beauty, nor would it address the greater harm he's done to the broader community. As for replanting the trees, even if he acquiesced, you'd not benefit: saplings take years to reach shady adulthood. Nor can his handing you some cash up the oxygen levels in the neighborhood.

Instead, your efforts should be expended on toughening local laws. And you'll have plenty of time to do that, now that you won't be squandering your weekends on backyard barbecues with the neighbor.

It is possible, if unlikely, that he had legitimate reasons for his clear-cutting. Is he plagued by allergies? Did those trees threaten his house? Did they make snarky remarks about his cat? But lacking such motives, he acted dreadfully.

**UPDATE:** Response to this question was particularly spirited. Many readers argued that property rights prevail: if J.T. wanted the leafy benefits he cherishes, he should plant his own trees on his own property. I'd considered that but dismissed it as impractical—saplings take years to reach privacy-producing height—and thus was undone not by my moral reasoning but my arboreal ignorance. Botanically savvy readers suggested varieties of trees, shrubs, and ornamental grasses that grow quickly. (A gleefully vindictive fellow proposed planting bamboo that would swiftly overrun the grounds of the tree-slaughtering neighbor.) One person suggested that a landscape architect could design small mounds or terraces to give young trees an instant boost in height. Others pointed out this happy consequence of J.T.'s planting his own trees: they would stand as a verdant rebuke to his neighbor. As Joyce Kilmer did not write: I think that I shall never see / a poem vengeful as a tree.

# Doctors & Nurses

PROMOTING HEALTH MEANS MAKING WISE DECISIONS ABOUT PUBLIC policy as well as wise decisions within the doctor-patient relationship. The remarkably successful effort to reduce smoking, for example, operated at both ends of this spectrum, and yielded enormous improvements in well-being. It is interesting to look at the sort of reasoning that operates in such choices—political arguments, scientific debates, and moral reasoning.

Consider proposals to tax sugary drinks as a way to fight obesity and finance health-care reform, an idea that has found support from medical experts and some interest from President Obama, while meeting resistance from the beverage industry in general and Coca-Cola CEO Muhtar Kent in particular. "I have never seen it work where a government tells people what to eat and what to drink," he told the Rotary Club of Atlanta. "If it worked, the Soviet Union would still be around." Is this sort of argument so dubious—and does it come from the maker of products so damaging—that Muhtar Kent should be dragged off in handcuffs?

Legal barriers notwithstanding, that might not be a bad response to such half-baked—or thoroughly deceitful—rhetoric.

Kent's assertion is fishy because it muddles a positive and a negative. The various plans under consideration do not tell us what we *should* drink; they are concerned with what we should *not* drink—sugary beverages, what critics call "liquid candy." Urging people not to drive short distances is different from commanding them to reach the corner store by hopping. Urging people not to drink cola is different from requiring them to drink cat pee.

And of course our government, like all others, does tell people what to eat and has for years. Perhaps *tell* is too coercive a term— no federal food police pound on your door at dinnertime demanding to see your broccoli. But *strongly recommend* is apt. Kent should check out the Department of Agriculture's ChooseMyPlate.gov or visit www .nutrition.gov, where jackbooted thugs engage in tyrannical meal planning—okay, no jackboots and no thuggery, but there are some tasty menus. (The recipe for cranberry-nut muffins looks delish.) Our government also tells people what to eat in other ways, both directly, by creating menus for public school cafeterias and military mess halls, and indirectly, influencing our diets through farm policies, tariffs, trade agreements, and food regulation.

Kent's evocation of the Soviets is entirely meretricious, deploying the cheap debater's tactic of deprecating something by linking it to what is widely reviled. The Beatles are bad because Pol Pot liked "Hey, Jude." Bowling is evil because Satan plays. On a team with John and George.

What is rightly and vigorously contested—by, for example, writer Michael Pollan, the documentary film *Food, Inc.*, the National Cattlemen's Beef Association, or the American Academy of Pediatrics—is not *if* government should involve itself in such things, but *how*. That's politics in the best sense. Well, second best. The Beef Association has its own economic self-interest at stake in a way that Pollan and pediatricians do not.

Kent's view of the legitimate function of government is curiously inconsistent. I hate to call it "hypocritical"—no, wait, I like to call it "hypocritical" for him to repudiate government action to influence soda prices when it comes to taxing sugary drinks, but to be complaisant about the many ways government strives to keep the cost of high-fructose corn syrup artificially low—in effect, to subsidize Sprite.

Kevin W. Keane, senior vice president for public affairs of the American Beverage Association, thinks it wrongheaded to single out soda: "When it comes to losing weight, all calories count, regardless of the food source." This is akin to saying that when I have only partial responsibility, I have no responsibility. If I was the triggerman on that bank job, I can't beg for a break because, after all, I wasn't also the lookout and the getaway driver and the caterer. (Are bank robberies catered? Must you pack a lunch? A healthful lunch?) Assuredly, many factors affect our weight. But it doesn't follow that because a policy fails to address all of them, it should not address any. That the feds devote few resources to going after counterfeiters who mint fake quarters doesn't mean they should decline to pursue those who run off $20 bills.

Nor are the multiple causes of a problem equally significant. Studies suggest that sugary beverages are a key contributor to obesity. The Center on Budget and Policy Priorities notes: "Americans consume about 250 to 300 more daily calories today than they did several decades ago, and nearly half of this increase reflects greater consumption of high-sugar soft drinks." So there's a case to be made for giving serious consideration to a soda tax even if other steps are not taken.

Such errors of reasoning might be seen as intellectual, not moral, failings, but it is difficult to extend that benefit of the doubt to Americans Against Food Taxes, which describes itself as "a coalition of concerned citizens—responsible individuals, financially strapped families, small and large businesses in communities across the country." As was reported in the *Times*, AAFT looks like a veiled industry organization: "calls to a media contact listed on the group's Web site go to the American Beverage Association." This smells like AstroTurf, corporate lobbyists posing as a grassroots organization. It is entirely suitable for interested parties to participate in public debate; it is not suitable to conceal who's doing the debating.

Now, I too engaged in some forensic high jinks, I'll admit. There are no actual proposals out there that call for a guillotine to be erected on the Washington Mall and for Muhtar Kent's head to be separated from his body. But to pose the question as I did is not deceit but a rhetorical device: I assume that readers recognize hyperbole. Of course, Kent should not be executed. Most moralists agree that a punishment must be proportional to the transgression (although it's often hard to agree on the terms). Nor should Kent even be imprisoned. I'd reserve that penalty for those who produce inarguably toxic products—the senior executives of tobacco companies, for instance. But it would be a fine thing if Kent and his cohort were ordered into a class on critical thinking, much as a traffic court judge can send recalcitrant speeders to driver-improvement school. There is a point at which a failure of reasoning is a failure of ethics.

### RACIST PATIENT

*I am an anesthesiologist at a metropolitan hospital. A patient scheduled for an operation one day requested a female anesthesiologist, a request we were inclined to honor. When the anesthesiologist's name was given to the patient, she wondered if the anesthesiologist was African American. When told that she was, the patient demanded a white anesthesiologist. It was 7:00 A.M., too early to contact hospital lawyers or the ethics board. What should we have done?*

*—D. W., Houston*

I admire your inclination to put a patient at ease, but such requests are not exempt from moral scrutiny. If a patient told you she would be more emotionally prepared for surgery if she could go out to the hospital parking lot and drive over a couple of puppies, you would not lend her your car. Similarly, you should have rejected her racist request, explaining that your hospital does not consider race when making assignments. (If it did, the hospital could face legal claims from rejected anesthesiologists.)

You were wrong even to grant her request for a woman anesthesiologist. We rightly consent to some such demands but not to all and not unthinkingly. Most of us would accommodate a woman's desire for a female gynecologist, deferring to the patient's sexual modesty. (Although I hope that this customary justification, too, will pass away as we advance toward true gender equality.) But few would honor her request for a female clerk in the hospital gift shop. Because an anesthesiologist's task does not intrude on sexual modesty, it was illegitimate to make sex a factor here. Surely other members of the surgical team were men but were not subject to patient veto.

UPDATE: Despite finding the patient's request objectionable, the doctors granted it.

This column received some dispiriting responses when it first appeared, among them several e-mails from women asserting that a surgery patient's being unclothed is in itself sufficient reason to preclude a male physician's attending her. And not all came from religious fundamentalists, or at least from those who made overt references to faith. It would be lamentable indeed if such prudery moved us to a two-tiered, gender-segregated system of medical care.

Even more alarming were the e-mails that dragged affirmative action into this discussion. Neither those readers nor the patient had the slightest idea if that African American anesthesiologist had entered school via affirmative action or gotten a leg up as the son of an alum or was a child genius who completed med school at age two. For all anybody knew, the replacement she demanded was an old white guy who, not having to vie with women or African Americans for a spot in med school, was less skilled. In any event, affirmative-action students tend to graduate at the same rate as their classmates and go on to lives of equal accomplishment.

## HALF A PILL IS BETTER THAN . . .

*Drug companies frequently charge the same amount for different strengths of a medication, such as 1, 2 and 5 mg tablets. I sometimes write patients a prescription for 20 mg tablets when patients take 10 mg daily. They can easily split the pills in half. No harm is done if the two portions are slightly unequal. (The local VA hospital does this with many pills, including Viagra.) The patient and the insurer save money, but the drug company makes less profit. Any thoughts?*

*—Lonnie Hanauer, MD, Millburn, NJ*

Several thoughts. My first is one of satisfaction that the VA is helping older vets enjoy a happy sex life. It's the least we as a nation can do for those who served so gallantly (or even lackadaisically) in the Spanish-American War.

My second thought—more power to you. Your clever thrift is akin to buying in bulk, and there's nothing wrong with that. Patients who want the convenience of pills in their precise dosage have the option of paying more for them. Those willing to do the work of pill splitting receive a discount. Ethics does not require us to buy retail. Some parents give their kids half an adult aspirin rather than buy prepackaged low-dose children's aspirin. In fact, pill cutters are sold openly at many drugstores, no skulking necessary. I know of no ethical system that requires us to maximize the profits of pharmaceutical companies.

My third is that the real solution to high-priced medication lies not in individual actions like yours, however ingenious and benign, but in policy changes. So I hope that in addition to the fine thing you're already doing, you and your colleagues are lobbying for legal reforms that would benefit your patients.

**NAUGHTY NURSES**

*I work at a hospital where several nurses practice therapies like Healing Touch and Therapeutic Touch, said to adjust a patient's energy field and thereby decrease pain and improve healing, although there is no significant evidence for this. If those nurses believe in these treatments, may they tell the patient they are effective? If the treatments provide merely a placebo effect, telling patients about this lack of evidence might undermine that benefit. Would that justify withholding the information?*

*—Name withheld, St. Louis*

Something needs to be adjusted here, but it is the nurses' behavior not the patients' energy fields. These nurses, however well-meaning, should not perform unproven therapies—if these are unproven; opinions differ passionately—on unwitting patients. To do so is to tell a kind of lie to patients, who reasonably assume that their care meets hospital standards. And while the placebo effect can be beneficial, that is insufficient reason to routinely deprive patients of pertinent facts. Patients cannot give informed consent to their treatment if they lack honest information about it.

That the nurses sincerely believe in the efficacy of their methods is of no account. People sincerely believe all sorts of things. My imaginary Uncle Milt sets great store by the potions he whips up in the bathroom sink under a full moon in his underwear. It is evidence, not sincerity, that is wanted here. (Or in the case of Uncle Milt, trousers.)

What these nurses could do is explain that these techniques are unproven and unendorsed by the hospital (if that is the case; hospitals vary), offering patients, in effect, the sort of supplemental treatment available outside the hospital. But this approach is not without risk. A therapy provided in the hospital by its staff carries a sense of official approval, no matter what disclaimers the nurses offer. In any case, these nurses must alert their colleagues and hospital administrators about such things. Both groups need to know how patients are being treated if they are to do their jobs well.

---

## IS THERE A DOCTOR ON THE PLANE?

*During a transatlantic flight, I heard an announcement: "If any doctors are on board, please make themselves known . . ." At this point, I had worked in the hospital for only eighteen months, but no one else came forward, so I treated a crew member with chest pain. As the crew thanked me, one pointed out that there were other doctors on the plane. Did I have an ethical obligation to care for a person at 35,000 feet?*

*—Kenneth Christopher, MD, Brookline, MA*

You did the right thing. While U.S. law does not compel you to render aid in an emergency (although some states do have Good Samaritan laws), the American Medical Association, among other organizations, imposes an ethical obligation to do so, a policy that is both reasonable and humane.

Your being a relatively new doc doesn't come into it. Once you're licensed to practice medicine, you are expected to be able to do just that. And it's not at all clear that older physicians provide better care than those newly minted. Medical specialty, however, is relevant. You might have sought some backup, asking the crew to announce, "Is there a cardiologist on board?"

Some physicians are skittish about lawsuits in such situations, an understandable but insufficient reason to stare obdurately at the in-flight movie while the pilot keels over and the plane plunges into the sea. But this concern is misplaced. A medical professional—doctor, nurse, EMT—traveling on an American flight is shielded by the Aviation Medical Assistance Act. Unless he or she is grossly negligent, there's little risk of a successful liability suit, even if something dreadful happens to the patient.

Your legal position in midair in the mid-Atlantic is slightly hazier. (What if a Thai doctor treats a Nigerian passenger in an Italian plane flying over Argentina?) No international convention protects you from a malpractice suit, notes Dr. Claus Curdt-Christiansen, chief of the aviation medicine section of the International Civil Aviation Organization, but many airlines themselves offer legal coverage to a doctor who comes forward.

However, any legal uncertainty is superseded by your ethical obligation to assist in an emergency. Physicians are trained, often in part at public expense, not just to make money or to keep their insurance premiums down, but to apply their skills to those in need. It is laudable that you did so and a rebuke to those who didn't.

---

### NO LESBIANS ALLOWED

*As OB-GYNs in a not-for-profit clinic, we gratefully accept donations for our underserved community. A patient offered a machine, to be used first in treating her own infertility, with one contingency—that it never be used for lesbian inseminations. We found this condition abhorrent and did not accept the machine. Were we wrong to reject a gift that, while excluding a minority, would benefit the vast majority?*
*—Scott Resnick, MD, and Shanti Mohling, MD, Taos, NM*

You did the right thing. As you put the question, however, it almost sounds like an innocuous case of someone wanting to give a high-tech hair dryer beneficial to many but useless to a few bald guys. But imagine your donor had offered medical equipment with the stipulation that it not be used by African Americans. In that case, you'd more aptly phrase the question: can I cooperate with racism? The answer would be obvious, as should the answer to this question: can I cooperate with homophobia?

It is frustrating to reject this equipment. But that's the tricky thing about moral reasoning based on the greatest good for the greatest number:

it has a discomfiting way of allowing a majority to bully a minority. And it can bring us into conflict with our fundamental values. We might find that hanging an innocent guy in the town square each day deters crime, a fine thing for the honest majority of the community, but the hanged man is likely to object. People can be so selfish.

## MD & KID

*I am a medical student on a pediatrics rotation. Recently, we diagnosed an eleven-year-old boy with leukemia. He was treated and will continue as an outpatient. Throughout his stay, his parents refused to divulge his diagnosis to him. He is a bright boy, interested in science, and curious about his treatment. Does he have a right to know his own diagnosis?*

—*E.L.*

Physicians have an ethical obligation to inform patients of their conditions and treatment, but parents have the legal authority to make medical decisions for their minor children and, by implication, to decide what information those children receive. How to harmonize these two duties can be controversial among medical ethicists (in questions of reproductive rights, for example). In this case, I believe that your young patient has the right to know what he's being treated for.

Ignorance breeds fear, an emotional state deleterious to one's health. A knowledgeable patient can more fully participate in his own care and thereby improve its quality. Thus, to act in the best interests of this patient, the physician must respond to the boy's curiosity.

The patient's age is a factor, certainly. Legally there is a crisp distinction between minor and adult but for actual children, attaining maturity is a gradual process. The older a child gets, the more entitled he is to be treated like an adult. A bright and inquisitive eleven-year-old can grasp much about his sad circumstances.

This child's physician should begin by talking to the parents and perhaps persuade them that, ethics aside, deception is a doomed strategy. Smart kids figure things out eventually. When their son learns he was lied to, at least by omission, he is apt to feel hurt and anxious, undermining his trust in his parents and his doctors, and making his treatment more difficult.

A physician may not perform any medical procedure without the parent's consent. The flow of information is not so unambiguously restricted. I, of course, hope that the parents can be convinced not to leave their son in the dark, particularly when the matter is presented to them with the help of a child psychologist and other members of the hospital team. But if they remain adamant, I believe that ethics (although not necessarily law) gives the son a right to this information.

---

## GYNO SILENCE

*I am a gynecologist. A new patient, referred by a Catholic hospital, told me, "I'm so happy to find a doctor who doesn't perform abortions." But I do perform abortions. Apparently she made an assumption based on that referral. Unsure how to reply, I left the examination room without directly commenting. I seldom discuss pregnancy termination unless asked by a patient; I have no desire to see picketers outside my office or snipers outside my kitchen window. Must I correct this misunderstanding?*
*—Name withheld, Fairfield County, CT*

You need not discuss this further. Your patient can reasonably expect you to respond to questions about her own care, but you have no duty to give her an account of how you care for your other patients.

I sympathize with your discomfort. You stumbled into a kind of tacit equivocation. Although you intended your silence to indicate only silence, you know that your patient took it as confirmation. But there are matters about which you may keep your own counsel. You need not satisfy a patient's curiosity about your religion or your national origins or whether or not you yourself are pregnant: some information is simply out of bounds. If a patient misconstrues your silence on such subjects, so be it.

Even if the patient inquires directly, you need say only: I don't discuss my treatment of other patients.

---

### TOO INTRUSIVE?

*I am a physician. In a weekly class I attend as a hobby, there is a young man with the body habitus of Marfan syndrome: he is tall and thin with long arms and legs. If he has this syndrome, he is at risk for serious cardiovascular damage. He is not my patient and is certainly entitled to his privacy. However, if he is uninformed, his life may be in danger. Should I speak to him?*

*—Name withheld, New York*

Ordinarily it would be impertinent to accost a stranger on so personal a matter, but in this case, you should. There are several guidelines to help you decide when to do so.

Do you possess information he is unlikely to have? This would rule out telling a size XXL at McDonald's to ease off the supersizing, but it would prompt you to give your young man medical guidance he may lack.

Does he face a serious risk? This would proscribe your advising a passerby that the mullet is a haircut that flatters few, but it would induce you to act in your situation.

Would your warning enable him to take action? If you passed a burning house and saw someone dozing on the couch inside, you'd awaken him so he can flee, not merely gape at the fire. Similarly, your speaking to this fellow would allow him to consult his physician and, if necessary, receive treatment.

And so, adhering to these guidelines, speak tactfully, but speak.

---

**SLIDER**

*In my solo medical practice, I treat children from diverse socioeconomic backgrounds. I don't participate in any insurance plans, but I routinely use a downward sliding scale to help parents in financial difficulty afford care. Many of my patients come from families with extremely high net worth. A friend suggested I charge them more. Is it ethical to use the sliding scale in both directions?*

*—Name withheld, New York*

You already use the sliding scale in both directions, and reasonably so. To give one person a price cut is tantamount to giving everyone else a price increase. There is no price sanctified by the gods that serves as an unvarying standard of comparison, as long as people are paying variable prices, it's all relative. If one person pays $90 for a service and another pays $110, whose payment have you reduced and whose raised?

Here's another way to look at it: Surely your fees have risen over the years. You're not now charging for a flu shot what you did in 1810 (if you are a Faustian health care professional who will live for a thousand years, and had there been flu shots in 1810). From that perspective, everybody's fees have gone up over the past 200 years, some more than others.

If you thought about your fees in another way, as a percentage of patients' income, you might conclude that you persistently charge wealthy patients quite a bit less than the needy. A bill for $10,000—it's a lovely nose job—represents 1 percent of the income of someone making a million dollars a year, but it is 33 percent of the income of someone making $30,000 a year. Why are you overcharging poorer patients? Why is someone with such a meager salary squandering it on a nose job? What was wrong with her old nose?

And remember, we already accept other sorts of variable pricing. The cost of an airline seat can vary depending on when you buy it. The cost of a movie ticket alters with your age: kids and seniors pay less.

Despite there being no mathematically meaningful distinction here, psychology plays its part; it can *feel* different if you apparently lower a price—that's generosity—than if you seem to raise one. That's gouging. And so you should be transparent, perhaps appending a general statement to your bills: "Fees may vary with ability to pay."

---

### BUYING AN ORGAN

*My elderly father would have died without a kidney donor. He was on various recipient lists, but the wait can be years. Family members were either unable or unwilling to donate. My father arranged the illegal purchase of a kidney from a foreign man, which required lying to immigration and hospital authorities. My loyalty is to my father, but I regret his actions. What should I do?*

*—Name withheld*

Your father should not have bought an organ for transplant. But if you were unable to dissuade him, to donate yourself, or to persuade other family members to do so, then there is little you can do now.

I understand his desperation. There are many more people in need of transplants than there are available organs. Each year thousands of people die while awaiting donors. It is tough to fault somebody for taking extreme measures to survive. And yet, the consequences of your father's actions are grim. To permit the buying of organs is to allow those with money to harvest the organs of those without. It's tough to imagine Donald Trump selling a kidney. (Even tougher to imagine anyone wanting Trump parts inside them, but that's an aesthetic not an ethical matter.)

In India, where organs were bought and sold, it was indeed the poor who sold and the wealthier who bought. If a system of acquiring organs is to be ethical, it must be equitable, not the case when one economic class is exploited (and put at significant medical risk) for the benefit of another. And exploitation it is when the seller is not making a truly voluntary decision but responding to financial desperation. Thankfully, the American way of organ transplantation relies on voluntary donors.

I should add that the hospital and doctors collaborating (if only passively) with your father should be censured and may find themselves running afoul of the law, even though their motives may have been benevolent.

There is something you and your father can do now if you want to make amends for his imperfect behavior: volunteer with one of the many organizations striving to expand the donor base.

**UPDATE**: The father is doing fine. The donor, minus a kidney, has returned to his home country.

This column generated vigorous disagreement. Many readers argue that one solution to the shortage of organs for transplant is to let people choose to sell what is, after all, a part of their own body. But what proponents of such sales call a "choice," I call the right to be dangerously exploited. Democratic societies have always limited our ability to harm ourselves, hence workplace-safety laws or child-labor laws or minimum wage laws that forbid a five-year-old to "choose" to take a job in a lead-smelting plant. Even when someone faces dire poverty, we do not permit him to sell himself into slavery.

It's true that we need to expand the pool of organs available for transplant, but there are ways to do that without endangering the most vulnerable members of society. One plan would make the use of cadaveric organs routine, switching from the current opt-in system to allowing those folks with, for example, religious objections, to opt out. Such systems are in place in several countries with impressive results. It's curious that those who resist such an approach here show more concern for the sentiments of the dead than the health of the living.

# Civic Life

EMERGING TECHNOLOGIES HAVE TRANSFORMED THE IDEA OF COMMUNITY— from a group of people we regularly see in person to a group we encounter only online. The comments section of the *Times*, like that of other newspapers, was meant to be not just an enhanced letters-to-the-editor page, but a sort of public gathering place, where we grapple with the issues of the day. Unfortunately, a comments section can, at times, also be a foulmouthed and loutish gathering, generating insults rather than civic engagement.

The *Times*, like most papers, does not publish unsigned letters to the editor, but it does run unsigned comments. This inconsistency is less a planned policy than a clash of two traditions, newspapers versus the Web. But should newspapers continue to post unsigned comments?

Which is to ask: what codes of etiquette and ethics should govern a comments section? What sort of community should we foster?

To promote the social good of lively conversation and the exchange of ideas, transparency should be the default mode. And that goes both for lofty political discourse and casual comments on Amazon. "Says who?" is not a trivial question. It deepens the reader's understanding to know who is speaking, from what perspective, with what (nutty?) history, and with what personal stake in the matter. It encourages civility and integrity in the writer to stand behind her words. There are times when anonymous posting is necessary, when disclosure is apt to bring harsh retribution—I'll come to that—but more often, anonymous posting sustains a culture, or at least a subculture, of calumny and malice so caustic as to inhibit the very discourse the Web can so admirably engender. Writers should not do it, and Web site hosts should not allow it.

My ex-wife, writer Katha Pollitt, told me, "I get a ton of hostile, misogynist, idiotic comments from anonymous trolls when I blog at the *Nation*. Sometimes I feel like I am dancing on the table for an audience of drunks. Not only is it dispiriting—and let's not forget that women writers on the Internet receive vastly more hateful comments than male writers—it has nothing to do with the brisk and vigorous exchange of ideas often said to be the reason for anonymity. Because there are no ideas and no exchange."

My own experience was marked by greater cordiality, but then again, I had a virtual bodyguard. The *Times* employs moderated comments, declining as a matter of policy to post those that include "personal attacks, obscenity, vulgarity, profanity (including expletives and letters followed by dashes), commercial promotion, impersonations, incoherence, and SHOUTING." But the very necessity of filtering such comments illuminates the by-products of anonymous posting.

Were it merely a matter of taste or tone or social style—etiquette— the anonymously obnoxious would be unimportant; we could all just lament the rising tide of boorishness and get on with it. But those who offer invective rather than argument discourage others from speaking. People who might be inclined to express an opinion grow reluctant when to do so may mean having some stranger call you a . . . well, judging by some of the unsigned e-mails I received in response to "The Ethicist," there is no limit to the epithets we face. (I should note that most responses were courteous, but I did have to toughen up.) It is the conversational version of Gresham's law: bad discourse drives out good.

Sometimes anonymity is legitimately practiced—by political dissidents in repressive regimes, for example. Donna Lieberman, executive director of the New York Civil Liberties Union, told me: "We've defended the right to anonymous speech successfully on some occasions," including "Iranian students in masked protest at the time of the shah." Journalists reasonably use anonymous sources when doing so is the only way to obtain significant information. Rate My Professors and the like, though not without their faults, are useful enterprises that rely on the shield of anonymity. Without it, what student, mindful of the wrath of a teacher scorned, would post? (But with anonymity may also come diminished credibility. It's tough to distinguish the astute from the vengeful.) Even in more casual online settings, students are vulnerable. Lieberman noted that "lots of school districts have discipline codes (to which we object) that punish out-of-school Internet speech by high school students." She also mentioned situations in which it is important to identify an incognito poster—for instance, to thwart harassment or bullying. So how are we to determine when anonymous posting is proper?

Here is a guideline: The effects of anonymous posting have become so pernicious that it should be forsworn unless there is a reasonable fear of retribution. By posting openly, we support the conditions in which honest conversation can flourish.

To take this approach is to break from the past. We are a nation founded on anonymous postings, or their eighteenth-century equivalent, pseudonymous pamphlets. The authors of *The Federalist Papers*, including Alexander Hamilton and James Madison, published under the name Publius. Among Benjamin Franklin's many pen names are Silence Dogood, Harry Meanwell, Alice Addertongue, and, most famously, Richard Saunders, better known as Poor Richard. Justice Clarence Thomas, concurring with the majority in a 1995 case, wrote a celebration of anonymous publication in eighteenth-century America.

But conditions change, and what once was benign now may be malignant; that's why we no longer allow people to wander the streets of our cities carrying guns. (Okay, we do allow that. But we have a good reason: to protect ourselves from marauding dinosaurs.) What has not altered is the importance of the free exchange of ideas. Ethics urges us to act in ways that promote this social good, that except when facing a genuine threat means writing with civility and signing your name.

When I published a version of this argument in the *Times*, a few comments asserted—yes, anonymously—that barring unsigned posts is "censorship." I don't agree. It has not stifled the letters pages or op-ed columns of newspapers to run only signed work, nor has it proved an insuperable barrier to book publishing for an author's name to appear on his or her work.

It was disheartening to note how many comments saw the ordinary expression of opinion in modern America as apt to invite physical violence. This seems, if not utterly without foundation, overwrought and self-dramatizing. But during the eighteenth century, the great age of the anonymous pamphlet, such robust responses were more common. When Samuel Johnson denied the authenticity of the Ossian poems, allegedly ancient works James Macpherson claimed to have discovered and translated, Macpherson threatened Johnson with a thrashing. Johnson replied in the newspapers, "I received your foolish and impudent letter. Any violence offered me I shall do my best to repel;

and what I cannot do for myself, the law shall do for me. I hope I shall never be deterred from detecting what I think a cheat, by the menaces of a ruffian." And he signed his name. Then he equipped himself with a stout cudgel.

I should add that I personally benefited from one use of anonymous expression. In an exception to the *Times*' policy of running only signed letters, those printed in "The Ethicist" sometimes appeared over "name withheld." People chose this option when their query included a confession of wrongdoing or revealed information about other people's behavior that could have had unfortunate consequences for the sender or his friends, family, or coworkers. People sometimes would be justifiably reluctant to offer such revelations without this protection. Given its bailiwick, the column couldn't have functioned without this exemption. But most online exchanges can and should operate unmasked.

## COFFEE FOR COPS

*Years ago, while working in a Philadelphia coffee shop, I was told not to charge policemen for their drinks. The idea was to encourage them to hang around and deter crime. In Washington, DC, recently, I noticed that my local café employed the same policy. Sure enough, a couple of latte-sipping cops were often stationed outside. But isn't this a form of bribery and hence unethical?*

*—Thomas Catan, London*

If you're right, and those cops are comped, this is indeed petty bribery, precipitating not only bad policing—patrol assignments should be based on the needs of each locale, not the availability of free mochaccino—but bad ethics. Nobody wants to live where bribery is endemic, where you have to pay off the mailman to get a letter or "tip" the sanitation men if you don't want to live within a wall of garbage. You should not act in ways that promote corruption and undermine the predominant honesty of municipal employees.

It's not only the coffee shop that's at fault, of course: so are those overcaffeinated cops. Officer Kenny Bryson, a media liaison officer with the DCPD told me, "The regs say that they are not to accept any gratuity. That's what it says in the manual." This is a reasonable proscription. Surely we expect police officers to have sufficient moral fiber to resist a three-dollar blandishment. (Notwithstanding the five New York City cops recently charged with accepting a street peddler's bribes of Coach handbags, as well as counterfeit Coach handbags. In pink. Or the apparently endemic ticket-fixing among the NYPD, blithely—can a cop be blithe?—denominated "professional courtesy.")

Officer Bryson points out that the café has an honest alternative. His department sometimes establishes mini-stations at convenience stores and fast-food chains, to provide a visible presence where there's been a crime problem.

Any query that includes the word *latte* is apt to be comic (and delightfully so), but petty corruption is a serious global problem that is particularly hard on the poor, for whom it can be a barrier to getting an education or a job or a house. We are fortunate to live in a country where this sort of thing is not pervasive; let's not grease the skids for its adoption (with a slippery skim-milk decaf Frappuccino).

UPDATE: Responding to this column, several readers argued that this practice is often meant benignly as an expression of gratitude to first responders. (Although in this case its intent was not without self-interest.) Yet it remains poor social policy, tainted by a history of less savory attempts to influence police procedures and of police demanding petty bribes from those on their beat. What's more, there need be nothing as crass as an explicit quid pro quo for such conduct to be undesirable or, as here, a violation of departmental regulations.

A better way to express appreciation of hardworking public employees is to do so at the polls when it's time to vote on pay raises (and I hope those efforts will extend to admirable nonuniformed workers like teachers).

### VOTING RIGHTS?

*I am a student at Kenyon College. Some local residents were upset that hundreds of students were allowed to vote for a property tax that will fall entirely on the permanent residents. Many students favor the measure as a way to fund the local elementary school. Students also note that they are called upon for jury duty. Was it ethical for us to vote?*
*—Name withheld, Gambier, OH*

Your voting was more than ethical; it was admirable. Such civic involvement is to be encouraged in everyone.

It is irrelevant that few students pay property taxes. (Although it should be noted that their room rent pays a portion of their landlord's property taxes.) We long ago eliminated economic requirements for voting: you needn't own property; you needn't pay a poll tax. Even people too poor to pay nearly any taxes may vote. Nor is it significant that most students eventually leave town. In four years, many Americans will have moved someplace new, but that does not strip them of their voting rights now. And what about the very old, those who may not be alive four years from now to pay those property taxes? Ban them from the polls? All voters should strive to act in the best interests of their communities, but owning property is not, nor should it be, a requirement for voting. If you meet the legal requirements to vote, go gaily to the polls. (There will be time for remorse when you see who's on the ballot.)

I understand local residents not wanting to enfranchise people who don't "really" live there (and thus dilute their own voting power), but what does that mean? After all, a nonstudent who spends four years in town is permitted to vote. Defenders of student voting rights have suggested it isn't *who* votes but *how* they vote that rankles critics: student populations are sometimes more liberal than the rest of the town. What's more, by living in a college town for four years, many students do not meet residency requirements to vote in their old hometowns. Surely they must be permitted to vote someplace.

## RELUCTANT JUROR

*When I asked to be excused from jury duty, the judge berated me for leaving my civic duty to the "poor." I did not oppose her diatribe, but I make good money and feel it's more efficient for society if I work, pay taxes, support*

*charities, and leave jury duty to others. Isn't this like leaving other essential functions—trash pickup, policing, dentistry—to others? Alternatively, couldn't I defer service to a less onerous period, like retirement?*
*—Name withheld, San Francisco*

No. Some obligations fall to all of us—or should, like military service in times of crisis, or driving the speed limit. We do not exempt those with greater incomes from either. Apparently, you would prefer to return to the Civil War–era practice of allowing the wealthy to buy their way out of inconvenient duties by hiring replacements. As for your willingness to serve decades from now, the obvious problem is the court can't count on your still being in San Francisco. Or still being.

Disconcertingly, your proposal places a greater value on the lives of those who earn more than those who earn less. An ill-paid nurse or librarian would serve jury duty, but a tobacco lobbyist or PGA star would not. Income is hardly a reliable guide to one's societal value, let alone the value of a life in a broader sense. If you are as smart as you imply, shouldn't the accused have the benefit of your (and Tiger Woods's) insights? Jurors should be a cross section of the community, not just those below a particular income level or above retirement age.

Jury service is not only a civic duty; it is also an opportunity— not merely onerous, but edifying—to glimpse a part of life you do not regularly see. Your plan erases a shared experience of American life, one of those things that helps create a community, like attending public school or going to the local library or swimming in a neighborhood pool. Granted, jury duty always arrives at a maddeningly inconvenient moment and is sometimes dogged with inefficiencies, but efficiency is not the summum bonum. Much that is worthwhile is notably inefficient: it takes hours and hours to listen to all the Mozart concertos; it takes years to raise a child.

Incidentally, you were wise not to tell the judge that her recounting the law was a "diatribe." Judges can be so pesky about the whole contempt-of-court thing.

---

### SINGLED OUT

*My same-sex partner and I are legally married in another country, a marriage not recognized by our state or (obviously) federal government, with significant negative consequences to our modest financial situation. My partner would be eligible for some government aid if she applied as a single person, but it feels disingenuous to do so, because as a family, we make well above the poverty line. In some sense, however, the government owes us this money since it unjustly disregards our marriage. Should she apply?*
*—Name withheld, Portland, ME*

There's no ethical obstacle to her doing so. As you realize to your dismay, in this context *single* is a technical term with a precise meaning defined by law. Your partner's duty is to meet the criteria for aid and fill out those applications honestly. If, for the purposes of, for example, health-insurance subsidies, the agency administering the program regards her as single, she has every right—ethical and legal—to apply as such.

*Family* has diverse meanings—to a religious body, a state legislature, a boss who hopes his employees won't unionize, Don Corleone. I take it to be a synonym for *insipid* when it precedes the word *film* and for *inedible* when followed by the word *restaurant*. Context shapes meaning. Marriage has long been, among other things, an economic institution. Your partner may take that into account when considering these applications.

This decision has nothing to do with the government compensating her for rough treatment or being evenhanded or mitigating any injustice marriage law imposes on you both. Nor could you argue that because federal marriage law discriminates against same-sex couples, denying them equal treatment, that you have an ethical right to balance the scales by cutting the line at the post office or punching a homophobe in the snoot, however appealing those actions might seem. But you have no duty to set stricter standards for such programs than the law itself. Similarly, although I favor a more progressive income tax, one that might compel a nice fellow like me to write a bigger check, I am not morally obliged to send the IRS more money than current law prescribes.

## STATEHOUSE BETRAYAL

*I am a state legislator. This last session I had an excellent student intern. But at the end of his stint, he announced that he was running against me and intended to from the start. (He had total access to my office, files, etc., but there is no evidence that he misused that.) His college adviser was horrified, probably worrying about the willingness of legislators to accept interns in the future. Are we being too sensitive? Should I have been more alert to this possibility?*

*—Phyllis Kahn, Minneapolis*

That's quite a story, a statehouse version of *All About Eve*. As both you and Margo Channing learned, you must be alert to the ambitions of young aides. Of course, your unwariness does not exculpate your ex-intern. It would be one thing if, upon joining your staff, he'd found your office to be a sink of corruption and incompetence, and vowed to unseat you. It is another for him to have deceived you from the start.

What you should do now is establish an intern ethics policy. It might, for example, clarify the restrictions on handling confidential information. It could also require would-be interns to pledge that upon leaving the job, they would not run against a former boss for a short period, perhaps one term. This is akin to senior executives agreeing not to work for competitors when they leave their employers, or government officials being restricted from lobbying their former agencies. Establishing such guidelines does more than serve an abstract good. It creates the conditions necessary for mutual trust, without which no satisfying joint endeavor is possible.

There is a bright spot in this disheartening episode. In the movie version, you'd be played by Bette Davis, if the producers can solve the problem of her availability, and if the public will accept a shift in the setting from the glamorous world of Broadway to the no doubt equally glamorous world of Minnesota politics.

## OUTING

*I have always believed that an elected official's private life is not a part of the public record. Before and after the Mayor Jim West episode, I have heard colleagues discuss outing legislators who oppose gay rights but are rumored to be gay. What is appropriate ethics in this case?*

*—State Senator Ken Jacobsen, Seattle*

Your colleagues may ethically out an official only if that official's being gay is germane to his policy-making. A person who seeks elected office, voluntarily entering the public arena, surrenders some claims to privacy. (Financial disclosure comes to mind.) Some, but not all. An official's private life should remain private unless he or she makes it relevant to a public position freely taken. A cross-dressing secretary of agriculture who voiced no opinion on the sexual high jinks of soybeans—do legumes engage in high jinks?—would not meet this standard; a gay state senator who opposed marriage equality would. Similarly, the assault weapons stockpiled by a gun-control advocate would be pertinent, his nude trout fishing would not be.

Determining when this imprecise standard has been met is admittedly difficult. Is a single vote on a single bill enough? My guideline is this: The more aggressively, the more centrally, an official participates in a policy struggle, the more reasonable it is to out him.

A counterargument could be made in defense of hypocrisy or more precisely for its irrelevance; a policy should stand on its merits, not on its advocates' conduct. That may be so in the dispassionate discourse of academe (at least idealized academe), but in the hurly-burly of political life, the human factor is meaningful and often invoked by politicians themselves—their military service, their religious observance, their grim-lipped stand-by-their-lying-man wives.

Neither of these positions permits spreading false rumors; the obligation to be truthful remains. And it should be noted that Spokane's mayor, Jim West, is in hot water over accusations of favoritism and of having molested two boys (which he denies), not for being gay per se (which is, of course, not remotely discreditable).

A clarification: my outing protocol would also apply when an official unhypocritically supports a policy. It would be worth mentioning if a senator who champions, say, tax breaks for cattle ranchers is himself a rancher (or a cow). Self-interest is noteworthy in public debate. But it is hypocrisy that more often inspires the urge to out; it is denying others the right to do what we ourselves enjoy that provokes contempt.

## CAMPAIGN CONTRIBUTION

*Friends and I have been contributing money to a leading Democratic presidential candidate. We are, however, Republicans. We feel that President Bush has a better chance of reelection running against this candidate. We considered donating to the president's reelection campaign but concluded that it had enough money and this would put our dollars to better use. This could go awfully wrong, but is it unethical?*

*—R. Rothschild, New York*

No election law demands sincerity from campaign contributors. Of course, there are legal campaign tactics that most of us would regard as unethical—appealing to racism, for example, or hammering at the private conduct of an opponent's family members. But the target of such actions would surely object to them, and that's not a bad test, one that your financial maneuver would pass. Were you to reveal to, for example, Howard Dean your real motive for donating to his campaign, he would still cash your check.

Perhaps you feel uneasy because your contributing to a Democrat is a kind of lie, an expression of admiration for someone you actually condemn. By contrast, directly supporting your true candidate or openly attacking his opponents is honest and straightforward. To game the system by trying to promote a pushover for the president to flatten in November requires a falsehood, or at least a bit of trickery.

Although this is not the lofty version of democracy we imagine Jefferson applauding, it is no rougher than ordinary political life. Such things are not unknown among those of varying ideologies. It was both pro- and antislavery factions who rushed people to Missouri so they could vote for that state's constitution. More recently, LBJ was not above employing arm-twisting tactics to pass civil rights and antipoverty legislation. American democracy can be a bloody business, and while one has an obligation to do no harm, one does not have an ethical obligation to campaign according to a more demure set of guidelines than one's opponent. I detest the influence of big money in politics, but I can't imagine how a presidential candidate can take a vow of poverty and still prevail.

As you suggest, there is the conscience-cleansing possibility of an unsuspected outcome: fueled by the massive funds you've provided, Dr. Dean roars on to victory.

### NOISY AND NOSY

*Recently my future son-in-law, an electronics expert, adjusted my sound system. The result was a piercingly accurate rendition of jazz recordings, symphonies, and action-adventure cable movies, as well as several noise complaints from neighbors. When the police arrived for the second time, I demanded the name of the complainant but the policeman refused to provide it. Don't I have the right to face my accuser?*

*—David Graham Halliday, Naugatuck, CT*

You have the right to face your accuser in a court of law, but you have no moral right to know who complained about neighborhood noise. Such a complaint is just one person's opinion, meant to prod the police to see if there are in fact high-decibel antics taking place; you've not yet risen to the impressive status of the accused. At this point, there's real social good in not revealing who complained. To do so would promote tension between neighbors and, even worse, might leave some folks too fearful of retribution to make legitimate complaints.

"Anonymous complaints are common in police work," says David Feige, a former criminal-defense lawyer. But he adds that there is "a whole body of law surrounding the question of how much more than a mere anonymous tip is enough to search someone, etc." In your situation, I'd say it was reasonable of the police to ring your doorbell, but if that tip was all they had to go on, and they heard no racket, they'd be out of line to search your house without permission.

Having little to go on myself (beyond the repeated visits of the cops to your place), I would add the general observation that we each have a duty to keep the volume low enough not to crack the plaster in the house next door or to threaten a neighbor's sleep, "the innocent sleep, sleep that knits up the ravell'd sleave of care, the death of each day's life, sore labour's bath, balm of hurt minds, great nature's second course, chief nourisher in life's feast . . ."—wait, sorry, where was I?—even if an electronics expert has "adjusted" our sound system to make that possible.

---

### GRAND JUROR

*I'm on a grand jury. We've been given cases involving someone who views pornography on his computer behind locked doors and someone caught in the presence of marijuana. The assistant DA indicates that I shouldn't abstain from voting, but my conscience won't let me sleep if I make felons out of such people. May I vote not to indict?*

*—L.D., Fountain Hills, AZ*

Yours is a common response to punishments deemed disproportional to the crime: jurors are often reluctant to convict—or in your case, indict—even someone they believe broke the law. In this way, legislators who respond to perceived social problems by increasing the harshness of the penalties are being counterproductive, making it less likely that transgressors will be punished and others deterred.

But where does that leave you? May you vote not to indict even when you think a crime has occurred? Ethically, you may. Legally, it's debatable. The attorneys I consulted were not unanimous, but most agreed that, unlike petit jurors who must convict if the evidence warrants, grand jurors "are entirely free to charge what the government proposes, to charge differently, or not charge at all," as Claudia Conway, a capital defender with New York's Legal Aid Society, put it. Even without disavowing the marijuana law, for example, you might honorably find it not applicable in this case. Another option you've overlooked: indict not for a felony but for a lesser charge.

One reason we use grand juries instead of going directly to trial is to forestall overzealous prosecutors. Just as a district attorney "is not obliged to prosecute every crime or seek an indictment in every case," according to Donna Lieberman, head of the New York Civil Liberties Union, grand jurors enjoy similar discretion. Thus, a sensible and ethical grand jury would discourage a DA from throwing the book at every jaywalker in town while he ignored murderers. Grand jurors should not merely rubber-stamp the government's wishes but should act as the conscience of the community—particularly important in a forum where the accused cannot present a defense or call witnesses or introduce evidence.

Such independence can be exercised ethically or unethically. Employing the more radical tactic of jury nullification in a criminal trial, some all-white juries in the Jim Crow South shamefully refused to convict white men for killing African Americans.

But again, honorable lawyers differ. Barnett Lotstein, a special assistant county attorney in Phoenix, articulates the conservative (and not uncommon) position: "The obligation and the oath a grand juror takes is to return an indictment if probable cause exists." Andrew G. Celli Jr., former chief of the New York State Attorney General's civil rights bureau, finds middle ground, allowing grand jurors to check a DA's imprudence but not to invalidate the law, saying, "You may not try to accomplish in the jury room what you've failed to achieve at the ballot box." Celli is persuasive: he respects the law but allows ethics to thwart its unwise application and you to calm a nagging conscience.

---

### KNOWN SPEEDER

*A friend was caught by police radar going 51 in a 35 miles-per-hour zone. In front of his children, he admitted that he was speeding but asked if I knew a lawyer to help him fight the ticket. I told him I thought he should accept the consequences, learn from the experience, and give his children a lesson in ethics. He looked at me as if I were from Mars. Shouldn't he just pay the ticket?*

*—Bruce Pellegrino, Far Hills, NJ*

Even those who think themselves guilty are entitled to their day in court, and there is civic virtue in their exercising this right. A trial is a way to hold officials accountable. Was the radar gun accurate? Was the speed zone clearly marked? Did the police officer behave properly? And what, given all the circumstances, is an appropriate punishment? Little of this could be scrutinized if everyone simply paid the ticket. It would be a court-clogging nightmare if each self-confessed speeder demanded a trial, but it is a fine thing if, now and then, some do.

The very process of traffic court encourages putting in an appearance. Here in New York even if you are unambiguously guilty, showing up in court often results in a lower fine than if you'd simply mailed in the ticket and a check. Some judges reconsider punishment, including points on the license, based on facts that emerge at a hearing. To go to court is not to hoodwink anybody or to work the system but is merely another legitimate response. If I were to endorse your more austere position, then why would I even wait for a cop to stop me in the first place? If I know I am speeding, shouldn't I just ticket myself and send in some money for the accompanying fine?

Yours is also a variation on a question sometimes put to lawyers, public defenders in particular, about the propriety of defending a "guilty" client. Another answer is that "guilt" in this sense is a legal determination that can only be made in a court of law. James Boswell, himself a lawyer, once asked his mentor about the propriety of a lawyer's "supporting a cause which you know to be bad," to which Dr. Johnson replied: "Sir, you do not know it to be good or bad till the Judge determines it. . . . An argument which does not convince yourself, may convince the Judge to whom you urge it: and if it does convince him, why, then, Sir, you are wrong, and he is right."

**UPDATE**: Pellegrino's friend paid the ticket, more as a matter of convenience than high principle.

**CONFIRMATION**: Pellegrino is not from Mars but was born and raised on this planet.

# *Money*

A COUPLE OF YEARS AGO, SINGER MILEY CYRUS, BELOVED BY TWEENS THE world over, announced that her forty-five–city tour would go paperless to thwart scalpers, the first major tour to do so. Ticketmaster, the company handling sales, offered only e-tickets and deployed other innovative anti-scalping technologies at each venue. But isn't scalping harmless, even beneficial—the very essence of American capitalism? Isn't it just another salubrious manifestation of the free market: people choose to exchange money for goods or services or innocuous acoustic treacle?

No. Cyrus is a teenage Joan of Arc (as was Joan of Arc, of course, though she was indifferent to the price of concert tickets). Scalping robs performers, bars less well-off fans from hot shows, and exacerbates the dismal effects of a money-talks society.

To give scalping its due, many states have legalized it. If Cyrus resented the prices that scalpers command, she was free to raise what she charged for tickets, which ranged from $39.50 to $79.50. It may vex her that someone who contributes no perky songs or peppy dances to the big tour should profit from her hard work, but scalpers and their advocates counter that they contribute by using the free market to distribute a scarce commodity efficiently. If it's okay to resell a car or a house, why not a concert ticket?

Here's why. Not every purchase involves a commodity. An airline ticket and a downloaded song, for example, are better seen as a license to enjoy a service. (If anyone can be said to "enjoy" air travel.) Also objectionable, particularly to Bruce Springsteen—like Cyrus, an ardent anti-scalper—are those occasions when scalpers raise prices and frustrate an artist's wish to perform for true and loyal fans, not just wealthy Mileyites or Bruce-come-latelies. (The tickets for his final shows in Giants Stadium were priced between $33 and $98, but weeks before they officially went on sale, scalpers were demanding ten times face value.)

Scalpers respond with a metaphysical question: who is a true Miley Cyrus fan? Anyone who watches *Hannah Montana*? Someone who shrieks ecstatically at the mention of Cyrus's name? Who swoons? Scalping provides a way to calibrate a fan's passion by what she is willing to pay for a ticket. "I love Miley $50 worth." "Well, I love her $100 worth."

It would be splendid if science could quantify desire, neatly settling many a lovers' quarrel (as Frank Loesser does in this lyric from *Guys and Dolls*, "I love you a bushel and a peck") but this remains a golden dream. Markets tend to allocate tickets not to the fan with the greatest passion but the thickest wallet.

A hypothetical $600 ticket—Cyrus's shows have commanded that— is a daunting purchase for most of us but a mere bagatelle to, for example, Michael Bloomberg, America's eighth wealthiest man. If a willingness to pay is to be the gauge of Mileymania, it must be measured not in absolute dollars but as a percentage of wealth. Would you give up a 20th of a percent of everything you own to see her? A 10th?

The median worth of an American family is roughly $120,000. To snare that $600 ticket, that family must spend half a percent of all it's got. Bloomberg is worth about $20 billion. To demonstrate equal ardor for Miley, half a percent of his worth, he must pony up $100 million. I hope he enjoys the show.

Such a proportional approach is not unprecedented. Courts consider ability to pay when determining punitive damages. Some countries peg traffic fines to income. Recently in Finland, a wealthy driver clocked doing 82 kpm in a 60 kpm zone received a ticket for 112,000 euros, a record. A speeder with a more ordinary income would have been assessed a more conventional fine.

But even if scalpers set prices this way, they would still do social harm. Earning power should not be the sole criterion by which the ordinary joys of life are allocated. There is much to be said for broad access to education, literature, drama. We are rightly proud of the New York Public Library, Stuyvesant High School, Shakespeare in the Park. Indeed, Olmsted and Vaux, the designers of that park, conceived of Central Park not only as an oasis of beauty and serenity, but also as an institution of democracy, open to all. Inclusiveness, community, an egalitarian society: these are the civic virtues that scalping corrodes. And while Cyrus tickets are not free, scalping unnecessarily expands the dominion of cash.

Here's my simple suggestion for ending scalping overnight: print the buyer's name on the tickets and then check the name against his ID at the gate. (Many venues—the Brooklyn Academy of Music, for example—already print tickets this way; no new technology required. And we're all used to having our ID checked to verify our name on an airline ticket or even to enter office buildings.)

Flexibility would be sacrificed when employing this solution. If something came up at the last minute that kept you from a show, you couldn't simply give your tickets to a pal at work. But you could still order tickets as gifts, the seller merely prints the recipient's name—your friend, your child—on the tickets at the time of purchase. In return for some small inconvenience, there would be big rewards: greater control for the artist, greater access for the ordinary fan, greater virtue for the community.

**UPDATE**: After I made this lucid argument, utterly exploding any moral justification for scalping, some readers inexplicably remained unconvinced. Many championed ticket reselling (the pretty term for scalping) as the wholesome operation of the free market. Here's the problem: Markets function best when supply can adjust to demand. But despite astonishing advances in biotechnology, science remains unable to increase the supply of Miley Cyruses. (Whether that is good or bad, I leave to music critics.) Given her popularity, her shows will necessarily be in short supply. The question of how to allocate that supply is inescapable. I'm not persuaded that virtue requires the most popular singers to perform only for the people with the most money, which is what market solutions, including scalping, generally amount to.

Some readers insist that concert tickets are in their very pith and marrow a commodity, as if that were a law of nature. Not so. We're simply used to thinking of them that way. There is no divine right to resell a ticket. Proposals to restrict or even forbid resales must be judged on their merits. Tickets to New York's Shakespeare in the Park, for example, are distributed free and may not be resold, a wise stricture intended to preserve an essential element of the experience: free Shakespeare for all. Or at least the many, not just the moneyed.

I do agree with those critics who note that things can come up at the last minute that keep even the most eager fans from attending a show. Why should they be out the cost of a ticket? One clever reader suggests a refinement to my proposal: "Make tickets fully refundable up to, say, twenty-four hours before the event for a small fee." If the fee is high enough to discourage folks from buying tickets they don't seriously intend to use, this should work well. It is akin to refundable and nonrefundable airline tickets or to travel insurance.

One common thread ran through the comments: everybody loathes Ticketmaster, for assorted reasons, with the wonderful diversity that makes our country so vibrant. If James Bond movies and other international thrillers weary of their casts of modern stock villains—drug dealers, terrorists, polluting corporations—Ticketmaster is waiting in the wings, universally despised. And if such a movie proved incredibly popular and were then transmuted into a hit Broadway musical, Ticketmaster itself could scalp—sorry, resell—tickets to it.

## RANDOM ACTS OF CHEATING

*As a friend and I left a museum, we spontaneously offered our stubs to a couple waiting to buy tickets so they could enter without paying. They seemed bewildered and reluctant to accept. Our motivation was not to cheat the museum but to give two random strangers an unexpected and pleasant surprise. Some of our friends think we shouldn't help anyone avoid paying the admission charge. What is your opinion?*

—*Kristin Fehlauer, New York*

When a friend and I broke into a Harley-Davidson showroom and handed out motorcycles to passersby, our motive was not to harm the dealer but, like you, only to perform an act of kindness for bewildered strangers. Or that would have been the motive had we actually done this.

Despite your benign intentions, what you call a "pleasant surprise," a less puckish person—me, for instance—could call "helping a couple of tourists cheat their way into the museum." And if they get caught and are tossed out into the gutter, they'll have one of those kooky "only in New York" anecdotes to tell their friends. They'll always remember your kindness.

Some argue that no museum should charge admission, certainly no museum that receives public funds. To do so puts an essential experience of civilized life out of reach of many families. Even when one can afford the admissions fee, the experience is transformed from a routine pleasure to a special event. Indeed, for many years New York's museums, like its libraries and parks, were free to all. In Washington, DC, the Smithsonian's museums on the Mall still charge no admission. However, what you and your friend were doing was not protesting the museum's ticket policy; it was an impromptu—if unintended—inducement to chicanery.

If you want to give someone a gift, you must pay for it yourself; so take out your wallet and buy a couple of passes. Or give a random stranger one of those Vermeer note cards, or a Vermeer T-shirt, or Vermeer pants; I know people are just nuts about Vermeer. And about pants.

### TAXING PROBLEM

*A self-employed person provides a service for me. If I pay cash, he gives me a 10 percent discount. He has confided that this cash is not reported to the government. Over the course of a year, the 10 percent discount saves me several hundred dollars. I know this is a long-held practice in many businesses, but is it ethical for me and the person I hire?*

*—B.H., New Hampshire*

If you know that this person is a tax cheat—and you do—it is unethical to abet his deceit and profit by doing so. Were you uncertain what this miscreant was up to, the situation would be murkier. Some businesses legitimately offer discounts to cash-paying customers so as to avoid credit-card fees. Some people simply find cash more convenient or enjoy wallowing in big piles of the stuff, like Scrooge McDuck. But there's insufficient murk in this situation to justify your playing along.

Ethics aside, there is another compelling reason to shun this little swindle. As a legal matter, says one accountant I spoke to, a business generally has "no tax code–related requirement to report his supplier's activities, unless he is an attorney or possibly a CPA or other tax professional." However, you may have an obligation to issue this person a 1099, which will certainly call attention to your transactions and may well get this cash fancier into trouble with the IRS.

Incidentally, a practice being "long-held" does not cleanse it; Viking raids were common for centuries. Typhus, same deal.

## SUSHI MONEY

*My friend and I met for dinner at a Japanese restaurant. The tab was $60, and we split it, paying $30 each. My friend told me that he'd expense his own share of the meal. (He gets reimbursed up to $25 by his boss.) Thus, he paid $5 for dinner, while I paid $30. Was this fair, or should we have divided the $25 reimbursement, thereby paying $17.50 each?*

—*Gregg Reed, New York*

You are each responsible for half the bill. How your friend got the money to cover his end is beside the point, whether he earned it as a job perk, inherited it from a long-lost relative, or got it by dancing on the sushi bar and encouraging patrons to toss coins (assuming he didn't run afoul of the health code or the estate of Bob Fosse). Further, you could argue that it is his employer's understanding that this reimbursement is to feed himself, not his pal.

## BEGGING: THE QUESTION

*I'm going to India in a couple of weeks, and I'm troubled by the prospect of children begging for money. Do I give them money or food or neither? If I give money, exploitative adults may take it. My family regularly contributes to Indian charities, but that is small consolation in these heartbreaking situations. What do I do?*

—*D.S., Minnesota*

Your desire to help a child in distress is commendable, whichever of those options you choose. The spectacle of a suffering child is so harrowing, our inability to relieve that suffering so demoralizing, that even experts differ about how best to respond. Martha Nussbaum, a professor of law and ethics at the University of Chicago, who has devoted much work to third-world poverty, told me, "My Indian activist friends have different views about giving anything to beggars. Some do it occasionally, some make a policy of not doing it."

It can be argued that giving money to beggars sustains a culture of begging and, in the most horrifying cases, motivates criminals to force children to beg and even to maim children to make their situations seem more poignant, and thus make their begging more profitable. But it is poverty itself, not ad hoc generosity, that makes begging persist. The real, albeit daunting, solution is to lift these children—these nations—out of poverty. That is the approach Nussbaum herself takes, as your family does, by steadily contributing to organizations with the expertise and commitment to take on this challenge. "I think that UNICEF is probably the best choice," she says, "since it has excellent programs in India." But there are many groups doing admirable work.

Less significant than how you give is that you give, despite the sense of futility that the spectacle of widespread poverty, particularly of children in poverty, can induce. "To wipe all tears from off all faces is a task too hard for mortals; but to alleviate misfortunes is often within the most limited power: yet the opportunities which every day affords of relieving the most wretched of human beings are overlooked and neglected with equal disregard of policy and goodness," wrote Dr. Johnson in the *Rambler* in 1751. As then, so now.

**UPDATE:** D.S. has returned from India where she responded "on a case-by-case basis." She sometimes gave money to a child whose parents were present and who seemed by their dress to be rural migrants, newly arrived in the city and struggling to find work. More often, she gave food, particularly to children she feared might be exploited by adults who would steal her donated money.

### BUMP COMP

*Flying from San Francisco to White Plains on business, I was involuntarily bumped from my flight, rebooked twenty-four hours later and, after lengthy negotiation, given $800, about $100 more than the cost of my ticket—there is a formula for such things—as compensation. Who gets the $800, me or the client who paid my travel expenses?*

*—Name withheld, San Francisco*

You. The airline compensated you for your hassle; it did not waive the cost of your ticket. That remained what it always was and must be reimbursed by the client. If you'd played a hypothetical in-flight scratch ticket—airlines are eager to find new sources of revenue—and hit, that money would be yours, too. Think of it this way: you won an annoying and inconvenient lottery.

**UPDATE**: This traveler kept the money, likening it to a gift from the airline. He informed the contractor who got him the job, who was okay with it, but the contractor did not inform the client.

### VIATICAL

*A friend and I disagree on the ethics of an investment he wants to make. The investment involves buying at a discount the life insurance of terminally ill individuals who want proceeds from their policies before their demise. My friend sees this as helping the "victim" receive funds now. I see it as making money from someone's death. You?*

*—Stanley Farb, Jeffersonville, PA*

Your friend would indeed profit from someone's death—as do morticians, limousine drivers, and florists. That in itself is not discreditable, assuming he does not hasten that death (by, for instance, running someone over with the limo or bludgeoning him with a bouquet). You might better see that insurance policy as akin to any asset a person sells to raise cash: a car, a savings bond, a record collection. If you buy it at a fair price—that ambiguous but significant term—you do no wrong.

Perhaps what disturbs you is the macabre aspect of this practice. When a company sells someone life insurance, it is betting that he is immortal: the longer he lives, the longer he pays premiums, the more money the company makes. It has an interest in his robust good health. When you engage in what is known as viatical practices, you hope the insured will die tomorrow, if not this afternoon. The more quickly he goes, the sooner you get paid. You have an interest in his swift demise.

Viatical practices expanded in the '80s as AIDS cases increased. Some patients, under dire financial pressure, sold their insurance policies, and some buyers were denounced for exploiting that dreadful vulnerability. Such censure presumes that the seller did not choose freely; indeed, he had no choice at all. Yet, responding to necessity needn't be dishonorable; we all require food but do not revile the grocer who provides it. We do, however, have little good to say about those who sell $10 hotdogs to airport travelers or $100 hotdogs to hurricane victims— those who take unfair advantage of our lack of choice. Thus, we must be mindful of the elusive distinction between profit and profiteering.

The real solution to this problem? Make affordable health care available to all, and the viatical market will diminish.

## KNOCKOFFS VS. COUNTERFEITS

*A friend tells me I must stop buying handbags from street vendors on Fifth Avenue in midtown. I never buy bags with logos on them—Kate Spade,*

*Louis Vuitton, etc.—just the nice generic ones. They're so much cheaper than in the stores. Must I stop?*

*—Valerie Brett, Monmouth Beach, NJ*

You are right to shun counterfeit handbags, but you may buy knock-offs, which are not the same thing. A knockoff apes the appearance of the original but does not represent itself as other than it is. It is not built around fraud (and probably not skillfully hand-stitched fine leather either). Nor does a knockoff run afoul of trademark law. Drawing on other people's work—in fashion, in art, in literature—is how ideas spread through the culture. (Is Eric Clapton a knockoff Robert Johnson? Is that a bad thing? Would absorbing the styles of three or four additional guitar greats make him more virtuous?) If absolute originality were the summum bonum, how would we get along without network television?

More potent arguments could be made against unlicensed street vendors—their sometimes lighthearted attitude toward paying taxes, your difficulty getting a refund from a merchant who is vigorously nomadic—but neither these nor your fear for the well-being of Louis Vuitton compels you to eschew them.

---

**LINE UP**

*I was at the counter of an Amtrak train café car, when a man entered, saw the very long line, and announced that he would pay five dollars to whomever would buy him two beers. A woman in line just behind me started to accept, when I told this man he should wait like the rest of us. He turned and walked out, either to the back of the line or to parts unknown. Was I right, or was his offer legitimate?*

*—David Brenner, New York*

Yes, you were; no, it wasn't. The beer-seeker tried to violate the fundamental law of the line—first come, first served—by leaping to the front on the springboard of his wallet. And while his five dollars might have compensated that one woman for being slightly inconvenienced, he offered nothing to those behind her who'd have to wait just a bit longer. Thus, she herself would have acted badly, in effect selling her place at the front of the line without actually vacating it.

Worse still, the line being long, Amtrak's beer supply might have run dry before satisfying all the thirsty and courteous passengers who were waiting their turns. The would-be line-jumper had no right to snatch up a possibly scarce resource.

There's another aspect of this situation that has nothing to do with ethics but is still disturbing to contemplate. Having money can spare us some hassles, and that's fine. But should every vexation in life be curable with cash, exempting those with money, and afflicting those without? True, this sort of thing happens often, first-class air travelers can avoid long security lines and inhumanly cramped seats. But do we want our country organized on the model of air travel?

An egalitarian democratic society must include shared experiences, even trivial ones like this. We are unlikely to feel that we are all in it together when it comes to weighty matters if we rarely are in it together when it comes to the hassles of daily life. Even if the man in the beer line had offered every single person in that line a few bucks to cut in front of them, they would have had the right to accept his bribe, but by kowtowing to his cash, that decision would have been unfortunate.

## RESTOCK THE MINIBAR

*When I checked into a hotel in California, I was starving, so I ate the $6 box of Oreos from the minibar. Later that day, I walked down the street to* *a convenience store, bought an identical box for $2.50, and replenished the minibar before the hotel had a chance to restock it. Was this proper? My view is "no harm, no foul." In fact, my box was fresher: the Oreos I ate were going to expire three months before the box I replaced them with.*

*—David Lat, New York*

I disagree. You might with similar logic stop by the Staples Center and present vendors with a bottle of the brand of beer you drank at the Lakers game last night. I don't think they would be inclined to refund your money.

The hotel is not providing just a product but also a service—the convenience of having cookies available right in your room, 24-7. To create this utopia of constant confectionary access, the hotel had to pay someone to travel the world and select the finest vintage cookies, order the Oreos, and stock the minibar. You enjoyed that service; you must pay the (ridiculously high) price.

It would be a different matter if you'd brought along that very same box of Oreos when you checked in—do you travel with a suitcase full of sweets?—and eaten them without ever unlocking the minibar. Although the final disposition of cookies would have been similar—a boxful in the minibar, a boxful in your belly—since you hadn't availed yourself of a hotel service, you wouldn't have to pay for it.

---

### MARRY AND DIE IN HASTE . . .

*Four months after he remarried, my father died in an accident. During his brief second marriage, he often told family and friends, "What's mine is mine, and what's hers is hers," indicating that he wanted his estate to go to me and my brother, as stipulated in his will. (My mother died from cancer about five years ago.) But New York law allows a spouse to claim about one-third of that, and his widow intends to, despite my father's wishes, although she has resources of her own. This is legal, but is it ethical?*

*—Name withheld, Long Island*

You might think your father meant to leave everything to you and your brother, but he chose to marry in New York, where he knew or should have known that the law sees it differently. And, since he had a will, surely the lawyer who drafted it was familiar with this law. I sympathize with your disappointment but do not agree that the widow has a moral obligation to renounce her inheritance or that there's something morally superior in the money going to you and your brother.

Had your father wanted to give less to his widow and more to his children, he could have consulted a trusts and estates attorney before he remarried and perhaps bestowed cars or cash or country houses on you fellows. But he did not. Joanna Grossman, a law professor at Hofstra University with expertise in wills and family law, says that your father had still more options, "If the father and his wife had in fact agreed that neither would inherit from the other, they could have cemented that agreement easily with a written waiver."

It is possible that he or his lawyer simply erred, believing that his written will would prevail, but you've no evidence of that. It is equally plausible that your father told you one thing and his wife-to-be something else and that she is acting in accordance with his wishes, however dismaying you may find them.

Grossman adds, "New York is actually quite stingy in providing for a spouse omitted by a premarital will; in most other states, she would be entitled to even more." So perhaps you're better off than you realize.

# *Animals*

IN WRITING THE COLUMN, ONE SURPRISE THAT I SUPPOSE SHOULD NOT have been surprising was how passionately people feel about animals. If you want more mail, write something—anything—about an animal. It will be ferocious mail—no matter how firmly you urge people to act kindly toward animals, you haven't done enough. If you suggest someone should get a second job to earn enough to care for her cat, you will be condemned for not insisting she take a third job.

We are also a gun-loving nation, shooting to death about 30,000 people a year; about 40 percent of those are murders, more than half are suicides. There aren't a lot of things at which America leads the world. For example, we do no better than seventeenth in any facet of a recent international study of educational accomplishment. Life expectancy?

Infant mortality? Nothing to be proud of. But we're number one in gun ownership and shooting ourselves and our fellow citizens. Throw in our third propensity, a devotion to religion, and it is astonishing that one seldom sees a bumper sticker proclaiming the primacy of "Guns, God, Cats."

It is when we think about shooting animals that our two primary passions collide. When I began writing the column, I wondered if this paradox could be resolved by recognizing two separate constituencies: animal lovers and hunters. But I no longer think that is the case, many hunters genuinely love animals. (Although the converse might not be true.) But perhaps ethical thought can reconcile these two loves, albeit to the detriment of hunting for sport.

A few years ago, the Interior Department ruled that wolves had sufficiently increased in numbers in the Western continental United States to once again allow some wolf hunting in Idaho and Montana, among other states. A moral argument might be mustered for the right to hunt for food and to manage wildlife populations, but surely some of the more than 14,000 people who bought wolf-hunting licenses in those two states are interested in neither wolf sandwiches nor animal husbandry: they simply enjoy hunting. Is it morally acceptable to kill a wolf for the fun of it?

Unsurprisingly, I believe it is wrong to inflict pain and death unnecessarily on a creature capable of suffering. While this belief might not compel us to be vegetarians, it does demand significant changes in the way we raise animals for food and precludes wolf hunting as a form of entertainment. I concede all putatively practical justifications for hunting and repudiate only the idea that hunting is a legitimate recreation. It is those who enjoy hunting as sport who must construct a moral defense for their fun; a wolf need not make a case for its not being shot in Montana. I'm not persuaded that hunters have made that case.

Some declare that hunting is a cherished tradition in their region or for their family. But having done something in the past is insufficient to justify its repetition. It was traditional in my family to be roughed up each spring during pogrom season, a time-honored custom in our part of Russia, and one we gladly abandoned when my grandparents immigrated to America.

Some note that hunting is a challenging activity. No doubt. But not everything difficult is desirable. Or ethical. Pickpocketing, too, is tough.

There are people who find it fulfilling to cultivate shooting skills, learn to track, take a walk in the woods, maybe bring the kids and make it a bonding experience, or bring a couple of buddies and make it a beer experience or just a chance to avoid spending time with the spouse. All of these might be amiable ways to beguile the time, but none need culminate with a killing. Inflicting death is not an acceptable leisure activity.

That hunting is widely regarded as a sport is undeniable. Indeed, an article about the Idaho wolf hunt ran in the sports section of the *Los Angeles Times*, in a subsection called "Outposts—outdoors, action, adventure." It sounds like a Jerry Bruckheimer movie. But this is a curious designation. In other sports, participation is voluntary. No sports fan, boozing happily at a tailgate party, is knocked on the head and shanghaied into the Green Bay Packers' defensive line, like a sailor impressed into Nelson's navy. But in hunting, the wolf doesn't get a say.

And while other sports are criticized for cruelty to animals—horse racing comes to mind—such diversions are at least potentially amenable to reform. Improvements in training, diet, veterinary care could be mandated. What would reform even mean in hunting? Should we genetically engineer a superwolf and teach it to shoot back? (Another Bruckheimer movie.) In any case, misconduct in one arena does not justify it in another.

Beyond what it inflicts on the hunted—pain and death—hunting damages the hunter. It coarsens us. It inures us to suffering. One measure of a society is how it treats the weak and vulnerable, including animals, including those deemed "wild" or outside the bonds of society. While it is hard to see the bleak parade of human history as an unbroken march of moral progress, there is something hopeful in Western cultures coming to regard animals not just as property, as things to be used any way we wished, but as beings entitled to legal protection.

We had room for improvement. As recently as the eighteenth century, various forms of animal torture were popular entertainments: bullbaiting, bearbaiting, cockfighting, dogfighting. Francis Place, British reformer and diarist, writing in 1835, describes a scene of recreation earlier in the century: "In the Long Fields were several large ponds; the amusements here were duck-hunting and badger-baiting; they would throw a cat into the water and set dogs at her; great cruelty was constantly practiced and the most abominable scenes used to take place."

The ensuing advance of animal protection law gives us cause for pride. In 1822, the British passed Richard Martin's Act to Prevent the Cruel and Improper Treatment of Cattle, perhaps the world's first parliamentary legislation for animal welfare. In 1835, the British banned bull- and bearbaiting as well as cock- and dogfighting. A 1911 measure ratified the legal concept of "causing unnecessary suffering." It is difficult to see hunting wolves for pleasure as other than a retreat from that ideal.

When I made these arguments in the *Times*, the reader response was—unsurprisingly—fierce. Many readers seemed not to have noticed that I conceded the pragmatic grounds for hunting and argued against it only as entertainment. These respondents went ahead anyway and championed hunting as animal management. (I blame the schools, maybe it was that flirtation with phonics.) Incidentally, *managing* is now my favorite euphemism for *killing*. I'm afraid your uncle was managed by a drunk driver. "Deranged Sociopath Goes on Cross-Country Managing Spree."

A few readers took the belligerent, mind-your-own-business-city-slicker approach. One wrote, "If you oppose hunting, don't hunt." But it would be a curious moral code that said only, "If you oppose burglary, don't burgle."

I was surprised how many comments asserted that wolves themselves kill other animals in grotesque ways and with dubious motives, as if our hunting them were a form of social justice: they get what's coming to them. They're no darn good.

Some comments made a broader antigun argument. I did not. Disclosure: when my sister and I were young, our dad taught us to shoot; we quite liked it and did it often. He grew up in rural South Carolina during the Depression and hunted for food. But in eastern Pennsylvania, where he and my mother raised us, and where there was a big dip in the population of my high school each year when deer season began, I never knew my dad to hunt. He did not confirm this, but I always believed it was because he'd seen enough killing during the war.

## FIGHTING LIKE CATS AND BIRDS

*Our backyard bird feeders predate our cat, who has turned out to be quite a hunter. Once in a while he will kill or trap a bird; he often brings them alive into the house and we've rescued quite a few. Is it inhumane to fill a bird feeder when the possibility of attack may occur?*

—*B. A. McCann, San Jose, CA*

It is inhumane to use a feeder as a snack bar for cats, luring songbirds to their doom. Indeed, those firebrands at the Audubon Society assert that if you use a feeder, you must never let your cat outside. John Bianchi, a spokesman for the group, notes that cats kill millions of birds every year, and there's nothing natural about it. "Domestic cats are not wild animals," he says. "They were bred to hunt and kill even when they are not hungry, to protect granaries." The invocation of nature red in tooth and claw is okay for some predators but not cats. Feeders attract raptors, Bianchi says, but "a hawk will take one songbird and fly off with it—a cat will stay near the feeder all day and kill five or six birds."

The Audubon Society advocates that cats always be kept indoors, even if you have no feeder—not just to protect birds but for the cat's own good. "Cats allowed outdoors live much shorter lives," says Bianchi, "and feral cats the shortest of all, only three years on average."

However, many people believe that their cats are happier if allowed to roam. And while it is tough to gauge an animal's contentment, a consideration of quality of life is a necessary part of this decision. If you do allow your cat to roam, then consider the classic solution: bell the cat. A big heavy bell that slows it down. No, no—a regular-size bell that gives the birds a fighting . . . no, flying, chance.

England's Royal Society for the Protection of Birds takes a more moderate line. Spokeswoman Sarah Niemann says, "Unless predation at a feeding station is high, then with care there is surely no reason not to feed the birds." Feeders should be positioned so that a cat cannot lie in wait, unseen by the birds, and that cats sometimes be kept indoors— "when the birds are most vulnerable, at least an hour before sunset and an hour after sunrise."

The RSPB's call for peaceful coexistence is reasonable, allowing you and the birds to enjoy your feeder without turning it into a tiny gladiatorial arena for bird-cat combat, a blood sport that tends to be awfully one-sided.

## ROAD KILLER

*When I'm mountain biking, I sometimes find a small animal (e.g., snake or lizard) that was accidentally injured by another biker or hiker and appears to be suffering. I want to help, but I am far from the nearest veterinarian. Usually I move the creature off the trail and hope it will live, but I wonder about putting it out of its misery. What should I do next time?*

*—S.S., California*

Dr. Rebecca Campbell, a veterinarian, shares your view of the situation, noting that a seriously injured small animal "will almost certainly die an agonizing death by starvation, dehydration, or predation. The best thing to do is get the creature to a vet, but if that's not possible you should humanely kill a little creature like a snake or lizard found on a trail." Campbell suggests doing this quickly. "Breaking its neck is best, but he risks a snakebite if he tries that. Unfortunately, a trail biker would probably have to crush its little head with a rock, unless he carries a machete in his pack."

A limitation of this advice is that it asks an ordinary person to diagnose an injury, assess the chances of recovery, and kill a small creature, something even those who accept euthanasia in principle may find disturbing in practice. And it leaves unanswered this question: how small is a small creature? Certainly, if you found an injured person on the trail, you'd take extraordinary measures to render aid. Most of us value the life of a human being, a creature with self-awareness and a sense of its past and future, more highly than that of a lizard. Yet while you may be willing to euthanize a lizard, what about a fox, a cat, a dog?

That said, given the actual circumstances you've found yourself in, Campbell's recommendation, while stringent, is reasonable and humane. Where death is inevitable, minimizing suffering should be your first concern.

---

### SWIM WITH DOLPHINS

*On my list of things I've always wanted to do before I die is swim with dolphins. But I am a devout vegetarian and concerned about animal rights and conservation. Would it be wrong for me to swim with dolphins if they were bred in captivity? Would I be a hypocrite and be giving my money to perpetuate something I was against?*

*—K.S., New York*

I sympathize. It's been my lifelong dream to swim with Meg Ryan, but I've come to realize that she—or any of our beloved actors—ought not be conscripted in such ways for my pleasure. The Humane Society of the United States, like other organizations concerned about animals, has a similar stance on dolphins. It asserts that swim-with-dolphin programs "pose an immediate threat to the safety of both human and dolphin participants." And while, as you suggest, the HSUS regards the capture of wild dolphins to entertain humans as a greater sin than exploiting dolphins raised in captivity, the organization condemns both practices, asserting that these marine mammals suffer and sometimes die in such programs.

You needn't be a vegetarian to embrace this argument. There are times when we may exploit animals—for example, for food (although vegetarians might argue this point) or essential medical research—but vacation fun is not such a case. Are there no water parks? Are there no casinos? Are there no underwater casinos?

Some say that a dolphin swim offers autistic children therapeutic benefits unobtainable elsewhere. Were that so, the good done to children might outweigh the harm done to dolphins. But neither claim, of benefit or uniqueness, is persuasive. And indeed, dolphin encounters have been touted for a flamboyantly broad assortment of maladies—manic depression, Rett syndrome, Tourette's syndrome, ADHD, Down syndrome, etc., according to one entrepreneur. This is not alternative medicine; it's hucksterism.

═══════════════════════════════════════════════════

## CAT CUSTODY

*Five years ago, my girlfriend went to Australia for a vacation and left her cat with me. She fell in love with Australia and decided not to come back, leaving me and the cat stuck with each other. Over time this cat has become a beloved part of my life. Now the ex-girlfriend has moved back to the United States and has hinted that she wants the cat back. Should I return it?*
*—Sean Eddy, St. Louis*

This custody question should really be directed to the cat, but alas, it can't declare whom it would prefer to live with (except by clawing the furniture to bits if you pick the wrong house).

As a matter of law, cats are property. If your girlfriend paid for it, she owns it. (Although you might now regard it as abandoned property.) As a matter of ethics, your cat may be less than a person but it is more than a thing. You may rightly consider the relationship that developed between you and the cat, from both your and its point of view. That's not something property law should preempt.

Interestingly, the law does suggest a way to take that relationship into account. Neeraja Viswanathan, a lawyer I consulted, e-mailed me, "Arguments can be made that the person who contributed the most to the pet should own the pet. If someone paid all the vet bills then you could argue that he 'improved' upon the property and should therefore get custody." (Is there a cozier phrase than *cat improvement?*)

If you love the cat, and your ex cares so little about it that she could abandon it for years while she went swanning about the antipodes, then you should get to keep it. After all, there is no shortage of cats needing good homes. Your ex should stop by an animal shelter and adopt one of those. Or, given her love for Australia, perhaps she'd prefer a wombat or a eucalyptus or a giant can of Foster's.

---

### DISEASED DOG

*I am a pediatrician who frequently treats children with kala-azar, a disease transmitted to humans from dogs by sand flies. Treatment of dogs and humans is painful, prolonged, and not very effective. Euthanizing infected animals is the best way to curb the spread of the disease. A stray dog, Lisa, established herself outside our house, and we fed her daily. When she was diagnosed with kala-azar, we reluctantly euthanized her. Ethical?*

*—Dolores Protagoras, Athens, Greece*

This sad action was permissible, given the facts you present. You rightly imply a moral distinction between humans and nonhumans. No disease, no matter how horrific, would justify murdering human beings to prevent its spread. We sometimes impose such things on animals, however, destroying some fowl, for example, to protect others—and us—from avian flu.

To take so drastic a step, the threat must be serious, and there must be no other way to counteract it. You may not destroy an animal to curb a trivial malady, like the spread of fleas, or a disease that can be countered by quarantine or inoculation. And in every case, suffering must be minimized.

This position accords moral standing to animals but places a higher value on people, something that Peter Singer, professor of bioethics at Princeton University and author of *Animal Liberation*, for one, does not automatically do. In an e-mail, he wrote, "Maybe killing Lisa was justifiable, if there was really no other way of preventing the spread of a painful disease to other dogs and humans. But I don't think that mere membership of one species rather than another can make a sharp difference to whether it is, or is not, right to kill an individual for the benefit of many others."

To confer higher status on human beings is not simply to champion the species to which we happen to belong. Rather, it is a willingness to consider intelligence, self-awareness, and the capacity for suffering, among other qualities. It is an imperfect argument. An infant or a person in a coma might lack these qualities. But it does suggest that we value a dolphin over a mouse, a mouse over an earthworm. There remains a duty to avoid harming any animal, but there are circumstances, like that of Lisa the dog, when doing so may be justified.

## GERBIL

*When we got our kids a dog, it supplanted their gerbil in their affections, and worse, took an instant dislike to the gerbil. Now we are moving. Rather than bringing both animals on a cross-country drive, I'm thinking of setting the gerbil free. He was raised in captivity and would be at a disadvantage in the wild, but I think he'd be happier, even if it shortened his life. What do you think?*

*—Pat Loeb, Garrett Park, MD (soon to be of South Pasadena, CA)*

You're correct that a gerbil raised in captivity "would be at a disadvantage in the wild," if by that you mean would be killed by predators or, never having learned to forage, would starve. Even if you enrolled it in a crash course for the about-to-be feral, you'd still be stuck.

"Gerbils are Mongolian desert rats," Dr. Rebecca Campbell, my go-to veterinarian, told me. "Unless you plan not only to reeducate your pet but fly to Mongolia to release it, you may not set it free." (Incidentally, if there's a prize for pet marketing, I'd like to nominate whoever changed *Mongolian desert rat* to *gerbil*. That's even better than "compassionate conservative.")

Having adopted a pet, you have a duty to care for it. If you no longer can, you must find someone who will. In the extraordinary circumstance that no neighbor or kindergarten class or pet shop can take in the gerbil, painless euthanasia would be preferable to the suffering your pet would endure in the suburban wilds.

**UPDATE:** Happily, Hershey the gerbil found a new home with a neighbor.

## DECEIVING THE DOG

*Sometimes my normally obedient dog, Ornette, escapes our fenced yard and will not return on command. We open the car door and tell her excitedly that we will take her for a walk, her favorite activity, to entice her into the car. Then we put on the leash and take her home, no walk. Although dogs don't really understand language in the way that humans do, I'm worried about the ethical propriety of our misleading ploy. Should I be?*
*—David Schade, Victoria, British Columbia*

I share your skepticism that your dog understands the precise meaning of "walk" (an assertion some animal lovers will repudiate, but please, no e-mail about how much your dog enjoys *Pride and Prejudice*). For all you know, when you excitedly say walk your dog hears, "I like you!" or "Let's drive home and watch *Lassie*." Yet clearly it is possible to deceive a dog (by pretending to throw the ball, for example) and in your case, fortunately so.

What's the alternative? You can't offer even the most linguistically gifted dog a cogent argument for returning to the yard. You could bribe her, if you carry meat in your glove compartment, but bribery, too, raises moral questions. Fortunately, what you are doing is innocuous; it is not akin to telling your kids they're going to Disneyland and then taking them to the dentist. (Or telling me I'm going to my dentist, a skilled and eloquent fellow, but instead subjecting me to the nausea and fear of an amusement park.) If you remain determined not to fool her, then give her a firm command—"into the car!"—and make sure she's trained to obey it, for the benefit of you both.

Alternatively, if you become convinced of your dog's verbal ability, give her bus fare and tell her to return home when she likes. Be sure to mention the stop where she gets off so she doesn't get lost. Maybe write it down for her.

## BIRD BRAIN

*My husband and I spent substantial time and money to entice bluebirds to our yard. This included a squirrel- and snakeproof bluebird house, special tasty food (which entailed keeping mealworms in my refrigerator), available water, and other amenities. Then an interloper nested in our bluebird house and laid five eggs. When is it permissible to destroy a nest of undesirable feathered folk? We want bluebirds, not common yard sparrows.*

*—Judy Barrett, Greensboro, NC*

If it were permitted to bust up the houses of creatures deemed insufficiently appealing, who wouldn't live in fear? Anne Hathaway, perhaps, but we mortals would be on edge. As I suspect you know, you may strive to attract bluebirds, as some people admirably do to protect that species, but you may not smash sparrows' nests simply because you find those birds "undesirable," that is, unattractive. In ethics, cuteness doesn't count.

You also face legal restraints. The Migratory Bird Treaty Act of 1918 protects more than eight hundred species from assorted rough stuff, including messing about with their nests. And while it exempts the house sparrow—its nest, eggs, and young may be removed or destroyed—other sparrows are protected. (You should, of course, consult state laws.) It's worth noting that some bluebird enthusiasts think it better to have no bluebird box at all rather than let house sparrows reproduce in one.

There are circumstances when ethics allows you to destroy a nest or eggs or even birds themselves if less lethal methods prove futile. Even protected species may legally be destroyed if they pose a significant threat to people, property, or the food supply (and proper permits have been obtained).

Government officials capture and gas geese deemed to threaten flights to and from New York, a matter of safety not aesthetics. (Although critics argue that gentler tactics have not been adequately explored.)

A friend and avid naturalist—among other things, he conducts bat tours for the American Museum of Natural History—went further, and persuasively so, "An environmental ethics that considers the 'big picture' compels killing some animals to protect native species and habitat." He mentions the damage "feral pigs, rats, cats, and goats" have done to island ecosystems. He does not mention your yard.

UPDATE: "Lest we be considered the Torquemada of the avian world, we decided to adopt the 'squatters rights' philosophy and allowed the interlopers to hatch their clutch of eggs," Barrett e-mailed. "We plan to be more vigilant next nesting period." She later told me that she'd have no trouble destroying a nest under construction, but would not tamper with eggs.

After this column ran, several readers argued that sparrows meet the criteria my Natural History museum pal laid out: they are a nonnative species that threaten endangered bluebirds. (Although some birders exempt native birds like wrens or chickadees from any forced relocation.) Some readers proposed a solution far better than my austere and ignorant nay-saying. Install a second bluebird house about a dozen feet away. Bluebirds won't live this close to each other, but sparrows will happily claim the vacant house and leave their cuter neighbors alone.

---

**BAD KITTY**

*I believe in having compassion for all sentient beings; therefore, I do not eat meat. If I feed my cat meat-based pet food, I am supporting the slaughter of other animals. Assuming it will not impair his health, is it ethical for me to feed my cat vegetarian food, depriving him of what he would naturally eat and giving him no choice in the matter?*

*—Annalisa Lazzaro, New York*

Fish gotta swim, birds gotta fly, and you gotta provide your cat with a healthful diet even if that means letting a carnivore be a carnivore. If this could be done with vegetarian cat food, that would be fine, but alas, what your vet is almost certain to tell you is that unless your cat gets taurine from its food—and it cannot get it from vegetables—it will go blind, among other horrible consequences.

The cat doesn't get a say (except by refusing to eat the Soy Chow) any more than it does about, for example, getting vaccinated. As to what it would do naturally, if released into the wild, what your cat would do is lead a short and unpleasant life. This is not to exempt the cat's behavior from moral consideration. You should, of course, prevent it from, say, loitering around a bird feeder and from using nuclear weapons.

---

### FUR IS MURMURRED

*Cleaning out the closets of the house we inherited from my husband's great-aunt, we found several fur coats. It didn't seem right to stuff them in the Goodwill bag, so we kept them. I would never buy a new fur, but is it wrong to wear an old one I didn't pay for, as a parody of fashion-conscious women who do? (Does parody count if I'm the only one who knows it's parody?) If it's wrong to wear the furs, what should I do with them?*

*—Hattie Fletcher, Pittsburgh*

You certainly should not wear a new fur. A case can be made for some exploitation of animals—as food or in important medical research—when there is no meaningful alternative, and when their suffering is minimized. But there is no justification for harming animals to produce something as frivolous as a fur coat. An old fur, however, is a different matter, although not for the reasons you offer.

It's insignificant that the fur was a gift; the animals in pain don't care who pays the bill. And you are rightly wary of the parody defense, too easily invoked by those who, for example, construct a racist parade float and when criticized say it's satire. How does an ordinary fur suddenly become a parody of itself? Are the words "I Am Heartless and Vain" shaved into the back? Now a coat made of live weasels or raw beef . . .

A more persuasive rationale for keeping the fur is that an attic coat can be grandfathered in (great-aunted in?). It already exists, you do no good by tossing it in the trash; you do no obvious harm by wearing it. Except this harm—appearing in fur announces that doing so is acceptable. You are voting with your feet (if the coat is much too long for you). Your wearing the great-aunt's fur does not injure any animals, but it does injure us, it coarsens our sensibilities as it declares our values.

Thus, if we concede the moral high ground to the Fur Is Murder (or at least Wanton Cruelty) crowd, you may not wear any new fur, but you may use—discreetly, privately—an old fur, a found fur. Make it into fur socks or a bathroom rug or an unseen lining for a cloth coat— utility without propaganda. If everyone follows that rule, the fur trade withers.

**UPDATE**: When this column first ran, I invited readers to suggest other uses for this old fur; more than five hundred people did. The most frequent idea by far was to make that old fur into a teddy bear— a collectible, a fond memento of the great-aunt, a toy kids love. Several Web sites list seamstresses who perform these coat-to-bear conversions professionally. This seems to meet my criteria for fur reuse—utility without propaganda—but does convey an odd message to the child cuddling that former coat (and former mink). Perhaps that's why I'm uneasy, this smacks too much of taxidermy. My objection may be aesthetic not moral, but I can't help wondering what materials these hobbyists would use to construct a baby doll.

The next most popular idea was to give old fur coats to the homeless, an altruistic act to be sure. However, if wearing fur endorses its use, then even the poor should not wear them. There is no shortage of wool or down or Thinsulate coats to be donated. And there is something redolent of crumbs-from-the-rich-man's table about dressing legions of the desperately poor in ermine. (Although it may well deglamorize fur to distribute it to poor folks.)

Surprisingly, such gifts are acceptable to PETA; that organization has itself sent fur coats to earthquake victims in Iran and refugees in Afghanistan. Those who are put off by the thought of a war victim huddled in my imaginary Aunt Minna's fox stole may be comforted to know that PETA also uses old fur coats in educational displays and for animal bedding. This last use is similarly endorsed by the Humane Society of the United States, which sends old furs to licensed wildlife rescuers who make nesting materials out of them for orphaned and injured animals.

Other oft-submitted suggestions: donate that old fur to a local theater company; make it into a pillow or fur throw; give it to a science teacher for static electricity lab work.

# *Sports*

NO SPORTS-RELATED SCANDALS OUTRAGED MY READERS MORE THAN the use of steroids, human growth hormone, and other banned substances. But even if a baseball player's use of performance-enhancing drugs is a moral transgression, the most effective way of discouraging it may not be to put a scarlet S on his jersey. As challenging as it is defining correct conduct, devising ways of getting us to embrace it is even trickier, requiring tactics other than moral suasion.

There are potent arguments against the use of these substances: respect for the law, esteem for baseball's history, regard for the players' health, and concern about being poor role models for young fans. But to frame this problem as one of individual moral failure is neither persuasive nor likely to yield the most effective solution.

Some critics assert that drugs can so alter player performance as to threaten the game itself. There is some basis to this apprehension. Assumptions about player prowess are reflected even in baseball's physical design: the height of outfield fences, for example, was set long before hitters bulked up on steroids. The distance between the bases, 90 feet, elegantly balances human running and throwing ability. There would be fewer successful plays at first if a drug-fueled hitter could run 80 miles per hour—with players so swift, the base paths would have to be extended by, oh, let's say half a mile, making it a tough toss from third and a disappointing view for people in the stands, even from the good $50,000 seats at the new Yankee Stadium. (I may be off about the price. They could cost $100,000.)

But drugs do not enable players to run 80 miles per hour, or make them invisible or able to fly. (The game would be more entertaining if they did.) The boost that performance-enhancing drugs provide is significant, particularly for athletes competing at the highest levels, but limited. Even with the infiltration of banned substances, the single-season home-run record climbed from Babe Ruth's sixty in 1927 to only Barry Bonds' seventy-three in 2001—not to six hundred.

Sports evolve, and technology plays its part. In modern professional basketball, peach baskets are out and video replay is in, as is footwear so high-tech that James Naismith, the game's inventor, would barely recognize those things on LeBron James' feet as shoes. For that matter, Naismith would be astounded by the size, strength, and speed of today's players and the transformation they have wrought upon the game, changes that do not bespeak ethical failure or foretell the game's demise.

It is difficult to see a profound moral distinction between pharmaceutical science and other equally sophisticated technologies that yield more dramatic results. In some sports, the most advanced approaches to training and diet apply biological research and computer analysis. As a consequence, Sir Roger Bannister's four-minute mile is now Hicham El Guerrouj's 3:43. Bicycle racers train in wind tunnels, and bicycles themselves have gotten lighter and stronger, going from steel to aluminum to titanium to carbon fiber. Many athletes wear contact lenses, and there's nothing natural or traditional about that. More extreme still is Tiger Woods' LASIK surgery, a deliberate and successful attempt to improve his vision to 20/15—better than normal. If laser surgery is ethical, why aren't steroids?

Here's one possible response: LASIK surgery is relatively safe, whereas steroids pose serious health risks. And while an individual player may make a rational choice to accept that risk, by doing so he unethically imposes that risk on all other players, who simply cannot compete against this incredible, drug-altered specimen. In professional football, for instance, the number of 300-pound players increased from ten in 1986 to more than three hundred by 2004.

Even if you regard such developments as morally dubious, the way to curtail them is not by denouncing putative failures of individual rectitude—baseball has tried that for years with unimpressive results—but to recast the issue as one of workplace safety.

Hockey shows what can be achieved by this shift. An NHL player who wore a helmet was once mocked as timid. Helmet use is now required and catcalls of "sissy-boy" are rare, in English or French. This change was not achieved by congressional bloviating about the players' duty to be role models for the kids or to stop endangering teammates by pressuring them to conform to a manly bareheaded style. Instead, hockey's authorities—owners and unions, managers, coaches and officials—established and enforced a helmet rule as a matter of employee health and safety. To refuse to wear one today would seem not immoral but dim-witted (perhaps a consequence of frequent blows to the head).

The absence of a helmet is easier to detect than the presence of HGH, but the same strategy is applicable: clear rules, consistent enforcement (with requisite testing), appropriate penalties, and a moratorium on consigning transgressors to eternal hellfire. If those who govern baseball show a persistent concern for the well-being of the players and a respect for the fans' faith in the integrity of the game, they can create conditions in which right conduct can flourish, something the owners have failed to do with their a-few-immoral-apples approach.

We admire athletes who work hard, even risking injury, to improve their play. It is oddly paradoxical to damn those who do just that— albeit pharmaceutically. Instead, baseball authorities must prohibit actions that are unduly dangerous, whether taking drugs or playing after a concussion, or that mar the beauty of the game (jet packs worn by outfielders, handguns for pitchers who want to intimidate a batter), not because such things are unethical but because they are unwise.

Some readers responded to this disquisition by countering that using banned substances is against the rules and thus, cheating. Well, sure, it is against the rules to break the rules. That assertion is delightfully circular, but it assumes that to violate a rule must be a moral transgression. Not so.

Some rules are ethically neutral. If a wide receiver runs out of bounds to stop the clock, he breaks a rule, but nobody condemns him for moral turpitude. If a basketball team schemes to (gently) foul the opposing team's worst free-throw shooter, nobody calls for that team to be purged from decent society.

Sometimes the rules themselves are patently egregious. For decades, Major League Baseball barred African Americans. Yet few readers, even those who are fretful about comparing modern drug-enhanced performers to their ostensibly clean-living forebears, call for adding an asterisk to pre-integration records to indicate that they were achieved by white players who did not vie with many of the era's best athletes.

If we are to condemn steroids on moral grounds, their use must be significantly different from other activities we accept as ethical—whether within the rules (taking ibuprofen) or not (a runner advancing despite failing to make contact with a base).

### ANKLES AWAY

*I play soccer for my town-club team, and we are about to face our biggest rival. Their best player, a midfielder, just got over a sprained ankle. Without him, we have a great chance to win, but if he plays, we'll likely lose. Some of our defensemen are talking about hitting the ankle so he gets hurt again and can't play. Is that dirty play or just part of the game?*

*—T.H. (age fourteen), Connecticut*

Deliberately hurting an opponent is part of the game, but it is a dishonorable part. To purposely inflict an injury on any opposing players—even those with two good ankles—is indeed dirty play and should be renounced; that's one reason so few soccer leagues permit the use of swords and truncheons.

You needn't treat this midfielder with exceptional tenderness. If he can't handle the rough-and-tumble of routine play, he shouldn't be on the field. And you may cheerfully exploit his debility; you certainly needn't slow down to allow that hobbled Hermes to catch you. You may even celebrate your good fortune if he inadvertently becomes too banged up to play. But you may not willfully harm him. In ethics, intent counts.

### ALL-STAR

*I coach a youth all-star baseball team. After tryouts, our league director chose the thirteen best players for our team, leaving about six kids unselected. Among those is a boy whose father recently died of cancer. The boy is not very good at baseball, about the worst among those who tried out. The community is pressuring the director to "do the right thing" for the boy and a family coping*

*with tragedy. They say some things transcend baseball skill. But what about the better player whose spot he'd be taking? What is "the right thing"?*
— *Name withheld, California*

Your community's desire to respond to a family's misfortune is admirable, but I'm not persuaded that they have found the best way to do so. This well-intended gesture could be seen as condescending to the boy who is to be helped—it says he can't succeed on his merits—and unfair to the better player, whose spot on the roster is not the community's to bestow elsewhere.

Assuming this boy isn't stuck on the end of the bench and actually gets into a game, it will take him about three pitches to realize he's not good enough to hold his own among the all-stars. It will not be a pleasant moment. His well-wishers may be setting him up for failure, the queasy sensation of his not deserving to be there, and the resentment of teammates who genuinely earned their place on the squad. Some gift.

The community should consider alternatives that will bring this boy more satisfaction and do the other children less harm. Perhaps there's another way he could be involved with the team, practicing but not playing, for example, or working with the coaches. His benefactors should discuss this with his family and find out what the boy would most enjoy. Excluding my TV set. That, too, is not theirs to give.

**UPDATE:** The league director put this boy on the all-star team. League rules say all on the roster must bat but only nine will play in the field. In his first few games, he never got a hit and did not field. In recent games, he's gotten on base and caught a fly ball. He enjoys playing, and his teammates—and coach—have accepted him.

### FAIR WAY

*As a frequent golfer, I often find other people's balls in various corners of a course. I sometimes take these balls to the lone driving range here in Manhattan—known for its exorbitant prices—and hit them there, in effect giving them perfectly good golf balls while evading the rip-off ball fees. Am I stealing or donating?*

*—Billy Bloom, New York*

Quite the self-serving rationalization. (And for you kids at home, eager to detect self-serving rationalizations, look for words like *rip-off* and *exorbitant.*)

If your ball-donation scheme is as advantageous to the driving range owners as you maintain—and it certainly seems to be—then surely they will accede to it when you ask permission, which you must do. That you regard their prices as too high doesn't allow you to cheat the place. That you consider donating a bucket of balls to be fair compensation for teeing off doesn't make it so. I think that my presence at any NBA game adds to the fun, but Madison Square Garden perversely insists that I buy a ticket. For barter schemes like yours and mine to be distinguishable from theft, they must be accepted by both parties in the transaction.

### NO FLY ZONE

*After seven years as a catch-and-release fly fisherman, I have decided to give it up because I believe it is wrong. Would it be ethical to pass on my flies and equipment to friends and family who are already fishermen? I don't need to impose my beliefs on others, and they fish whether I give them anything or not.*

*—D.P., Orondo, WA*

Is fly-fishing immoral? That is something about which honorable people differ, but you believe that it is, and so you should not give your gear to your fishing buddies. When a cowboy-movie gunfighter has an epiphany, he hangs up his pistol; he doesn't sell it on eBay.

If you forswore eating sweets, a morally neutral act, you could give away your pie pans. But were you to donate your muddler or soft hackle, your krystal bugger or philandering Schwarzenegger—this last may not be an actual fly; I'm a confirmed indoorsman myself—to other fisherfolk, you'd be abetting what you regard as misconduct.

Declining to donate your gear is not "imposing" your beliefs on others. You make no attempt to stop anyone else's fishing; you simply refuse to abet it, even indirectly.

## TENNIS COURT OATH

*My girlfriend and I found the public tennis courts occupied by a single person practicing his serve. I said this was unethical or at least selfish, since there were people waiting and his court could have been used by two or even four others. My girlfriend countered that since there were no posted rules, all tennis-related uses were appropriate. Who is right?*

*—Goutam Jois, Cambridge, MA*

She is. Assuming this fellow practiced his serve only for a reasonable amount of time, he used the tennis court legitimately—i.e., for tennis. A solo workout is not the wisest use of shared public space, perhaps, but inefficient need not mean unethical. If it did, then those playing singles would have a moral obligation to yield the courts to those eager to play doubles, as you imply, who would in turn have to make way for those keen to play my innovative game, octuples. (The injury rate from rackets swung in close quarters is an admitted disadvantage.)

Sometimes customs evolve to resolve such conflicts. For example, it is an unwritten rule on many New York City playground basketball courts that pickup games take priority over casual shootarounds. Total strangers tend to honor this practice with remarkably little bickering. But where custom fails, formal rules are helpful. You would do well to propose your entirely reasonable preference to the officials in charge of your local courts.

---

**PAY PAL**

*I officiate youth hockey. In nonleague games, it is the coaches who pay us two officials. At one game, the team's coach (whom I knew) paid the other official the normal fee but tucked away extra money for me. When my co-official asked if I had gotten the same wage, I said yes so he would not feel cheated. Was it ethical for this coach to pay me extra when the other official and I are the same age, have the same experience, and both did the same amount of work?*

*—A.M., New Jersey*

That's why I lie to my (imaginary) wife about the (hypothetical) jewelry I give to my (fictional) mistress; so my wife won't feel cheated.

Both you and that coach acted badly. He denied your fellow official the expected pay parity, and you covered up for him. But it is the other team's coach who has the bigger gripe. How can he be confident that the game will be officiated fairly if his rival might slip an official a few bucks? For obvious reasons, few sports permit a coach to give an official a pregame tip. (Or a postgame Buick.)

It is unfortunate that this coach directly paid you at all. It would be better if both coaches contributed to pay packets not designated as coming from either of them individually, to avoid the possibility of an official, even unconsciously, favoring the team that put money in his purse.

## REFFING LACROSSE

*I referee lacrosse for girls in grades three through eight. To keep a strong team from running up the score, if a team is up by four points, instead of starting with a face-off after a goal is scored, the losing team gets possession of the ball. Sometimes when I've imposed this rule, the winning team continues to encourage their girls to score. Should I speak to that coach about being disrespectful?*

*—Kelly Seeger, Westfield, NJ*

If a coach, giddy with victory, defies this rule, you should talk to her. The idea is not to keep the score close as an abstract exercise but to prevent one team from demolishing the élan vital of the other. (One sign that you should act: several players are weeping openly.)

The essential point of this endeavor, of young kids playing sports at all, is fun. If one team humiliates the other, that fun is much diminished (for half the participants, at least). A ruthless coach deprives the victors, too, of worthy lessons: an appreciation of fair play, the value of treating an opponent with respect.

How these laudable ends are to be achieved is less clear. Learning to lose without despair is also a part of sports. (Professional athletes sometimes say that losing a blowout is easier to shake off than dropping a close game.) If a stronger team benches its best players or discourages them from scoring, some on the weaker team may resent it as condescending. Many a child has eyed an adult with suspicion—over the chessboard or at the mini-golf course (or, for devil-may-care parents, on the dueling field)—and accused, "Did you let me win?"

Coaches and officials should be mindful not just of the rule's letter but its spirit, shaping the play to respond to the kids involved. And your league should reexamine its rules from time to time and perhaps try other measures, like reassigning players to better balance the teams.

---

### SOCCER? SACK HER?

*One of the Lions, a team in our recreational men's soccer league, approached us officials about a female player on the Dream Center, the team they'd face next. Several of the Lions are Muslim, he said, and their religion forbids contact with a woman in this way and they wanted to avoid the possibility of injury. And they did join a men's league. The Dream Center's manager said the Lions could forfeit if they wish. Should we back his decision? Bar that player for this game? Change the matchups to avoid the conflict?*
*—Andy Zmugg and Craig Meller, Peoria, IL*

Let her play. While this is nominally a men's league, you allowed her to join the Dream Center and compete in previous contests; how can you bar her now? Consistency has its claims. And while the Lions' concern for her safety might be well meant, that is a matter for her to decide; the Lions may not impose safety upon her.

Next you must clarify the rules for the future. In doing so, be wary of men's eagerness to protect women, something that can be indistinguishable from simply restricting women's activities and cultivating segregation. Nor should you invoke religious strictures to regulate a secular pursuit in a pluralistic community.

There are legitimate reasons for considering sex in sports as it relates to physical factors—size, strength, speed—but not to ideology.

(Nobody would deny the legitimacy of the Ladies Professional Golf Association; everyone should reject a No Jews Allowed Golf Association.) It is a fine thing to create conditions for well-balanced contests, but players should have a chance to vie in a more competitive league if they wish—female golfers in PGA events, for example.

**UPDATE:** The woman player agreed to sit out that one game. The conflict reappeared when these same teams met in the playoffs. The Dream Center defended its player's right to compete; the Lions demurred. The league matched each against a different team in lieu of a championship game. Going forward, the rules will define this as an "adult league" open to men and women. The Lions will probably withdraw.

---

**FOUL BALL**

*At my son's Little League game, a foul ball sailed over the fence and shattered the window of a parked car. Signs at the ball field specify that the league is not responsible. One parent argued that the hitter's family should replace the window. Our family thinks the player and his parents have no such obligation: foul balls are part of the game. Who is right?*
*—Steve Fram, Palo Alto, CA*

Posting a sign doesn't shield you. If it did, I'd post one waiving my responsibility for, well, nearly everything.

As an ethical matter, the car's owner should pay for his own window. He knew he was parking beside a ball field and that foul balls are a routine part of the game. By choosing to park there, he assumed the risk of such a mishap. The city did nothing wrong by providing convenient parking and a fence around the field; it need not deploy some kind of anti-foul-ball missile system to guarantee total parking lot protection. And the player did just what he is meant to do on a ball field: play ball. Although he might want to choke up on the bat, follow through, and hit only standard softballs. Were you to knock, say, flaming cantaloupes into the parking lot and set your buddy's car ablaze, I'd revise my answer.

Fortunately, there is a real-world solution or at least a California-world solution. Vanessa Wells, safety officer for the Palo Alto Little League, explains, "California insurance law generally treats auto damage involving a falling object as a no-fault claim on the car-owner's insurer. A baseball is regarded as such a falling object." Like plummeting aircraft parts. Briefly lofted into the stratosphere by a muscular Barry Bonds.

Wells adds that the league does worry that a foul ball may hit a passing car and cause an accident, but so far that's never happened. The league might want to provide, or require each team to provide, insurance against such mishaps.

---

### FLOODED SOCCER FIELD

*My daughter plays soccer where opportunities are uneven. Some teams have better facilities and coaching and draw on a larger player pool. Weaker teams have difficulty competing and sometimes compensate by adjusting the playing field for home games. They grow the grass extra long or hose down the turf to create mud, neutralizing the superior ball-handling skills of the stronger team's players. My daughter's team has encountered such tactics. Are they ethical?*

*—Maureen Steinberger, Portland, OR*

Similar maneuvers are seen in many sports. In baseball, groundskeepers have been known to tend the grass along the foul lines to accommodate the home team's strengths: balls are likelier to roll foul when the grass is kept short and stay fair when it is long. In basketball, the old

Boston Garden was said to have dead spots on the floor that were easily avoided by the Celtics but confounded visiting teams. A certain amount of gamesmanship is okay in any sport, but there are limits, ambiguous but genuine, and your daughter's rivals have transgressed them.

Here's one guideline: you ought not manipulate the field of play so as to destroy a fundamental part of the game. Those hose-happy, lawnmower-averse teams that nullify ball-control skill central to soccer undermine the essence of the game and thus, go beyond the pale. (The Celtics never actually flooded the Garden to eliminate dribbling.)

Because it's impossible to define precisely when a team has gone too far, judgment is best left to the officials. And while mud-making does not explicitly violate the rules of soccer, "the condition of the field and the determination of whether it is playable is the decision of the referee," Chuck Keers, the executive director of Oregon Youth Soccer, e-mailed me. "If the grass is too tall, or if the field is too muddy, then the referee can declare that no game shall be played." The wise official will realize that ethics is more than mere adherence to the rules, and sportsmanship more than an appeal to legalisms.

**UPDATE**: Several readers believed that I took too narrow a view of this situation. They're right. It is insufficient to evaluate only the on-field response to inequality; we must also discuss how to vanquish it. Rather than considering only this ad hoc aquatic solution, the daughter's team should press the league to become more egalitarian, instituting measures to even up the facilities and coaching among all teams. Indeed, we all should consider this broader question among teams in an amateur soccer league, public schools in neighboring towns, or in the broader inequities that exist throughout America. Ethics concerns not just how we act at a moment of decision but how we respond to the conditions that engendered that moment; ethics demands not just individual rectitude but civic virtue.

# 9/11, Iraq, Afghanistan

QUANDARIES ARISING FROM NEW TECHNOLOGIES BROUGHT ENDURING change to my Ethicist column; there were also shorter-lived trends, as readers reacted to the great events of the day. Among the most troubling queries I received were those concerning 9/11 and the subsequent wars in Iraq and Afghanistan.

Some questions arose from what was perceived as a clash between American values and certain forms of Islam, especially as practiced in less industrialized parts of the world, raising uncomfortable questions about the limits to religious tolerance, and ultimately asking: is ethics merely an expression of a particular culture, or do our beliefs express more universal principles?

These issues vigorously asserted themselves when online images showed a seventeen-year-old girl in Pakistan's Swat Valley being flogged in public for going outdoors with a man not her father, which some saw as a violation of Islamic practice. At that time in Afghanistan, a proposed law would have severely restricted the rights of Shia women, forbidding a wife to leave the house without her husband's consent and condoning marital rape. Both Pakistan and Afghanistan, like the United States, are signatories of the United Nations Universal Declaration of Human Rights, which forbids sex discrimination. For most Americans, gender equality is an indispensable tenet of our democracy. But we also profess tolerance for other people's culture and religion. Should we respond to these developments with tolerance?

We should not. Tolerance ends where harm begins. To flog a teenager or strip half the population of a basic right is unambiguously harmful and hence to be vigorously opposed. John Stuart Mill lays out this idea in his essay "On Liberty," declaring with understatement that those who injure others are "amenable to moral disapprobation."

An action is not exempted from moral scrutiny because it is designated "religious" or enshrined in sacred texts. Putting adulterers to death is prescribed by Leviticus, but such a punishment is unlikely to be deemed tolerable by even the most ferocious American fundamentalist.

Nor does an action receive a free pass because it is embedded in an enduring cultural tradition. Such an appeal is little better than announcing: we've always done it this way. Persistent need not be commensurate with desirable. Earthquake and plague, flood and famine, have persisted for eons. (And Glenn Beck has had a TV show for years.)

Indeed, in asserting such claims for tolerance, it is not always obvious what culture or religion we mean. Who defines such things? Sunita Viswanath, founder of the advocacy organization Women for Afghan Women says: "This law is not an expression of the culture that

I witness. Who says what a culture is? Culture is not a monolith. Culture evolves." As for religion, she says, "Many Afghan women say that even if we refer to the Koran, it endows women with more rights than does the Taliban."

Tolerance—live and let live—is a wise response to things that are morally neutral, that harm no one: variations in diet or dress, musical preferences, ways of observing (or ignoring) the Sabbath. It is particularly estimable in a nation of immigrants like the United States, home to people with diverse ways of life. Here tolerance is a call for civility, for humility, an injunction not to be a hick. The world is a big place, and not everyone does things our way. Not everyone likes burgers and fries. Okay, everyone does like burgers (veggie burgers in some cases) and fries (witness the global hegemony of McDonald's), but some people prefer to eat them while wearing a sari or a dashiki or a hijab.

This matter of clothing can be contentious. The French, for example, ban the wearing of religious symbols in school as an intrusion of religion into the secular arena. For similar reasons (and to avoid displaying what can be an emblem of subjugation), women in Turkey are forbidden to wear the hijab—to cover the head as an expression of Islamic obligation—on public campuses. But to some students who wear the head scarf, the hijab is a badge of independence. Others see the issue as one of free expression. Soli Ozel, who teaches political science at Istanbul's Bilgi University, makes the latter case. "I find the ban a violation of a fundamental right," he told me, "and I always allowed such students to come to my class that way even if it was forbidden by law."

A different approach to resolving an apparent conflict between social goals was taken by Betty Brown, a Texas state legislator, who proposed that Asian Americans would run into less trouble when they go to vote if they took new names that are "easier for Americans to deal with," a reform unlikely to be embraced by Steven Chu, secretary of energy; or Eric Shinseki, secretary of veteran affairs; or Yo-Yo Ma, secretary of cello; or Ang Lee, secretary of movies. (I may have misstated some of these job titles.)

Tolerance can seem a dubious virtue. We speak of someone having a high tolerance for pain, not a tolerance for delight or cake or Jane Austen novels. It is a slightly seedy ideal, always a bit condescending. We tolerate downward, to our inferiors in class, in customs, in taste. We abide our neighbors even though they are wrong about everything: their ideas, their values, their inadequate lawn care. But we do not burn their house down, and that's no small thing.

There are bigger things that tolerance provides. Although Americans practice an array of religions—and some of us practice none—we have avoided, if not all religious bigotry, actual religious warfare. European history is a chronicle of faith-based slaughter, from the Crusades through the St. Bartholomew's Day Massacre to the ethnic cleansing in Bosnia. India has been beset by blood-soaked Hindu-Muslim conflicts since its founding; the riots of the early 1990s were particularly grim. The Middle East has its own sad saga. Elevating religious tolerance to a national virtue has helped us escape these horrors. And if this virtue (and, for that matter, our commitment to gender equality) has sometimes been more honored in the breach, it is not unimportant that freedom of religion is written into our Constitution, and it may be a sign of progress that President Obama held a seder at the White House. It will be more progressive still when our tolerance extends to electing a nonbelieving woman to host the White House seder.

Tolerance is not passivity. We may criticize—courteously—ideas with which we differ. We must combat those that do harm. Happily, in Pakistan, reinstated Chief Justice Iftikhar Mohammed Chaudhry ordered an investigation of the events in the Swat Valley. And the Afghan Justice Ministry is reexamining its odious new law. (Less hopefully, President Hamid Karzai explained away Western outrage as a misunderstanding, the result of "a not-so-good translation" of the law.) Ethics obliges us to resist such affronts to basic human rights, to demand adherence to an elemental moral precept: gender equality. And it is particularly urgent that our leaders do so in response to two nations with which we are formally allied.

**UPDATE:** While I made this case in reference to two Muslim nations, I agree with those readers who responded by cautioning against generalizing about Islam and who noted that gender inequality is not unique to sharia. An ethical precept must be more than a means by which one country deprecates another; it must apply consistently. If we condemn religious sexism in Pakistan and Afghanistan, we must at least question the softer inequities of America's mainstream faiths. The Catholic Church closes its leadership—that is, the priesthood—to women. Orthodox Judaism does similarly with its rabbinate. Such things are not equivalent to flogging, of course, but neither are they immune to criticism.

One rebuke was both surprising and, I believe, unwarranted. Contrary to what some readers decried, I did not characterize rural folks as hicks. I characterized hicks as hicks: the unappealing connotations of that word were just what I was urging all of us to avoid. I did not slander rural life.

Incidentally, neither did Karl Marx, it seems. Apparently, his famous reference to "the idiocy of rural life" was a big misunderstanding, a translator's error. What Marx was getting at, according to the editors of the *Monthly Review*, was "*the privatized apartness* of a life-style isolated from the larger society"—in other words, the failure of rural folk to see themselves and their circumstances as connected to other people, to think and act politically. Marx was not alluding to the lack of musical theater in the countryside or to the inability to find a good cappuccino.

## DELI DOUBTS

*Over the years, I've become friendly with my deli owner, a youngish Arabic man. He has often expressed anger about U.S. policy in Israel and even displayed a Palestinian flag. I took our discussions with a grain of salt, even when he said, "Just wait, something big is coming. The Arab people are getting angrier and angrier and they will strike back." Before 9/11, this never rose to a reportable suspicion, but now, while I dread making trouble for an innocent person, can I let it go?*

*—Name withheld, Brooklyn*

If you had a genuine reason to believe your deli man was involved in or has information about this catastrophe, then you should contact the authorities. But by your account his remarks sound less like subversion than invective, so you ought not make that call. Instead, talk further with your friend. You'll reconnect on a human level and can better gauge whether his words were a personal tirade or foreshadowed an actual attack. Many law-abiding people have strong views about all sorts of things. Some fundamentalist Christians are given to doomsday pronouncements—God's wrath will rain down upon us. I myself have walked out of the movies cursing a certain actor, and no one reported me to the feds (or that inept action hero to the Screen Actors Guild).

The FBI takes a different view. A spokesman, while noting the importance of free speech, believes you should report your deli man, adding that few of those they contact are ever accused of a crime. "He may be innocent, but unless we have a chance to investigate, we can't know if the information is relevant," he says. Many Americans concur: within four weeks of the attack, the bureau had received 294,000 tips, nearly all of which contributed nearly nothing to public safety but consumed police resources.

While the FBI may not intend to stifle dissent, that's what often happens. A visit from a government official can be intimidating. Such calls paid to suspected "subversives" in the McCarthy era cost people jobs, broke up friendships, destroyed lives. Recently, hundreds of people, not accused of any crime, have been jailed or detained for unspecified periods.

We as a nation are responding to a genuine threat, and it is understandable that many of us have a heightened—and not always rational—sense of danger. But it would be sad if in defense of America, we abandoned what is best about America.

---

### STOCKPILE CIPRO

*Caught up in the anthrax scare, I filled a prescription for Cipro, which I won't actually take unless there is a widespread outbreak. Friends criticize me for "hoarding," unjustly putting my fears above those with an immediate need for the drug, e.g., cystic fibrosis patients. But don't I have the right to protect myself and my family? Isn't this similar to stockpiling food or water for an emergency?*

*—Name withheld, Brooklyn*

I'm with your friends: hoarding Cipro is wrong. You protect you and yours at the expense of me and mine, and that is not an ethical course. Stockpiling food or water endangers no one—neither is in short supply.

While Cipro is one of several antibiotics used to treat anthrax, it is, as you note, the preferred treatment for some other diseases. If, as you fear, Cipro is in short supply, then you imperil those with an immediate need, just so you can ward off a purely hypothetical danger to yourself. And of course, if Cipro is not in short supply, then there's no reason to stockpile.

While you suggest that you will take Cipro only if you are certain you've contracted anthrax, not everyone is as fastidious. Hoarding, and the self-treatment that often accompanies it, is associated with the unnecessary or improper use of antibiotics, which contribute to the development of antibiotic-resistant bacteria—and that's another health risk to me and mine.

I can understand your anxiety. Anthrax represents a real, if statistically minimal, threat, and public officials have not been entirely forthcoming, as many postal workers can tell you. Maybe a better approach is for you to become a member of Congress: you will apparently receive swift preferential treatment, obviating any need to hoard medicine. Few people in authority ever regard themselves as nonessential, particularly when it comes to the distribution of medication or parking permits.

---

### CONVOY DUTY

*As a convoy commander in Iraq, I had serious reservations about the effectiveness of a young single mother in my unit, but what really appalled me was the thought of her leaving a child orphaned. When she was assigned to a particularly dangerous convoy, I replaced her with an unmarried man. He didn't know he was replacing anyone; I just said I was shorthanded and asked for volunteers. Did I act ethically?*
—*Ray Doeksen, Chicago*

You did the right thing for the wrong reason. Were this female soldier unqualified for the assignment, she would be a danger to herself, her comrades, and the mission. You could replace her on those grounds— but not because of her home life. Few commanders have sufficient knowledge of the private lives of all their troops to consider such a factor equitably. Perhaps one of your soldiers was a single dad. Another might care for a dozen siblings. And even if you knew all that, how would you balance such diverse circumstances?

David Perry, professor of ethics at the U.S. Army War College, concurs. Responding as a private citizen, he e-mailed "It's too much to expect commanders to make such complicated calculations. . . . How can any commander know how much their soldiers are loved and valued by their parents, children, siblings, friends, fellow soldiers et al?" Indeed, as Perry implies, such reasoning comes uncomfortably close to valuing some lives over others.

That you replaced this young woman with a volunteer doesn't get you off the hook. Because you withheld pertinent information, the replacement was unable to make an informed decision.

When deciding who is eligible for military service, it is reasonable to consider domestic obligations. But such decisions should be a matter of policy that can be applied consistently and transparently. It should not be an ad hoc matter for individual commanders, who would do better to treat all their soldiers equally.

## SCREENING LINE

*I flew out of Denver International Airport shortly after a bad storm and spent three hours in the security line. First-class passengers had no wait because the Transportation Security Administration allowed them to skip to the front of the line. Security costs are shared by the airlines and taxpayers. Should preference be given to first-class passengers?*

*—Allison Moule, Broomfield, CO*

While airlines share the cost of passenger screening, they also share the cost, through their taxes, of state troopers. But when a first-class flyer gets a speeding ticket, he is treated like everyone else. Passengers submit to screenings because they are legally obligated to do so; therefore, all passengers should be treated equally in this regard. To establish a short line for those who pay more and an endless line for those who pay less violates the spirit of equal treatment under the law—unlike when an airline provides comfy first-class seats and miserable coach seats, which is not a legal matter (but, I assume, a perverse psychological experiment).

If we must have a caste system in America, let's make our Brahmins not those with fat wallets but those who give joy to millions. At the Randyland International Airport, Aretha Franklin would sashay through security. Billionaire Walmart Waltons—Rob, Jim, and Alice? We thank you for your patience.

---

### SELL WTC TICKET

*I have an unused ticket for the World Trade Center observation deck. If I sell it on eBay, I'll likely get many times what I paid for it (and I have a lot of student loans), but to profit in this way just doesn't feel right. Would making money from such a sale be ethical?*

*—R.P., Chapel Hill, NC*

I understand your reluctance, but see no ethical barrier to your selling an artifact of the World Trade Center, although some will be offended by your profiting from a tragedy. People routinely trade in the remnants of calamity. Civil War diaries, paraphernalia from the *Titanic*, relics of Pompeii—all are steeped in suffering; all are bought and sold. What makes your proposed eBay activity seem ghoulish is the disaster's temporal proximity. It is a dictum of stand-up performers that tragedy plus time equals comedy. Perhaps the axiom here is tragedy plus time equals collectibles. But that is a matter not of ethics but of taste. On those grounds, there was a call to roust some souvenir sellers from the vicinity of the Trade Center, although few objected to the endless stream of lurid TV specials profiting from the disaster, the political campaigns that exploited it, the pop songs that invoked it, the upsurge in sales of American flags in a variety of forms—car-window stickers, bandannas, T-shirts (with and without jingoistic slogans), or the "authorized" souvenirs associated with police and firefighters, for example.

Beyond questions of taste, there is the harsher charge that you would dishonor the dead. Most religions impose upon us obligations to those whose lives have ended. But that is the province of religion; ethics concerns our duties to the living. In that regard, you should be mindful of, but not governed by, the grief of those most affected by this tragedy, the family members of those who died. And so, the more intimate an artifact, the more reluctant you should be to trade in it. (Indeed, truly personal effects would likely be the property of family members and should be returned to them.) But your ticket is not such a relic, and so it may be sold.

---

### ANTIWAR & INVESTING?

*My friends and I ardently oppose the war in Iraq on both moral and political grounds. Would it be ethical to invest in oil futures, believing the war I oppose might increase their value? I say yes: my money would not fund anything directly war-related (as an investment in Northrop Grumman might), and these futures represent oil from places like Nigeria and the North Sea, not Iraq. My friends say such an investment would be war profiteering. What do you say?*

*—Andrew Miller, New York*

If you were Colin Powell or Donald Rumsfeld or Karl Rove, someone actually shaping foreign policy, it would be improper to make personal investments that could be affected by your official actions. Indeed, such conflicts of interest are forbidden by federal law. Richard Perle, the former chairman (and continuing member) of the Defense Policy Board, was accused of a similar transgression for accepting a six-figure fee to advise communications company Global Crossing on a Department of Defense matter.

However, because your views on the war are largely ignored by those in power, I see scant ethical objection to your scheme. Your obligation is not to shun profits related to the war—no enterprise can be totally insulated from such an enormity—but to be wary lest the giddy prospect of imminent wealth undermines your resolve to protest a war you revile, which is your civic duty in a democracy.

Alas, your get-rich-quick scheme may not give you a real crack at corruption. Unless you have insider info—for instance, from wire-tapping Tommy Franks' phone (in which case you could end up in jail)—you're guided only by the same information available to all other investors, and so you are unlikely to make a killing in oil.

---

### JARHEAD WEDDING

*My twenty-three-year-old nephew is soon to be married, having postponed the event while serving as a Marine in Iraq. He plans to wear his uniform at the wedding. I am bitterly opposed to the agenda behind our involvement in Iraq and the long-term implications for our country, and so I am inclined not to attend rather than be confronted by a symbol of misguided patriotic pride. But am I inappropriately putting personal political convictions over family cohesion and loyalty?*

*—Hannes Vogel, MD, Stanford, CA*

You are. Attending your nephew's wedding, no matter his dress or his politics, is not an endorsement of U.S. foreign policy. It's not even an endorsement of his new bride. It's just a way to wish him well and renew family ties.

You would do better to see his wearing his uniform as pride in his profession, not a declaration of support for the war in Iraq, about which the troops, like other Americans, differ. However, if his vows include a pledge to "love, honor, and find those weapons of mass destruction"— or rather, if he opens a political conversation—you could respond politely, perhaps by toasting the joys of marriage with the words "long hard slog."

---

**MESS HALL MESS**

*During a tour in Baghdad, I befriended a man who, working for an Iraqi employer, emptied our trash, cleaned our bathrooms, and shared our danger. He learned that he could double his salary by working for an American contractor overseeing a mess hall, but he would have to show he had experience with menial kitchen work. As he had no such experience, he asked if I would prepare a false document saying he did. I refused. Was I right?*
*—C.M., Colonel, U.S. Army, Fort Hood, TX*

Experience doing menial work in a kitchen? Surely there are tasks a person can swiftly learn on the job. But dim-witted as is this prerequisite, you were right to decline your friend's request. The military and its contractors do not need more phony documentation. The lack of reliable record keeping, of conscientious oversight, has had lamentable consequences in Iraq. Nor will it benefit your friend to be nabbed with faked papers.

Nor need integrity have relegated you to inaction and remorse. You could have written an honest letter to the American contractor, attesting to your friend's ability to do the mess-hall job and detailing his true work history. (Cleaning a bathroom sink is not profoundly different from cleaning a kitchen sink.) You might have found ways to get this fellow the experience required for that better job or sought employment for him that lacked this ridiculous obstacle. Surely as an officer you knew both military and civilian officials who could have guided you toward legitimate options. Ethics requires not just the rectitude to refuse wrongdoing but the resourcefulness to devise an honest alternative.

**UPDATE:** Unassisted, the friend found a better paying job, four dollars instead of two dollars an hour, but in a more dangerous locale, a small combat outpost in a Baghdad neighborhood. The colonel does not know his current fate.

### I WANT YOU

*Our master's degree program in public policy requires students to devise solutions to a real-life policy problem—this year, the crisis in military recruitment and retention. The best paper will be forwarded to the Department of Defense. We students oppose the war in Iraq and the military's rejection of gay recruits, and see each as a cause of the recruitment problem. Is it ethical to require us to participate in an exercise aimed at assisting an institution whose policies we morally oppose?*
—*Heather Valdez Singleton and Alexa Kasdan, Cambridge, MA*

The school may require students to do the exercise but may not compel them to send their work to the DOD. They are students, not consultants, and are entitled to decide how their work is used. Their right to privacy cannot be ignored.

If, as it seems, the essential purpose of this exercise is to educate students, not to assist the Department of Defense, then it is legitimate pedagogy. Similarly, a student in the business school might be asked to devise an ad campaign for cigarettes, not to encourage smoking but to learn about a formidable marketing challenge (and about coping with sleepless nights when one is racked with guilt). A really good professor would see either assignment as a chance to discuss the moral implications of such work. There is a distinction between engaging in an academic exercise and abetting a dubious policy.

When executing this assignment, you can meet your obligations as students and remain true to your values by making them the focus of your solution to that policy problem: a truly egalitarian army, accepting gay soldiers, and fighting a just war with broad national support, will have fewer problems with recruitment and retention.

UPDATE: Singleton and Kasdan completed the assignment, emphasizing reforms including those described above. The school sent what it considered to be the best solution to the problem—not theirs—to the DOD with the consent of its authors.

## MEMORIAL

*At their fifteen-year reunion, my wife's high school class began raising money for a memorial. One former classmate, an honors student, active in the school and well liked, was killed on 9/11. Two others, neither of whom was particularly involved with the class, died of apparent drug overdoses. Must the class memorialize all three equally or can they pay sole tribute to their peer who was killed during that tragic event?*

*—Marc Stiefel, Richboro, PA*

Your wife's class has no ethical obligation to construct a memorial for every—or any—alum. To honor one student does not compel them to honor all. But they might reconsider the criteria by which they seem to judge some lives—some deaths—worthier than others. For your wife's classmate to be struck down on 9/11 in an act of horrific violence is heartbreaking, but it is not a demonstration of personal merit. That sad morning claimed the lives of the wise and the foolish, the generous and the greedy, the exceptional and the mundane—a tragedy deepened by the arbitrariness of death. Those who wish simply to mark the passing of former classmates should recall that those other two people are just as dead; those who loved them are just as grief-stricken.

If, however, it is not the manner of the honor student's death but the example of his life that inspires the class, if he is held in abiding affection, then it is reasonable to single him out for remembrance. The class might consider providing a prominent memorial to him and more modest commemorations for other classmates.

# *Work*

AN IMPORTANT PART OF DOING ANY JOB IS NOT DOING IT. TIME OFF refreshes us, improves efficiency, and augments contentment. And yet, Americans get far less vacation time than the people of other industrialized nations. In fact, we get far less than the members of our national legislature. Congress typically spends all of August on vacation. That's in addition to its week off in February, two more in April, and another in May. Most Americans get about two weeks a year, if that. There is something amiss in this four-to-one disparity.

It is unethical to exploit a position of public trust for personal gain, a reasonable characterization of our elected representatives awarding themselves a lavish vacation package (along with gold-plated health coverage, a hefty salary, and daily deep-muscle massage from the sergeant at arms, if I read the Constitution correctly, and I don't). It is unethical to slack off at work, arriving late and leaving early. Yet even when not on vacation, many in Congress are members of the Tuesday-to-Thursday Club, working only a three-day week and treating Mondays and Fridays as travel days. It's a long commute to Hawaii or Texas or Montana. If only it were possible to rent some sort of apartment near the Capitol.

"Do-nothing Congress" is a term of opprobrium neither recent—in 1948, Harry Truman ran against the "do-nothing . . . good-for-nothing" 80th Congress—nor left wing. Norman Ornstein, of the right-leaning American Enterprise Institute, has written that a modern industrial nation can't bumble along with a part-time legislature. His argument is one of practicality and governance, but there's also an ethical basis for his position. Our representatives took the job knowing there was much to be done—on energy, on the economy, on oversight; list your own priorities. It is not honorable to shirk one's responsibilities.

In their defense, some representatives regard these away days as work time, a chance to meet with constituents. That idea had some currency in the pre-e-mail, prephone, prehistoric days when this lackadaisical schedule evolved, but it's hardly convincing now. Those were also pre-air-conditioning days, when a Washington summer was even more of a miasma—I speak meteorologically, not morally—and the desire to leave town more urgent. Today there is AC in DC, a variety of ways to stay connected to the voters from afar, and nearly every representative has full-time office staff back home.

Although Congress grants itself a couple of months off each year, it guarantees ordinary Americans no paid vacation whatever. The European Union mandates at least four weeks off with pay, a fact cited in support of the Paid Vacation Act of 2009, a modest attempt to ensure many U.S. workers at least a one-week vacation. Its sponsor, former U.S. Representative Alan Grayson, a Democrat from Florida, believes that a wise vacation policy can increase productivity, stimulate the economy, and improve employee health. It is also an issue of social justice, he notes on his Web site "In other countries, it's a matter of right. Everyone is entitled to it. In our country, it is a matter of class." You'd think every representative would pause before leaving town to endorse it. The number of cosponsors Grayson lined up? Four. Not to mention that he didn't get reelected.

Denying others what you grab for yourself is hypocrisy, widely regarded as a moral failing. In Canto XXIII of the *Inferno*, Dante sentences hypocrites to the eighth circle of hell and assigns them a wardrobe unsuitable for DC in August:

> *Caps had they on, with hoods, that fell low down*
> *Before their eyes, in fashion like to those*
> *Worn by the monks in Cologne. Their outside*
> *Was overlaid with gold, dazzling to view,*
> *But leaden all within, and of such weight,*
> *That Frederick's compared to these were straw.*
> *Oh, everlasting wearisome attire!*

There is a counterargument to the charge of hypocrisy: to entice top people to public office, we must offer appropriate compensation, including vacation time. But do we attract such luminous legislators? When the first Congress met in 1789, its members voted themselves a pay package of six dollars a day (over the objections of fiscal conservatives pushing for five dollars). That year, John Adams presided over a Senate that included James Monroe; among those in the House were James Madison and Elbridge Gerry. Current Congressional base pay is $174,000, and we've attracted . . . draw up your own disheartening roster.

In theory, if we disdain the vacation status quo, we can throw the rascals out. But we do not choose officials on a single issue; our failure to renounce this crowd need not signify approval of their eagerness to pack a bag. What's more, we can't vote them out, not really. The advantages enjoyed by incumbents win them reelection roughly 95 percent of the time. A sitting representative has a greater chance of dying in office than losing at the polls.

In an egalitarian society, lawmakers do not exploit their office to vote themselves lavish perks but live much like the people they represent. Congress should get the same health coverage enjoyed—can that be the right verb?—by a typical American. Congressional pay should be pegged to the median for a family of four, currently $70,354. And Congress should receive the same vacation time as an average American, which right now is thirty-seven days. No wait, I'm thinking of France, that terrifying example of all that is to be shunned: attractive clothes, delicious meals, widespread human happiness. American workers average twelve days a year. Oh, everlasting wearisome attire! Even on Casual Fridays!

Some readers found the preceeding argument unconvincing, noting how hard those in Congress work. No doubt. But so do coal miners, janitors, and commercial fishermen. The question I posed—okay, the complaint I made—concerned the disparity between the vacation time our representatives bestow upon themselves and the vacation time the average American worker receives. My hope is not that Congress gets less but that the rest of us get more, something Congress itself could guarantee.

One other thought about the wrangling over pay in the first Congress: There were forceful arguments for high pay. Here's one in a letter from an anonymous member of Congress to the *Pennsylvania Gazette*. If proper wages were not paid, "your government will be administered only by a few aristocratic nabobs, who can afford to live without wages upon the income of large estates."

As it turns out, allowing Congress to award itself not merely decent but fat pay packets has not resulted in a government of ordinary citizens. It yielded a government of nabobs, a plutocracy, or something close to it. In 2008, two-thirds of our senators were millionaires, as were 39 percent of those in the House. Among Americans who are not legislators, about 1 percent are millionaires. The other 99 percent really could use a vacation.

## TEMPTING THE MAID

*My mother wants to hire someone to clean house and handle the laundry. To assure herself of this person's integrity, she plans to leave loose money around as "bait" during the house cleaner's first few days of work. Here in Brazil, those stray bills can constitute a significant percentage of a house cleaner's wages. My mother sees this "trap" as a perfectly ethical precaution. Do you?*
*—Daniel Hutchins, Juiz De Fora, Brazil*

Your use of "trap" implies one distasteful feature of your mother's scheme: it tiptoes toward entrapment, if not legally, then certainly ethically. The target of her little sting is minding her own business, only to be lured into crime. Theft is clearly wrong, but there is a well-known injunction not to put temptation in someone's path. ("Tempt not a desperate man," says Romeo to Paris.) That's why I don't wear a sport coat made of hundred-dollar bills. That and because I look so sickly in green.

People are not crudely divisible into honest and dishonest; different circumstances elicit different behaviors in us all. (Millions of otherwise law-abiding citizens have illegally downloaded music.) As a prudent employer, your mother should not strew cash around the house; as a sensitive human being, she should be mindful of the economic gulf between her and her housekeeper. We do not wave food in the faces of the hungry.

This sort of integrity-testing might be justifiable were there probable cause of serious wrongdoing and no other way to confirm it—for example, in a police precinct plagued by bribe-taking. But it should be a last resort, not a routine part of the job application. Your mother would do better to check references and hire someone of demonstrated honesty.

## SELF-OUTING

*I am a supervisor at a large corporation in the Bible Belt. I am gay and out and, while the company has no formal nondiscrimination policy, my colleagues and supervisors generally have no issues with my sexuality. I am to interview a potential employee in his early twenties who hunts, drives a truck, and did not attend college. I want those who join my team to be of a tolerant disposition. Would it be appropriate to tell this applicant that I am gay?*

*—Name withheld*

It would not. By bringing up your sexual orientation in a job interview, you could give the applicant the impression that his is a factor in hiring, a policy that would be abhorrent. Instead, talk about your company's amiable, tolerant workforce and your eagerness to add someone to your team who is similarly broad-minded. That is, discuss the company's practices, not your personal life, something relevant only to those who might date you.

It is a fine thing to demand that an employee be complaisant, not so fine to demand—or seem to suggest—that he be gay (or, for that matter, straight). What's more, your company's hospitality toward its diverse workforce is something an applicant should want to know, something that should make him even more eager to come aboard.

**UPDATE**: The interviewer did not disclose his sexual orientation. He hired this applicant who later learned from someone else that he, the interviewer, is gay. The applicant, now a new employee, had no problem with this (and mentioned that he has a cousin who is a lesbian). The interviewer acknowledges, with becoming humility, that he learned something about his own preconceptions.

## DECEPTIVE COVER LETTER?

*When my husband, a native of Venezuela, began seeking work as a Web site manager, his résumé was full of grammar, spelling, and punctuation errors. I stepped in, and now nothing goes out until it is perfect. Indeed, I often rewrite whole sections of his cover letters. Am I duping potential employers, who may find out only after they hire him that while his spoken English is just fine, he can't write to save his life?*

*—Christy White, Oakland, CA*

As long as the information in these letters is scrupulously honest, you may improve its presentation. Job candidates and employment agencies do so routinely, sometimes using professional résumé-writing services. A cover letter is not an editorial test; it is meant to be a forthright expression of suitability for a job. If you fear that you might be misleading, you can have your husband state that he has dazzling technical skills, potent low post moves, strong rebounding ability, and real court savvy—if he is applying for a job as a New York Knick, say (and if he has those skills I hope he will apply immediately)—but that he is a native Spanish speaker whose writing ability in English is limited. He should not, of course, apply for jobs in which writing well in English is essential, or hoodwink a potential employer about his lack of that latter ability.

## NAME CHANGE

*I am an African American male looking for Web programming work. When I used my ethnically identifying first name on my résumé, I got few calls for job interviews. Now I use my middle name instead, and I've been getting more interviews. My résumé is accurate about my education and experience. Is it wrong to change my first name to conceal my ethnicity?*

*—Malik Raymond Singleton, Brooklyn*

This name change is a reasonable defense against racial bias. A potential employer has no right—ethically or legally—to refuse an interview because of an applicant's race. Thus, you are not withholding information that is even remotely relevant. The disheartening thing is that such a tactic may be called for. It would be unethical—and often illegal—to change your name to commit fraud, but you are not doing any such thing.

One argument against the practice of hiding one's identity as a member of a minority is that it can augment oppression by concealing how accomplished and ubiquitous a particular group is—closeted gays, for example. This may in part explain your discomfort, the feeling of letting down the side, to in any way act as if being African American is something discreditable that should be concealed. But that's not what your action implies. There is not, of course, a thoroughgoing parallel between sexual orientation and race: when you show up for an interview, it is apparent that you are an African American. In any case, it is not the victims of discrimination but those whose bigotry prompts such measures who should feel shame.

If you persist in your name change, you'll be in good company. Actors Tony Curtis, Kirk Douglas, and Winona Ryder; singer Barry Manilow (okay, I'm not sure he's really good company, not on a long car trip, not if he insists on singing "Mandy" for thousands of miles); and architect Frank Gehry, to name only a few, changed their names to avoid the most onerous effects of discrimination. Woody Allen and Mel Brooks also adopted stage names, but more to gain a patina of showbiz glamour than to conceal the ethnicity so central to their work.

Incidentally, another simple solution: use your initials.

## SALARY LIST

_My boss accidentally left a document on my desk listing the salaries of all the company's employees. I read only the header, not the contents, then returned it. I felt I did the right thing, but now I'm not so sure. Reading it would have harmed no one, and the information would have helped me negotiate a long overdue raise. But would it have been ethical?_

—_J.H., San Francisco_

More than ethical—admirable. In your place, I would have read the document, made sure my own salary was listed, and circulated it (anonymously—I'm reform-minded, not self-destructive) to everyone in the company. The one who benefits most when such information is suppressed is your boss, not you or your colleagues. It can help an employee to know that the person at the next desk makes twice as much money for performing the same task. If salaries are reasonable, employees will understand and accept them. If they are not, secrecy helps sustain that injustice.

Transparency is necessary for good governance—why not for good management? It is a wise policy that requires publicly owned companies to disclose certain financial information, including compensation packages offered to many senior executives. In money matters as in many others, knowledge is preferable to ignorance. It is thieves who operate under cover of darkness.

Broadcasting salaries may be sensible and benign, but don't expect your boss to see it that way, or your colleagues, or the company's lawyers. Money is the last bastion of prudery. People who post videos online of themselves having sex blush demurely as they draw the veil over their 1040s. Some are embarrassed because they make more than you might think, others ashamed because they make less. But while this fiscal priggishness is understandable, you have no moral duty to play along (legal constraints notwithstanding).

And don't be so sure that you are underpaid and due for a raise. If you tear away that veil, you might not like what you see.

**UPDATE:** Many readers rejected my conclusion here, instead granting an employer broad rights to denominate anything as secret. I remain skeptical. Some claims to confidentiality are legit—genuine trade secrets or employee health information, for example—but others are not. This salary information is sub rosa simply because the boss wishes it so. But pursuing self-interest doesn't endow him with a moral claim to secrecy. That is, you can't accuse an employee of stealing information that is, at least as an ethical matter, already his.

Nor does it damn the employee to act anonymously, as some of my critics charged. We vote anonymously, and few people object to that. In both cases, anonymity is a way to be protected from bullying, not a confession of wrongdoing.

I was especially surprised by some readers' assertions that ignorance produces tranquility and knowledge causes turmoil. I'd counter that employees are reasonable people who will respect a fair wage structure. Public universities, for example, have made salary information available for years with remarkably little rioting.

I do agree, as was much bruited about, that some employees might prefer salary secrecy. But that doesn't mean they're entitled to it. Some people would like to keep their real estate transactions secret, but deed transfers are public record precisely because access to such information is deemed a public good, even if, from time to time, it discomfits some folks. So it is with salaries.

## FAIR PAY

*When I hire local teenagers to do odd jobs—weeding, hauling boxes—I pay about what they'd earn at a fast-food restaurant. I pay adults doing similar work at least twice as much and add a hefty tip, since they have families and basic living expenses. It's not the money but the message: I don't want the teens to think this sort of labor might provide a lucrative career. Is this pay inequality ethical?*

*—Joan Hess, Fayetteville, AR*

Two people doing the same job equally well are entitled to the same pay. How they spend it—on rent or video games or renting video-games—is not your concern. It might not be about the money for you, but I assure you it is for your hires. They're not hauling around your boxes for the career counseling you provide. Nor is your "message" even needed; few would-be systems engineers or surgeons are sidetracked by the giddy high-rolling lifestyle of the handyman.

Looked at benignly, you're giving a bonus to an older worker to help him meet his financial obligations. Looked at less generously, you're penalizing a teenager for not having a couple of kids. Is that what you mean by "the message"? Are you prepared to fully embrace your pay plan? If an employee wants to buy a second TV or have a third child, will you give him a raise? When one of his kids grows up and leaves home, will you cut his pay? Such thinking was once used to justify paying single women less than married men because while men had families to support, the women didn't "need" the money.

The ethical solution is to pay what in your area is considered a fair wage for the job—not just what the market will bear, but a decent living wage—regardless of who has it. That is, set compensation according to the act not the actor. What you engaged in is simply age discrimination disguised as generosity.

### DELIVERY

*Is it ethical to order food for delivery during a thunderstorm? If I'm doing it*
*to avoid going outside and getting wet or struck by lightning, isn't it wrong to*
*have somebody else (with little agency to refuse) do it in my place?*
                                        —*James J. Stranko, New York*

As someone who seldom mines his own coal, I'm in no position to condemn those who consign difficult, dangerous, or simply miserably uncomfortable jobs to others.

Here is how you can do so ethically—support efforts to ensure that those who do such jobs toil in decent conditions, with their health and safety protected, and that they earn decent wages and receive the benefits we all want and many of us expect in our wealthy nation: medical insurance, a pension, a vacation now and then. You can't always know such things, but you can make some effort to educate yourself about those you employ, and you can tip generously when someone works for you under unusually rough conditions.

### INTERNAL AFFAIRS

*I work for a media company. We're quite busy lately, and I would like to*
*send one of our interns, who are unpaid college students, on the occasional*
*coffee run, but it seems wrong somehow. I know they wouldn't be learning*
*anything, but wouldn't it be better for the company to have an unpaid intern*
*and not a paid employee do this?*
                                        —*Name withheld, New York*

If only "better for the company" were synonymous with "ethical," I would have an easier job. And Bernie Madoff would get less jail time. Alas, there are more reliable guides to right conduct, ones that discourage regularly asking interns to fetch your coffee or give you a pedicure.

The quasifiction engaged in by many employers and colleges is that interns will be paid little or nothing but will earn college credit because their experience is essentially educational. Having made that bargain, both parties—employer and college—are bound by it. Interns should be assigned tasks that are at least potentially edifying. If you want to hire people to run errands, do so and be candid about their duties.

Some flexibility is called for. Much can be learned just by hanging around an operation, and newbies must expect to do some scut work. And so, on rare occasions, when tasks pile up and deadlines loom, interns may be sent on a coffee run. Such chores can teach them how coworkers help out in a crisis. But this should not be a routine chore.

When my daughter was a college student, she had an internship with *The Colbert Report*, an experience she found genuinely illuminating. She told me, "If everything was busy, we might be asked to pick up coffee for the people in the studio. We were happy to do it, because we loved the show, and that was a way we could help things run smoothly."

In fact, knowing the coffee preference of Dave or Jay or Alex Trebek could be regarded as professional training for those whose first post-college job, given the dismal economy, will be at Starbucks.

---

### CHILD LABOR

*In the developing country where I live, it is common to have household help. A friend asked me to hire a fourteen-year-old whose impoverished family badly needs the money. If I don't, this child will find someone who will. In my house, her work would be age-appropriate—rinsing dishes, making beds, and dusting, what we call "top work"—and she would receive nutritious meals, kind treatment, and not be endangered. Or is it more ethical to forswear child labor while knowing that her need will drive her to a job that could be much more exploitative than the one in my house?*

*—Amita Chauhan, Mumbai*

It is a grim truth that many families face such dire poverty that they rely on the earnings of their youngest members. And so you might do some good by employing this fourteen-year-old, but you must be mindful that she is fourteen when determining what sort of work she does and how many hours she does it, considering not only her health and safety, but also her future. She may need to work, but she also needs to go to school to escape a lifetime of poverty.

Jacqueline Novogratz, CEO of the Acumen Fund, a nonprofit that takes an entrepreneurial approach to combating global poverty, suggests the "employer could help the girl pay for school fees so that she can attend school, and then have her come afterward to help clean the house. The combination of part-time work with full-time schooling provides the girl's family with a sense of dignity, and it gives the girl greater choice in her life."

Her suggestion is a good one for you and your would-be employee, transforming you from someone who would benefit from her being permanently impoverished into a partner in her having a brighter future.

**UPDATE:** Chauhan did not hire this girl. She e-mailed "I have a son who is the same age and thought it would be very difficult to see one child working while another was studying and playing."

## MATERNITY LEAVE

*My state does not mandate paid maternity leave, and federal law doesn't cover a business as small as where I work. Fortunately, my generous employer offers eight weeks paid leave and an additional four unpaid. I am not sure I will return to work after that. May I still accept this offer? If I accept but do not return, must I refund the money?*

*—Name withheld, New Mexico*

Maternity benefits are not an advance payment on future work; they are something already earned, akin to accumulated vacation days or, in more humane countries, simply something to which all workers have a right. There is nothing dishonorable in your not resuming work after your baby is born or unseemly about your uncertainty. Having a child, particularly a first child, is a life-changing experience. You cannot be sure how it will affect your feelings about the job.

Although state law did not require your employer to offer maternity leave, she chose to do so, making it a part of your compensation package. She did not include the condition that only those who return to work are eligible for paid leave. Now she must keep up her end of the bargain. She may not rescind it because she is unhappy with what you do after your leave is over.

What is truly ignominious is not just the meager benefits offered by any particular employer—and yours seems better than most—but our national policy. In 2007, *Inc.* magazine reported "In a study from McGill University's Institute for Health and Social Policy, the United States, Lesotho, Liberia, Swaziland, and Papua New Guinea were the only countries out of 173 studied that didn't guarantee any paid leave for mothers. Among the 168 countries that do, 98 offer 14 or more weeks of paid leave." Inexplicably, the proud chant, "We're number 168!"

is seldom raised in the halls of Congress, not even by those representatives who boast of their devotion to family values or who hector mothers about the importance of staying home to raise their children. And yet few of those representatives are ever struck by lightning. It makes you wonder.

**UPDATE**: A week after having her baby, the letter writer told her boss she was on the fence about returning to work. The boss changed the offer to two weeks of paid leave instead of eight.

# *Arts*

DOES COMEDY QUALIFY AS ART? I DON'T ALLUDE TO WILDE OR SHAKESPEARE; when it comes to the Immortals, nobody would argue otherwise. I mean something less highbrow—late-night television comedy, a field in which I worked and about which I have strong feelings.

The notion of ethical comedy was much discussed in 2009 when David Letterman joked "Sarah Palin went to a Yankees game yesterday. There was one awkward moment during the seventh inning stretch: her daughter was knocked up by Alex Rodriguez."

Palin was outraged, claiming that her fourteen-year-old daughter, Willow, had been slurred. Letterman explained that he had been referring to Bristol Palin—eighteen, unwed, and a mother. He declined to apologize but said ruefully, "There are thousands of jokes I regret telling." Sarah Palin, unappeased, called the joke "disgusting." A week after the original broadcast, Letterman apologized on the show, mollifying Palin but not the demonstrators outside his studio. They demanded that he be fired.

He was not, of course, and quite rightly. He should not even have apologized. His mordant and amusing discussion of the episode got it right: it was a lame joke, but no worse than what he's been doing for thirty years.

But while his initial response was appropriate, his analysis of that joke was imperfect. He properly acknowledged it to be "ugly" and second-rate—so lackluster that many comics had been telling essentially the same joke for months. Here's Jay Leno on Sept. 2, 2008: "Governor Palin announced over the weekend that her seventeen-year-old unmarried daughter is five months pregnant. And you thought John Edwards was in trouble before!" Similar gags were delivered by Conan O'Brien, Jimmy Kimmel, and Craig Ferguson, among others. Hack work.

Letterman's version had three targets—Alex Rodriguez for his sexual shenanigans, Sarah Palin for her abstinence-only politics, and Bristol Palin for personifying the futility of that advocacy. All three are fair game, including Bristol, who, unlike, say, the Obama kids, is now over eighteen and chose to be a public figure as a seventeen-year-old by participating in the presidential campaign and promoting teen abstinence. Audiences enjoy irony. Comics mock hypocrites.

Here's where things get cloudy. Palin declared that it was not Bristol but Willow who went to the ball game—ergo Letterman had scurrilously attacked a child. He explained that he had alluded to Bristol, and there's little reason to disbelieve him. He's an honest guy; he doesn't taunt children; the audience clearly took him to mean Bristol. Indeed, I doubt that many of them knew Willow was in town. Or that she exists.

A joke is a form of fiction, its punch line a contrivance: the bartender was not actually talking to the duck. A premise, too, can be invented; a man with a duck did not really walk into a bar. Letterman's premise was that Bristol attended a Yankees game. If reality muddied things, that is an aesthetic flaw, not a moral transgression.

Alas, the joke does have ethical shortcomings. Although Bristol is a legitimate subject, she is also a pathetic one—beleaguered by her family, pressed by her circumstances, abandoned by her boyfriend—making the joke a bit bullying.

More disheartening, sexism permeates the joke. Letterman has ridiculed Bill Clinton, Eliot Spitzer, John Edwards, and, here, Alex Rodriguez for licentious excess—embarrassing conduct, perhaps, but Letterman treats it with nothing harsher than a sort of smirking envy. Bristol is condemned on moral grounds—she's loose, she's easy, she's held to the standards of a 1950s high school. Nobody envies the tramp.

A joke is an expression of its teller's persona; context counts. The night Letterman told this joke, his Top Ten List was "Highlights of Sarah Palin's Trip to New York." No. 2 was "Bought makeup at Bloomingdale's to update her 'slutty flight attendant' look." Male politicians are not so relentlessly mocked for their appearance, and when they are, it is for being a fop or a doofus, vain or foolish. Women politicians are evaluated for their sexual allure; they are put in their place. In his initial response to this contretemps, Letterman said of No. 2, "I kind of like that joke." He should reconsider. He should retire the word *slut*.

In that wry, self-mocking, and often astute clarification, Letterman dismissed the entire kerfuffle by saying of his material, "They're just jokes." This is not so astute. Every joke is an assertion about the world—sometimes indirect, sometimes ironic, always open to interpretation. Neither Sarah Palin nor I must endorse Letterman's every (or any) assertion, but he must. Otherwise, he would be an unprincipled hack, expounding what he does not believe.

My exegesis is not that of the Palins; theirs was more baroque. Todd accused Letterman of making light of rape. Sarah rebuked him for his "sexually perverted comments." When Letterman ultimately apologized and Palin accepted, she managed to invoke "our U.S. military women and men putting their lives on the line for us to secure America's right to free speech." If you cocked your head, you could almost hear "The Star-Spangled Banner" and catch the faint aroma of . . . could it be eagles?

I wrote for David Letterman from early 1984 through 1990. I found my boss to be smart, funny, and worthy of respect—a practitioner of ethical comedy. No orders were issued to the writing staff, no rules inscribed, but as in most cultures, there was an unstated code the community absorbed. For example, much comedy attacks; the interesting moral question is whom and why. Our show's precept: assail the powerful; don't pummel their victims. And we were to mock only what was volitional: what someone does, not who he is. You do not ridicule a guy for having a huge nose; you do deride him for being an inept actor in a crummy movie. Did Dave fall short? Often, as do we all. But he lived in a moral universe, subjecting his staff, his material, and himself to moral scrutiny. Having subsequently worked on other TV shows, I learned that this is not universally so.

Soon after I started at *Late Night*, we did a spot with the Ridgid Tool girl, a curvy spokesmodel for a tool company that publishes the kind of calendar once ubiquitous on gas station walls. Unsurprisingly, she was less than eloquent, and Dave came across as exploitative, as if he'd invited her onto the show to humiliate her. After the taping, he and the senior staff reviewed the segment, and we never again did another like it. I don't want to overpraise Dave, he was surely concerned with his image, with how the audience saw him, but he was also determined to do the right thing, which is one of the reasons I was proud to be part of the show. That, and a chance to write "Monkey Cam" and work with one very talented chimp.

There is another aspect of comedy that affected me more directly in writing the column. Some readers thought that it was unseemly to write about serious subjects in an amusing way, arguing that to do so trivializes important matters. But the opposite of *funny* isn't *serious*; it's *somber*. To use humor is to choose a rhetorical style, a particular tone. George Bernard Shaw wrote "Life does not cease to be funny when people die any more than it ceases to be serious when people laugh." Samuel Taylor Coleridge put it this way, "The true comic is the blossom on the nettle."

After I made this argument, some readers berated me for wasting time on something as trifling as a comedian's joke. One even suggested a few worthier topics: "the looming conflict in Iran and the impending threat of North Korea." Let me reassure those so concerned that the news pages of the *Times* devote much attention to those things. And I hope it is not tactless to mention that my topic was not so picayune as to prevent those critics from bothering to comment on it. But I quite like these putatively unimportant matters. They are a culture's unguarded moments. Examining them can yield glimpses of our assumptions about—as here—power, family, and gender. In any case, the persistence of murder doesn't require us to ignore burglary.

Some readers blamed Letterman for his choice of subject matter, asserting that teen pregnancy is "nothing to joke about" because "it is a serious problem in our society." We rightly distinguish between fair and unfair targets for a joke, but as a general matter, all topics are inbounds, even the most troubling or profound. Especially the most troubling and profound. It is tears that create the conditions for laughter—the sort of laughter that counts for something. Much Jewish humor, for example, responds to centuries of suffering. Here's how John Milton, a man who inexplicably never got his own talk show, translated a couplet from Horace:

> *Joking decides great things,*
> *Stronger and better oft than earnest can.*

Some readers charged that I violated journalistic ethics by writing about someone I'd worked for. That might be true for a reported article: a journalist generally should not write about someone with whom he or she has a close association. Covering events in which you participate is fraught with potential conflicts of interest and distortions of perspective. But that is not true for an opinion column like mine. I hoped that my personal experience with Dave and his show would provide some fresh insights into comedy in general and his sort of comedy in particular. I had to be transparent about my history, and I was. Writing for *Late Night* is not something I "admitted," as one reader put it, but something I'm proud of and feared I was boastful about.

Here, some nettlesome questions from both the makers and consumers of art, high and low.

## NUTCRACKER NUT

*Last Christmas I took my grandchildren to* The Nutcracker, *a ballet I love. My enjoyment was severely marred by the appearance of a black snowflake and then, even worse, a black Snow King. The aesthetic incongruity was inconceivable. The entire ballet was spoiled. It is analogous to a one-legged midget playing Tarzan. Does this make me a racist?*

—*Name withheld, Sewell, NJ*

This does make you a racist—not in the sense of exercising a virulent antipathy toward African Americans, but of being, like most of us, affected by feelings about race.

Here's one way to think about your reaction. When you see *Gladiator*, the hero is not portrayed by a citizen of ancient Rome; he does not speak Latin. He is a New Zealander, and nobody complains (except a few carping movie critics who are just jealous of Russell Crowe). When you go to *The Lion King*, the title character is not a lion. Movies, theater, ballet—all are artificial. To experience them is to accept many contrivances. In Shakespeare's day, men played the women's roles and people did not see this as an "aesthetic incongruity," but as a theatrical convention.

What prevented your doing likewise at *The Nutcracker* were your ideas about race. Remember, we're talking about dancing snowflakes, yet none of the dancers were crystalline specks of frozen water. The entire event eschewed any pretense of naturalism, of strictly corresponding to the real world. What you call an "aesthetic" response is invariably more complicated than that, a product of many of our ideas.

Not so long ago, some folks would have reacted similarly to a Jewish singer in a leading role at the opera. But as anti-Semitism waned in America, so did such attitudes. As race-neutral casting becomes commonplace, I think you'll no longer see it as incongruous; you'll judge a dancer by her skill, not her skin tone.

## NASAL CHORUS

*I sing in the chorus at Lincoln Center. One evening while the baritone performed a particularly difficult solo, an emotionally demanding a cappella passage, an audience member in the first-tier box, only five feet from the stage, started blowing his nose loudly and continued to do so throughout the solo; even his companions were gesturing for him to pipe down. Making disruptive noises at a concert is certainly rude, but if you are sitting close enough to distract the performers, does it rise to unethical?*

*—J.C., New York*

There is no way to precisely calibrate when *rude* changes state to *unethical*, like water to ice. But to annoy those few audience members near you is bad and to hinder the performers is worse, potentially undermining the concert for everyone.

What's significant is when this fellow's affliction hit. We do not condemn people for things over which they have no control, like the unexpected onset of a cold or a sudden attack of hay fever. But if the honker knew, or should have known, before arriving at the concert, that he was apt to be a nasal nuisance, even just to those around him, he had a duty to gulp down powerful decongestants or simply stay home.

There are ways to respond to the surprising onset of something dreadfully phlegmy; that's why theaters have lobbies to which one can flee, and why the muse Terpsichore is so often depicted proffering Nyquil, or should be.

## PICTURE THIS

*I am a street photographer, which means I photograph people in public places, sometimes without their knowing it. I'm not a full-time professional, but I've had gallery shows and do sell my work. Do I have an ethical obligation to get people's permission before taking their picture?*

—*Todd August, Houston*

There are few legal barriers to your shooting first and asking questions later. In fact, you seldom need to ask at all. Someone strolling down the street has no reasonable expectation of privacy, so you don't need permission to take his picture. Commercial use without consent is forbidden—you can't snap a skateboarding Luciano Pavarotti and put him on a Wheaties box—but the law recognizes society's interest in the free exchange of ideas, including artistic ones. Hence, explains Adam Liptak, a lawyer for the *Times*, "authentic artistic uses are pure speech as deserving of full First Amendment protection as news reporting is." And while newspapers and photographs, of course, have a commercial dimension—both are sold—their essential identity is the expression of ideas, unlike that Wheaties box.

However, while the state should not restrain your photography, there are times when you yourself should. Being an artist does not exempt you from considering the consequences of your behavior. If early one morning, bleary-eyed and unshaven, I am walking to the deli for a quart of milk, I might not want a photo of myself taken that would end up on display in an art gallery. Yes, I have chosen to appear in public, but that's where they put the grocery stores; a guy's got to eat. That should not compel me to pose for you. My interest in not looking like a goofball ought to carry some ethical weight. By ignoring the feelings of your involuntary models, you reduce them to mere things, like rocks or clouds shot by a nature photographer. Thus, you should indeed ask permission to photograph someone—before, if practical, after, if you're going for something candid. Should the subject refuse, consider finding another one.

More troubling than the vanity of a pampered person like me is the more complicated issue of involuntary subjects with whom there is a significant power imbalance—a homeless person sleeping on the street in New York, for example, or the wretchedly poor of Calcutta or Mogadishu. It can be important, both morally and artistically, to photograph these people, but you must be mindful of the humanity of those who have no meaningful choice about participating in your art.

You may one day capture an image of such transcendent truth and beauty that you're willing to override a subject's wishes. So be it. You'd not be the first artist to behave like a ruthless egomaniac, nor your subject the first to believe his life was ruined by his portrayal in a work of art, nor I the first to enjoy such a work. Unlike law, which must try to lay down adamant and precise rules, ethics may limn general principles, which in this case urge you to give your subject genuine consideration but not absolute authority.

---

### STEALING—SAVING?—PUBLIC ART

*I live in a city where artists display their work on abandoned buildings and fences around empty lots. Is it ethical for me to take home these items that face certain ruin? I concede that the artist's intent was for the pieces to be on public display, not to hang in my living room. But in the 1800s, Lord Elgin brought Greek statuary to London for safekeeping. So am I a preservationist or a looter?*

*—Name withheld, Chicago*

Comparing your swiping neighborhood street art to Lord Elgin's bringing the Parthenon marbles to England, while playful, does suggest that you are, alas, a looter.

Elgin couldn't get the okay of the Parthenon's creators, because they were long dead, but you can consult the contemporary artists whose work you covet. And while the Parthenon marbles ended up at the British Museum, available to all, there is, presumably, less open access to your living room. Exacerbating your misdeeds, much street art is meant to be ephemeral; your taking it undermines the work itself. Thus, your actions are analogous to stealing flowers from a public park where they were planted for the enjoyment of all: they too will wither and die, but that doesn't mean you should swipe them.

It is undeniable that the marbles Elgin brought to England are in better shape than many of those left behind, which have been through several armed conflicts and endured the ill effects of Athens' auto emissions. But by that justification, the ghost of Aristotle can walk off with Ellis Island or the USS *Constellation* or Edison's Invention Factory, which have all been on the most endangered list of the National Trust for Historic Preservation. And in fact, the Greek government is eager to have what it regards as its statuary returned, and many nations and arts organizations support its desire. Such advocates are less apt to use the term *safekeeping* than *plunder*.

And so Elgin's behavior may have been as dubious as yours. Byron certainly thought so, excoriating Elgin in "The Curse of Minerva" as a man who should be turned to marble himself:

> *So let him stand through ages yet unborn*
> *Fix'd statue on the pedestal of Scorn.*

Count yourself lucky that Byron doesn't write an ethics column.

Elgin's supporters make a more potent argument—or at least raise nettlesome questions—when they challenge the primacy of geographic proximity. Does a locale have a claim to a work of art merely because it was created there? The contemporary Greek nation-state has little in common with the Greece of the Periclean Age, when the Parthenon was built. Surely these artifacts are the common cultural heritage of the entire world. Perhaps. But history grants this claim: viewing a work of art in its original setting (albeit one with more cars and iPods around) can deepen our understanding of that work. The pyramids would not be the pyramids if moved from Egypt to San Diego. Although the access to good surfing beaches might be adequate compensation.

## GRANTED

*As a writer midway through a long project, I'm considering applying for a small merit-based grant. I don't need the money to complete my project, but it would be gratifying and helpful to receive it. If I win, however, I might deprive another artist of the means necessary to complete a project. Is getting this grant just getting greedy?*

*—C.C., Ithaca, NY*

If this grant is meant as alms for artists, forgo it. But not every grant is established to aid the indigent; some are intended to laud the accomplished. Both goals are admirable. The Nobel Prize, for example, is hardly needs-based, and while it is not, strictly speaking, something for which one can apply, people have been known to lobby vigorously for it. Reasonable enough; winning such recognition can be a boon to a writer's morale and a boost to her literary career. No one thought less of V. S. Naipaul, not a poor man, for accepting this honor and the fat check accompanying it.

The obligation persists—for the grant-giving body, for you, for us all—to aid those in need, artists and others. But forsaking this grant is not your only way to do so. Should you find yourself with a bit of extra cash—from a grant, the Nobel Prize, or the lottery—it would be a fine thing were you (and V. S. Naipaul and I) to remember the less fortunate.

---

### GULLED

*I waited over eight hours in line to see Chekhov's* The Seagull *in Central Park. Each person is allowed two free tickets; I saw the play with one and sold the other for $80. A coworker says this is unethical, but I say I provided a service to the buyer. What do you say?*

*—J.B., New York*

I say your coworker is an astute and honorable person you'd do well to emulate. Selling your ticket subverts one of the most appealing qualities of free theater in the park: it's free, a summer pleasure for all, including those who cannot afford $80 a ticket. While you are allotted two tickets, they are to admit you and a companion, not provide an entrepreneurial opportunity. With tickets in short supply, your taking an extra to sell almost certainly meant that someone who waited in line behind you for eight and a half hours did not get to see the play. Thus, while you may perform a service to the buyer, it is akin to the service a burglar provides his fence, selling something to which he is not entitled.

What's more, your behavior clashes with the intent of the theater and those actors who agreed to appear because this is a free performance. Indeed, the theater explicitly bars your selling those tickets. Kenny Burrows, the theater manager, told me he "had people arrested every day" for scalping.

But the real villain here is *Seagull* director Mike Nichols, who turned a populist New York institution into a celeb-fest. Surely the long lines were less a reflection of New Yorkers' hunger for Chekhov than our eagerness to glimpse (the by all accounts splendid) Meryl Streep, Kevin Kline, et al. And this doesn't even take into account Nichols' making that movie about dolphins who talk, mostly about themselves, at tedious length.

---

### FOUND DIARY

*My son found an adolescent girl's diary, an amazing sociological and cultural document, in front of a McDonald's. I'm an artist and writer and want to reproduce it in a limited edition down to its spiral binding, drawings, and coffee stains. I take the postmodern position that I can do whatever I want with it, though I would respect the diarist's privacy (her name is nowhere in it) and change any identifying factors. Is reproducing someone's innermost thoughts permissible in the name of art?*

*—Rita Sirignano, Calgary, Alberta*

It is not permissible to publish someone's work, particularly her most intimate thoughts, without consent. Indeed, it is disturbing that you apparently made no effort to return this diary to its owner by leaving word at that McDonald's, for example, or putting up posters in the neighborhood.

Your editing might protect the diarist from some embarrassment, but not all (surely the people who know her well would deduce her identity). But even if she were impervious to embarrassment, you may not peremptorily publish. *Postmodern* is one word for what you propose; there are others that are more accurate and less self-serving.

The law coincides with ethics here. One lawyer e-mailed me "In countries that adhere to the Berne Convention (and that would be most of the world), the diary gained copyright protection at the moment each entry was written; thus, reprinting it (i.e., copying it) would be copyright infringement, pure and simple. In the United States, such willful infringement is not just a tort but can be a federal crime."

---

**FOSTERING RACISM**

*I'm learning the old-time clawhammer-style banjo playing that accompanies fiddlers in traditional Appalachian string bands. When I gather with other musicians, some of the old songs we play include the offensive N word. Should we play these songs as they have come down to us or change the offensive lyrics?*

*—J.R., Toledo, OH*

The Stephen Foster problem. Its solution depends as much upon your audience as on you. You ought not perform these songs for a skinhead crowd as a way to supercharge its racist sing-along and rock-throw. Even if you're performing for a genial and rockless audience, you should either provide some context or skip the disturbing parts of this repertory, noting your omissions and briefly explaining why you've made them. Honesty compels you to give your listeners some sense of the original odious lyrics; discretion sometimes compels allusion rather than expression. To spring bigotry set to music on the unwary is to violate an implicit agreement between performer and listener. You wouldn't offer to provide a movie for a five-year-old's birthday party and show the kids *Psycho*.

You may sing the unalloyed originals when you're performing for an audience that knows what it's getting into. It is important to preserve and understand the relics of our past, even the most shameful aspects of that past. No good is served by creating a cleaned-up, artificial America. You simply need to make sure that an audience has a choice about what they'll be hearing. If they've been alerted—via your posters and program, perhaps—and wish to listen to historically accurate material, then discuss and sing. That is, give it not just the songs but some historical context, some real understanding.

Even when you are playing only with fellow musicians, you have an obligation not to perform these songs naively, but with a sense of their historical meaning. And you'd be wise to consider the coarsening effects on your own sensibilities of casually using such epithets. There is a moral obligation not to be a blockhead and an even more potent duty not to be the cause of blockheadedness in others.

Years ago I saw a bowdlerized "My Old Kentucky Home" on a Kentucky Fried Chicken box. As I recall, the lyrics as presented by Colonel Sanders were "'Tis summer, the young folks are gay." I was put off by this falsification of history, this willingness to dissemble to sell chicken. (And the gravy was kind of gluey, too.)

---

### JUDAICA

*Traveling in Poland, I visited antique stores offering Jewish items—menorahs, mezuzahs—that seemed more than sixty-five years old, suggesting that they were looted in the Holocaust. I saw things I wished to make part of my own Jewish home but found myself unable to pay for what was probably stolen property. Part of me wishes I had stolen (liberated?) some of them. Would that have been justified?*

*—Randy Malamud, Atlanta*

It would not. While these objects undoubtedly have a tragic history, it is less certain that they were stolen, explains Marilyn Henry, a columnist for the *Jerusalem Post* who has written much about such sad relics. She e-mailed me to say that "while the items may have been looted during the Nazi era, they may have been treated as legally 'abandoned' when the family was deported; they may have been sold at fire-sale prices by the original owner/family to raise funds to flee; they may have been held with the best of intentions by neighbors in anticipation that a Jewish family would return, and the family did not return."

Nor is it clear that the shopkeepers you encountered were culpable in acquiring these objects. As you note, the enormities that befell the owners of these objects occurred before all but the most elderly of these shopkeepers could have been involved. But even if a shopkeeper was knowingly trading in contraband, that would not justify your theft. Instead you should report such things to the authorities.

If an object can be traced to its rightful owner or community, you should try to return it, perhaps through an organization like the Commission for Art Recovery. You might be able to do so for objects of great financial value, but more often, Henry wrote me, "as beautiful as these objects were, many of them were mass-produced, or did not have decorative features or imprints that would make it possible to associate objects with a particular Jewish family or a Jewish institution such as a synagogue."

In this likely case, you could purchase an object and donate to a Jewish institution or use it in your own home, reverently and respectfully, much as you wished to do; "restoring it to the Jewish life for which it was destined," in Henry's words.

There can be unintended consequences if we all forswear buying Judaica so steeped in suffering and death. Agnes Peresztegi, director of the Commission for Art Recovery, Europe, said in an e-mail "it would not serve our purposes to eliminate the market, because if silver Judaica cannot be sold due to the issues of questionable ownership, they may get melted for the silver." She, too, agrees that to put these items to their intended use can be an honorable commemoration.

UPDATE: Several readers responded to this column by pointing out another possibility—many such objects merely seem old but are newly manufactured for the tourist trade. This may not be actual fraud, but it certainly relies on and intends to profit from unsophisticated and unwary buyers.

---

### PLAYWRIGHT'S RIGHTS

*The theater group at my mother's seniors' community typically does a lot of editing—removing expletives and cutting scenes so plays don't run too long. If they didn't, they could not do the plays at all. But what's worse, my mother recently changed a line in a play she is directing, Neil Simon's* California Suite, *to improve it. Isn't she wrong to do these things?*

—*Lane Galloway, Seattle*

Most playwrights license their work to be performed only as written— no cuts, no "improvements." Fortunately for your mother, some authors offer condensed, cleaned-up editions of their plays for groups like hers. I've been told that A. R. Gurney has such a version of his *Sylvia* in which the eponymous dog curses far less than in the original. If no short-and-sweet Simon is available, your mother should seek his permission for her changes; many writers are accommodating, particularly with small, nonprofit productions.

But if this approach fails, and you're willing to take your chances with the cops, let the cutting begin. Copyright law might bar it, but ethics does not. People have done the same to *Hamlet* for centuries, why not to *Mamma Mia?* Shakespeare's works are in the public domain, obviating legal constraints, but ethical concerns remain about the plays' integrity. Why restrict theatrical thought? It is a fine thing to loose more ideas, albeit some foolish, upon the world. If your mother read *Portnoy's Complaint* aloud to her cronies, trimming it to her standards of length and luridness, who'd be hurt? What's fair for Philip Roth is fair for David Mamet.

One objection to these unauthorized versions is that they can damage an author's reputation with the unwitting. But if a play is well known, no production, however nutty, can do its author much harm. (People's indelible memory of *The King and I* won't be effaced by my version featuring a drunken, bitter Anna and some fabulous naked kickboxing from Tuptim.) Your mother can defuse this danger by customizing only solidly established works and by alerting the audience that they're watching a play by Neil Simon as revised by her. The audience can decide which version it prefers—an aesthetic judgment, not an ethical one.

**UPDATE**: Many people, including many playwrights, vigorously disagreed with me on this one, none more eloquently than John Patrick Shanley, recipient of the Pulitzer Prize for his play *Doubt: A Parable* and the Academy Award for his screenplay *Moonstruck*, among numerous other honors. I reproduce our e-mail exchange as written (and with his generous consent).

Jan 9, 2007
Dear Sir,
How is it ethical to advise people to break the law, not as a matter of conscience, but as a matter of personal whim? How is it ethical to encourage people to alter and/or deface artists' work BECAUSE IT'S NOT IMPORTANT TO YOU? It's sad to see this kind of narcissistic drivel being passed off as ETHICS.
Not Very Respectfully,
John Patrick Shanley

Jan. 10
Thanks for the note. My task with the column is not simply to remind people what the law says but, from time to time, to suggest that, legal considerations aside, ethics might not preclude a particular action. When considering the mom who wanted to

trim a Neil Simon play, my approach was to note that the law forbids this and then make a case that ethics does not. There are many reasons one might knowingly break the law—as indeed, many people do—conscience, as you suggest, being perhaps the most admirable but by no means the only one. (Would you regard it as unethical to smoke pot, for example, hardly an act of conscience?) I did not argue that what she did was unimportant but that it was ethical.

If you are arguing on ethical, not legal, grounds, would you extend this same stricture to Shakespeare's plays? (In the public domain, of course—a legal matter—but the integrity of the work itself is an ethical concern.) Each is to be performed only as written? Out goes Kenneth Branagh's stirring *Henry V*, Baz Luhrmann's witty *Romeo + Juliet*? Why Shakespeare but not Neil Simon? If you're arguing the law, well sure, as I wrote, there is no legal right to do what the mom did and I defended, but what's legal and what's ethical are not always synonymous.

Respectfully,

Randy Cohen

On Jan. 10

Dear Randy,

Thanks for the reply. It boils down to the concept of property. The plays you cite in your reply to me are owned by the public. They are in public domain. Neil Simon's plays are private property. The public doesn't own them and therefore does not have the free use of them. When you write wearing the mantle of an ethics expert, you have a responsibility in excess of a normal citizen. You must be scrupulous. I suggest that it is unethical to extend a free pass to people who abuse copyrighted material. I'm not sure I understand how you arrive at a different conclusion. It seemed clear to me, in reading your piece, that your measure was simply your own idea of what property is important to protect, and what property is not so important; that is why I characterized your judgment as narcissistic. It was based on your feelings, rather than a governing intellectual concept.

John Patrick Shanley

Jan. 11

Dear John,

I agree. As a legal matter, what's at issue is the idea of property. But ideas and their expression are property only in a metaphoric sense. A play is not a car. If I swipe your car, you no longer have it. If the pencil-happy mom alters a Neil Simon play, the authentic version continues to exist for anyone who wants to produce it. Our idea of intellectual property is a recent one. Protecting that property was not the primary purpose of copyright law for the founders; rather, it was stimulating the creation of ideas. Article 1, Section 8, of the Constitution lays it out as "To promote the Progress of Science and useful Arts, by securing for limited Times to Authors and inventors the exclusive Right to their respective Writings and Discoveries." As the term of copyright continues to be extended well beyond that "limited time" (mostly at the behest of large economic interests), the moral basis of intellectual property law becomes debatable. So, while I concur—and wrote—that it is not legal for the mom to alter *California Suite*, the morality of the act is debatable. For me, a key question in making an ethical judgment is this: who's harmed? If she lets the audience know what sort of weird hybrid they're getting—i.e., if there's no deception—and if she pays Simon for his work (as apparently she did), then neither audience nor playwright are harmed. The results may well be rubbish and may make Simon miserable, but that would be an artistic, not an ethical disaster.

Thanks for your note,
Randy Cohen

On Jan. 11
Dear Randy,

All right, I admit it. I like your mind and you have won my respect. However, I will answer your question since it is pertinent. Who is harmed? I'll leave Mr. Simon alone and substitute myself in the situation. I am harmed. I am my reputation. I am my work. That's all we playwrights have. Copyright laws were written precisely because we are so vulnerable. People go and watch a play to which my name is affixed, and they form an opinion about my work based on that experience. Most people do not go to see a play multiple times. They see a play performed once and they feel they've seen it. "Have you seen *Doubt*?" "Yes." "Who wrote it?" "John Patrick Shanley." Some guys get to leave their children a house, a business. I leave my children my name and a few plays. It's their inheritance. And it deserves just as much protection as what you might leave your children.

Respectfully,
John

Jan. 12
Dear John,

You've had my respect and admiration since I first saw *Moonstruck*. (Although I might have been wary of exchanging e-mail with you had I read the second sentence in your Wikipedia entry: "He is famous for insisting in his contract that not a single word can be changed in the screenplays that he writes.") While I believe that my prescription—revise only solidly established plays; clearly inform the audience—guards an author's reputation, I realize that here we are at loggerheads, and I understand your determination to protect yours.

All best,
Randy

Jan. 12
Dear Randy,
What's left to say? Peace. By the way, you have an amazing amount of energy to deal with what I know to be a shitstorm of playwrights.

My Best,
Shanley

## CODA: RESPONDING TO ANGRY E-MAIL

A great pleasure of the previous exchange for me, in addition to John Patrick Shanley's insight and passion, was the gradual change of mood from angry to civil, even to affable. It took me awhile to learn that readers will accept—even enjoy—real disagreement as long as I am courteous and respectful.

For the first few years of the column, I tended to respond in-kind to angry e-mail. (I suspect many of us have a tendency to treat others as they treat us, for good or ill.) When I received a particularly hateful screed, insulting, ad hominem, SHOUTING AT ME IN ALL CAPS, I would think, You call that vicious? It's amateur work. I am a trained professional; I can compose something a hundred times more venomous. And I would.

Parents and teachers tell us that we'll feel bad if we respond brutally to someone who is brutal to us. It's not true. When I sent one of my tormenters a savage response, I felt great. It is a pleasure to thrash a bully. (And by "bully," I mean anyone who is unkind to me.) But it is an ineffectual pleasure, one that solidifies disagreement, makes enduring enemies, changes nobody's thinking, garners no dinner invitations. And so eventually I forsook the pleasures of the punch-up for another strategy: a soft answer turneth away wrath (Proverbs 15:1).

Turns out, it doth.

I began ignoring the tone of even the angriest e-mails and responding courteously to the sense of it. Just as an experiment. Often, even the author of a barbarous e-mail would then reply politely. Sometimes he'd apologize for his initial intemperance. My first, unworthy, thought, I'd hit upon a cunning way to make my tormenter feel guilty while I seized the moral high ground. Brilliant!

My second thought was to recall that Lincoln had invoked something similar in March of 1861, in his First Inaugural Address, in regard to a vastly graver conflict, urging "Though passion may have strained it must not break our bonds of affection," and appealing to "the better angels of our nature." Even for something as modest as an e-mail argument, that's excellent advice.

# *Technology*

THE MOST ENDURING CHANGE IN THE QUESTIONS SENT TO THE COLUMN derived from the ethical implications of new technologies. People found themselves in circumstances, in which no cultural consensus as to right conduct had yet evolved. Consider texting. You're having dinner with your teenage kids, and they text throughout. You hate it; they like it. At the office, managers are uncertain about texting during business meetings. Many younger workers accept it; some older workers resist. Those who defend texting regard such disputes as the clash of two legitimate cultures, a conflict of manners not morals. If a community—teenagers, young workers—consents to conduct that does no harm, does that make it okay, ethically speaking? Or, to put the question more broadly, is all ethics culturally relative?

Seek consent and do no harm are useful moral precepts that govern some doctors in their practice of medicine and some couples, that amorous community of two, in their erotic lives, but that dual doctrine does not validate ubiquitous text messaging. When it comes to texting, there is no authentic consent, and there is genuine harm.

Neither teenagers nor young workers authorized a culture of perpetual interruption. No debate was held, no vote taken at the junior high cafeteria or the employee lounge. Instead, like most people, both groups merely adapted to the culture they found themselves in, often without questioning or even being consciously aware of its norms, let alone considering alternatives. That's acquiescence, not agreement.

Few residents of Williamsburg, Virginia, in, say, 1740 rallied against the law that restricted voting to property-owning white men. For decades, there was little active local opposition to the sexual segregation in various Persian Gulf states. A more benign example: few of us are French by choice, but most French people act much like other French people, for good and ill. Conformity does not imply consent. It simply attests to the influence of one's neighbors.

So it is with incessant texting, a noxious practice that does not merely alter our in-person interactions but damages them. Even a routine conversation demands continuity, the focus of attention; it cannot, without detriment, be disrupted every few moments while someone checks a text. More intimate encounters suffer greater harm. In romantic comedy, when someone breaks a tender embrace to take a phone call, it's a sign of love gone bad. After any interruption, it takes awhile to regain concentration, one reason few of us want our surgeon to text while she's performing a delicate neurological procedure upon us. Here's a sentence you do not want to hear in the operating room or the bedroom: "Now, where was I?"

Experiments have shown the deleterious effects of interruption, including a study that, unsurprisingly, demonstrates that an interrupted task takes longer to complete and seems more difficult, and that the person doing it feels increased anxiety.

Mine is not a Luddite's argument, not broadly antitechnology or even antitexting. (I'm typing this by electric light on one of those computing machines. Newfangled is my favorite kind of fangled.) There are no doubt benefits and pleasures to texting. Quietly texting while sitting alone on a park bench harms nobody. (Although it cuts into your novel-reading time, opportunity costs.) But what is benign in one setting can be toxic in another. Chain saws: useful in the forest, dubious at the dinner table. As Dr. Johnson put it in a pre-texting age, "A cow is a very good animal in the field; but we turn her out of a garden."

Nor am I fretful that relentless texting hurts the texter herself. Critics have voiced a broad range of such concerns. Too much texting damages a young person's intelligence, emotional development, and thumbs. That may be so, but it is not germane here. When you injure yourself, that is unfortunate; when you injure someone else, that is unethical. I can thus enjoy reading about a texting teen who fell into a manhole. When a man is tired of cartoon mishaps, he is tired of life. And yes, that teen is fine now. Better than fine. In that manhole? Leprechaun gold.

A couple of years ago, a Massachusetts grand jury indicted a Boston motorman who crashed his trolley into another, injuring sixty-two people. He was texting on duty. A few weeks later, Patti LuPone berated an audience member who pulled out an electronic device during her show in Las Vegas. Theaters forbid the audience to text during a performance, a rule routinely disregarded. Perhaps stage managers could be issued tranquilizer darts and encouraged to shoot those who open any device during a show. At intermission, ushers can drag out the unconscious and confiscate their phones. Or we might institute Patti's Law: any two-time Tony winner would be empowered to carry a gun onstage and shoot such offenders.

These are the easy cases, of course, clearly it is unethical to text when doing so risks causing a train wreck. And formal regulation can easily address such gross potential dangers; a dozen states and the District of Columbia prohibit texting while driving, for example. But the problem of eternal texting in more casual settings cannot be solved by legislation. No parent will call the cops if a son or daughter texts at the table. Instead, we need new manners at home and at work, social customs to restrain this emerging technology.

Some folks regard incessant texting as a technological problem with a technological solution, proposing that offices, theaters, and restaurants install electronic devices to jam incoming and outgoing wireless transmissions. A college teacher who "used to regularly kick students out for texting during class" took that route. "I finally went online and bought a jammer from China. It sits silently in the corner, blocking all the cell-phone signals, and I never had to say another thing about texting again!" She is my hero, and I shall visit her every day in jail.

Alas, her tactics violate U.S. law, which bars phone jammers. Journalist Mike Elgan reported that this prohibition is not global, noting "Chinese and Indian schools use jammers to stop cheaters. Mexico allows jammers in churches and hospitals. And Pakistan allows jamming in banks and libraries." But in the United States, only federal authorities may deploy jammers, to the consternation of local officials anxious to, among other things, thwart cell-phone use by prison inmates.

The law notwithstanding, these gizmos are widely available on the Internet, from the powerful (able to block signals over a wide area) to the pocket-size (able to create a personal zone of textlessness). I've heard rumors of such things being discreetly deployed in upscale New York restaurants and in a Moscow theater.

One argument against them is that they would block emergency calls, including those to doctors, but this isn't much of an argument. A doctor could list the theater's or restaurant's landline as his emergency number and alert the proprietor or box office so someone can swiftly find him in a crisis. That's just what docs did for decades.

There is another limitation to wielding jammers in theaters. The determinedly inconsiderate would not realize that they have no signal until they flip open a device to text, distracting their neighbors with that flash of futile light. Perhaps during the transition to a more courteous age, we can all carry powerful flashlights—Maglite makes a particularly good one marketed under the sinister slogan "It's never dark in America"—and shine it in the eyes of texters, a bit of Old Testament eye-for-an-eye justice, a response the texter will no doubt greet with a quiet, gentle apology.

## WI-FI

*I accidentally discovered that the wireless Internet (Wi-Fi) card in my laptop lets me access the Web in my apartment. Clearly a neighbor has set up an access point with a signal strong enough to reach my kitchen. I use the Internet at home only to check e-mail, which will not affect my neighbor's usage. Can I use his signal? Should I offer to pay a portion of his monthly charge?*
*—Siona Listokin, Berkeley, CA*

If you regularly use the Web in your apartment, you should arrange for legit Internet access: that is, pay your fair share. Nor can you pay your neighbor for something that isn't his to sell.

But when you leave the apartment, things change. "If you're driving around town, and someone's left a node open, and you pop on and use it just to download some e-mail, feel free," advises Mike Godwin, senior technology counsel for Public Knowledge, a public interest group in Washington concerned with technology and intellectual property.

Godwin is persuasive. The person who opened up access to you is unlikely even to know, let alone mind, that you've used it. If he does object, there's easy recourse: nearly all wireless setups offer password protection. And while the failure to lock a door may indicate carelessness, not consent, in this case it does suggest indifference. Godwin does warn of the "tragedy of the commons," however, which here means you have an obligation not to use too much bandwidth, by downloading massive music files, for example, which would inconvenience other users.

But do you cheat the service provider, if not an individual consumer? Is there a free-rider problem? Time Warner Cable thinks so, and it has taken action against those who have touted the availability of an open Wi-Fi node on computer bulletin boards. The company argues, in effect, that while you may have a glass of water at a neighbor's, you may not run a hose from his place to yours.

Property rights, even as defined by Time Warner, are worthy of consideration, but overemphasizing them can stifle the public good that is universally available wireless Internet access. (Consider the interstate highway system or any public library: enormously useful institutions whose costs and benefits we all share and support through our taxes.) I prefer my prescription: everyone pays for Internet service at home, but when out and about, everyone may briefly use any available hot spots. Nobody's free riding, nobody's hurt, everyone has better service. Not as good as a publicly financed network available to all of us, but good enough.

"This is a period of transition, and the natural reaction of some institutions is to clamp down," Godwin concludes. He's right. But that does not create a moral imperative to defer to those who do. Rather, you may use but not overuse Wi-Fi hot spots you encounter around town as long as you pay your share to maintain the Internet.

## CELL MATES

*On the noisy ten-dollar Chinatown bus from New York to Boston, the girl behind me spent the entire four hours on her cell phone, telling the same inane story to five different people. I wanted to ask her to stop but didn't know if I should, considering the price of the ride and that I don't mind noise in general, just her nasal repetitive noise. What should I have done?*
*—Justine van der Leun, New York*

You should have grabbed her phone and pummeled her with it mercilessly while screaming "Shut up! Shut up! Shut up!" No, no. You can't do that. You should simply have grabbed her phone and thrown it out the window. And reveled in the cheers of your fellow sufferers.

Okay, not that either.

Her misbehavior falls between manners and morals and is difficult to rebuke because cell phones are a new—newish—technology; the social codes governing their use are still evolving. Here's my guideline: don't impose your cell phone conversation on people confined in a closed space—a bus, a restaurant, a commuter train. If your loquacity prevents those trapped nearby from reading or working or simply thinking their own thoughts, then cut it out.

You correctly suggest that different social settings permit different behavior. I can't ask everyone at a Jets game to pipe down so I can read *War and Peace*. And there are different expectations at McDonald's than at the Four Seasons. However, courtesy is not reserved for the wealthy. Even folks who can afford only the bargain bus are entitled to consideration.

As you imply, the ordinary conversation of one's fellow passengers may be as loud as the cell-phone prattler's, but it's not just a matter of decibels. We forbid playing radios or saxophones on the bus (and I trust you keep your iPod low); we can reasonably ban innovative sources of clamor and din like cell phones. Custom, too, has its claims.

You had every right to ask this passenger to curb her logorrhea, but she's not likely to have complied. The bus driver, if he'd had enough sleep the night before, might have had more success—he commands moral authority that passengers lack. Better still, the bus company should post this clear policy: one quick phone call to make travel plans, and that's it. Alternatively, I propose this federal law: unless your cell phone conversation is essential or amusing or intriguing, you must shut up.

---

## A VERY PRIVATE BABY

*After my niece's first birthday party, her parents sent videos and I uploaded them to YouTube for family members to view. My sister-in-law sent me a*

*stern note saying that unless images of my niece are accessible only to people approved by her and my brother, I may not post them. YouTube lets you restrict access, so I complied, but isn't her request overprotective and unfair?*
*—David, Los Angeles*

The only video subject more tedious than other people's vacations is other people's infants. (I quake at the prospect of vacationing-baby videos.) Does your sister-in-law really imagine a popular clamor for the newest niece pics? But while her ideas about privacy and child-rearing differ from yours, so be it. That is a mother's prerogative. Overprotective, perhaps, but not unfair. Her child, her rules.

In fact, her policy doesn't seem particularly extreme. She simply declines to have her family album published, i.e., posted online. If she applied this restriction not to Facebook but to *Entertainment Weekly*, nobody would bat an eye. Perhaps she senses, with a mother's intuition, that hers is a very private baby.

This conflict could prove more vexing when it comes to videos that include both you and your niece. May you not document your own life? Alas, here too the mother's wishes should have priority. But her policy is easily accommodated. As you suggest, you can limit access to approved visitors at a Web site or, more traditionally, disguise your niece's identity by printing the customary black bar across her eyes, lending her an air of criminality, quite advanced for a child her age.

## E-BOOK ACCESS

*I bought an e-reader for travel and was eager to begin* Under the Dome, *the new Stephen King. Unfortunately, the electronic version was not yet available. The publisher apparently withheld it to encourage people to buy the more expensive hardcover. So I did, all 1,074 pages, more than three and a half pounds. Then I found a pirated version online, downloaded it to my e-reader, and took it on my trip. I generally disapprove of illegal downloads, but wasn't this OK?*

*—C.D., Brightwaters, NY*

An illegal download is—to use an ugly word—illegal. But in this case, it is not unethical. Author and publisher are entitled to be paid for their work, and by purchasing the hardcover, you did so. Your subsequent downloading is akin to buying a CD, then copying it to your iPod.

Buying a book or a piece of music should be regarded as a license to enjoy it on any platform. Sadly, the anachronistic conventions of bookselling and copyright law lag behind the technology. Thus, you've violated the publisher's legal right to control the distribution of its intellectual property, but you've done no harm, or so little as to meet my threshold of acceptability.

To clarify, this is not analogous to buying the hardcover and cruising by the bookstore the next day to swipe the paperback, something that would impose new costs on the publisher. Ideally, publishers would institutionalize my prescription by offering multitiered options when you buy a book, perhaps including a free or discounted e-book to those who have purchased the hardcover, or even offering the hardcover version at a lower price to those who have already purchased the e-book.

Unsurprisingly, many in the book business take a harder line. My friend Jamie Raab, publisher of Grand Central Publishing and an executive vice president of the Hachette Book Group, says, "Anyone who downloads a pirated e-book has, in effect, stolen the intellectual property of an author and publisher. To condone this is to condone theft."

Yet it is a curious sort of theft that involves actually paying for a book. Publishers do delay the release of e-books to encourage hardcover sales—a process called "windowing"—so it is difficult to see you as piratical for actually buying the book ($35 list price, $20 from Amazon) rather than waiting for the $9.99 Kindle edition.

Your action is not pristine. Downloading a bootleg copy could be said to encourage piracy, although only in the abstract—no potential pirate will actually realize you've done it. It's true that you might have thwarted the publisher's intent—perhaps he or she has a violent antipathy to trees, maybe a wish to slaughter acres of them and grind them into Stephen King novels. Or to clog the highways with trucks crammed with Stephen King novels. Or perhaps King himself wishes to improve America's physique by having readers lug massive volumes. So be it. Your paying for the hardcover put you in the clear as a matter of ethics, forestry, and fitness training.

## COLLEGE OF MUSICAL KNOWLEDGE

*I produced a recording for a singing student's application to a college's professional music program. Her singing was passable but not great. Her mother asked, "Is there anything you can do with your equipment to make her voice better?" Computer technology enables me to make even the worst singer sound professional, but if I employ it, do I defraud the college?*

—S.H., Connecticut

You may help the student put her best foot (best throat?) forward; you may not abet deception. Simply recording her with a good microphone in a muted studio will make her sound better than taping her over the phone in a sawmill. But other techniques are more problematic. For example, to electronically alter the pitch of a note falsifies a basic fact, presenting her as singing what she did not (and perhaps cannot) sing. That is where to draw the line.

Admittedly, it is a blurry line. (Is it legit to compile several imperfect takes into one flawless version?) You might gain clarity by considering not only the acts of the producer but also the assumptions of the consumer. If you believe that admissions officers will be misled, then you've been a little too state-of-the-art.

Ideally, schools would provide technology guidelines (although enforcement would be tough) or ask producers to disclose their methods. While awaiting those reforms, be comforted that admissions officers are a savvy bunch, and that this recording is only a first step. Many professional programs require an in-person audition. This does not justify deceit but does mitigate its consequences.

**UPDATE:** S.H. gave the student two CDs. Both employed sophisticated audio techniques, including merging the best of several performances, but on only one did he digitally correct the pitch so the student seemed to hit notes she had not. He left it to her to decide which CD to submit. He says she chose the pitch-corrected version and has not yet heard from the school.

### ONLINE OR OUT OF LINE?

*Last spring I was a high school sophomore struggling with a research paper. My brother was a sophomore at a prestigious university with an excellent online library. He offered me his user name and password, providing access to resources unavailable to the public. Keeping in mind the thousands of dollars spent on his tuition, and that the university wouldn't lose anything by my getting an A on the paper, could I have accepted his offer?*
*—Sara Smolley, Florida*

If the library access your brother offered was, as I gather, unauthorized, then it wasn't his to give, and it certainly wasn't yours to accept. (He's not allowed to swipe pens and paper and send them to you, either. Too bad, I know.) Were he to have done the research for you—something rare in the annals of big brotherhood—that wouldn't change things. His library privileges, presumably, permit him to do his own work, not to set up a reference service. That he pays a lot of tuition is beside the point, those who shoulder Ivy prices must obey the rules, too.

The university could indeed lose if all students passed along their passwords to reference-hungry relatives. An overloaded system with concomitant delays for legit users is no boon to learning. But even if the school doesn't lose, you'd be on shaky moral ground. Yours is the same rationalization used by those who hook up their own cable TV or sneak onto the subway (or, more rarely, hook up their own cable TV on the subway). For these services to be sustained—libraries, HBO, or IRT—each user must pay his or her fair share.

On the bright side, there are many fine public libraries right there in Florida (if the legislature hasn't cut their funding), as well as many publicly accessible sites for online research.

**UPDATE:** Or at least there were when I drew this overoptimistic conclusion in 2003. Since then, the corralling of information by for-profit companies has become an ominous social problem, most flamboyantly in Google's efforts to scan—and control access to—every book ever written on this or other planets from the invention of printing until the end of time, if I understand their strategic vision (and I do not). Exacerbating this lamentable trend is the defunding of institutions like universities and libraries that make information available to the public. A Florida reference librarian reminded me that "many public libraries do not offer quality database coverage because of cost while many academic libraries do not permit public users because of contractual arrangements with vendors."

## DAUGHTER'S BLOG

*I stumbled upon my college-age daughter's online journal. I have always regarded diaries as off-limits to outsiders and have scrupulously avoided even casual glimpses of my children's personal writings. Now, however, my daughter is offering her daily postings to the world. I imagine that the idea of her father reading her innermost thoughts would lead to self-censorship, and I don't want to spoil a writing venue she enjoys. Is it ethical for me to read her journal without telling her?*

*—Name withheld, New Jersey*

Don't ask me; ask her. And respect her wishes.

Were this a stranger's online diary, you could read voraciously. When someone publishes, on paper or on-screen, it's fair to assume that she consents to everybody's reading her work—fair but not entirely reliable. Sometimes an online journal is accessible because its writer neglected to enable the password protection, an expression less of literary openness than technical naïveté. And sometimes what a writer is willing to reveal to a casual reader she is reluctant to reveal to her parents. What's key is that your daughter should not think herself unobserved if you are, in fact, observing her.

Age is also a factor. We grant a three-year-old little right to privacy. Her parents may keep an eye on her around the clock, watching what she eats, when she sleeps, how she brushes her teeth—even when she assumes herself to be unobserved. Few women your daughter's age would willingly submit to such scrutiny.

As the father of a daughter around the age of yours, I sympathize with your wanting to know what she's up to. But it would be no more ethical for you to read her journal surreptitiously than to skulk around her campus hoping to pick up snatches of her conversation.

I would add one exception to this rule. If you had reason to believe your child was engaging in truly dangerous behavior, and if less intrusive efforts to confirm this were unavailing, you could consider reading her blog. The parental duty to protect your child would supersede her right to privacy. But again, the older the child grows, the weaker the parent's authority becomes.

**UPDATE**: Seven years later, I add this thought, Blogs! How quaint! Today the daughter is probably on Facebook, where there are privacy settings that she's lax about. So while the popular technology of improvident self-revelation has evolved, the ethical guideline is unchanged: don't read your older child's diary without consent.

## GIVE ME A SIGN

*Is it piracy if you take your laptop into a library and download CDs or copy movies from its DVD collection? I travel the country continuously and frequent libraries. Never have I seen a sign that prohibits copying the material on their shelves.*

—*Adam Wasserman, Los Angeles*

I, too, frequent libraries, and never have I seen a sign that prohibits shooting a patron who jabbers into his cell phone in the reference section, but I don't take that lacuna as permission to open fire. While libraries exist to lend just the sort of material you describe, your duplicating an entire copyrighted work is forbidden.

Siva Vaidhyanathan, an expert on intellectual-property issues who teaches at the University of Virginia, explains that copying an excerpt for educational, research, artistic, or journalistic purposes is generally legal, "but copying an entire book or film would usually lie beyond any fair use of copyrighted material." That is, downloading a few moments of "Give Up the Funk (Tear the Roof Off the Sucker)" for nonprofit scholarly purposes is fine; duplicating all of *Mothership Connection*, the

Parliament album on which that splendid song is found, to save your-self the cost of buying it, is not. In judging such conduct, both motive and size count.

This guideline strives to balance the right of a creator to be paid for his work (and thus encourage his creativity) and the interest of the larger society in the dissemination of ideas. The fundamental goal of copyright is not to secure profits but to inspire thought—"to promote the Progress of Science and useful Arts," as Article I, Section 8 of the Constitution puts it.

Although copying an entire work is seldom legal, it is sometimes ethical—for example, if the work is not available for sale (remember: most books ever published are now out of print); if it is available only in an archaic form (a 78 recording, a Betamax tape, a clay tablet); if you already own a copy and want another in a more usable format (less scratchy, fewer coffee stains). But such reasonable situations might not inoculate you against lawsuits. The law is an expression not just of eth-ics but of power.

**UPDATE**: This column ran in 2006. Today the situation is, if any-thing, hazier and still very much in flux. One solution some libraries have adopted is to make digital versions of such things available for downloading in formats that are playable only for the traditional two-week rental period; not a bad approach. Library patrons have access to this material, while creators are paid for their work. But this tactic risks excluding people with less money, those who do not own Kindles or iPads or the like. Happily, some libraries now lend those devices, too. But for this system to work, libraries must be properly funded, a drum I realize I have been beating for more than the traditional two weeks.

## GOOGLE THE GUY

*My friend went on a date last week and "Googled" the man when she got home—that is, looked him up on the Internet search engine www.google.com. She found that he had been involved with many malpractice suits. (He's a doctor.) Her "homework" has now resulted in a discounted opinion of this man. What do you think about using Google to check up on another person?*
*—Shana Novak, New York*

I'm for it, at least in certain situations, but then again I have to be— I've done it. And many other people have, too; that's why the verb "to Google" is a familiar neologism. (It must demoralize those poor souls at AOL, with all their childproofing and spam and ads, that no one ever says, "I met an interesting guy and AOL'd him.") Had your friend labored all afternoon at the courthouse checking equally public information on her date, she'd have crossed the border between casual curiosity and stalking. Her Googling, however, was akin to asking her friends about this fellow—offhand, sociable, and benign.

The Internet is transforming the idea of privacy. The once-clear distinction between public and private information is no longer either/ or but more or less. While the price of a neighbor's condo may be a matter of public record, it's a very different kind of public if it's posted on the Internet than if it's stored in a dusty filing room open only during business hours and overseen by a scowling clerk. This distinction does not concern the information itself but the ease of retrieving it. (And new technology brings this corollary benefit: you can now be consumed with real-estate envy in the privacy of your own shabby home.) With this change comes a paradoxical ethical shift where laziness, or limiting yourself to insouciant Googling, is more honorable than perseverance, as in hauling yourself down to the municipal archives, say.

By calling such an act "checking up" on someone, you make typing someone's name into a search engine sound devious. But that is less a consequence of its malevolence than its novelty. Acceptable behavior is ratified by custom, and that takes time. As more and more people routinely Google their blind dates, nobody will feel uneasy doing so. This cultural adaptation is not arbitrary, but a communal determination that an action is harmless. So it might be better to think of this not as snooping but as curiosity. If someone set you up on a blind date with a poet, he'd most likely not feel offended but flattered that you were sufficiently interested in him to read his work. But this means the time to Google is not after your blind date but before. And it never hurts to search your beau's name along with the words "ax murderer."

While Googling is innocuous, it is not entirely reliable. For starters, people share names. You can't be sure if you're reading about one guy who has had a varied career (or who can't hold a job) or several people. And you can't be sure which one will be buying you a cocktail (the surgeon? the sock collector?). Googling myself—which sounds more perverse than it is—turned up an architecture prof at McGill University, a video editor, a broker of sports tickets, and a table-tennis champ; I'm now jealous of all of them.

Even if you sort out the names, you can't rely on the veracity of online information. So while your friend did nothing unethical by Googling her guy, she'd be unwise to discredit him too quickly (as a date or a doctor) or, for that matter, to marry him, based only on a cursory search.

**UPDATE:** This unaltered exchange from 2002 now seems quaint. Who wouldn't Google under such circumstances? Who'd even ask if doing so was legit? Today the idea of *not* Googling seems prudish if not irresponsibly rash, considering how much ideas of privacy and propriety have been transformed in just a decade. Although as I understand it, it would still be considered impertinent to install hidden cameras in the guy's house. Or trousers.

## CRIME AND PUNISHMENT

*I am an Internet technician. While installing software on my company's computer network, I happened on a lot of pornographic pictures in the president's personal directory, including some of young children—clearly less than age eighteen, and possibly in their early teens. It is probably illegal and is absolutely immoral. Must I call the police? I think so, but I need my job.*

*—S.M.N., Vancouver*

There is a profound moral obligation to protect children from harm, but in your situation calling the cops is not the way to honor that obligation. And while it is a crime to possess child pornography—understandably, the sexual exploitation of children is reprehensible—you have no legal duty to call 911.

There is a more powerful argument for not calling the cops. The punishment for mere possession of these images is grossly disproportional to the crime. We should act vigorously against anyone who endangers a child, but we should seek a more appropriate response to those who are only remotely connected to such heinous acts, whose only crime is looking at a forbidden picture. What's more, these photographs might depict—legally—not children but young-looking adults. The images could be digitally altered. Your boss may have acquired free (albeit illegal) images rather than buying them and providing a financial incentive to those who harm children. Someone other than your boss may have downloaded the pictures.

And so, while protecting your job—i.e., narrow self-interest—should not forestall your calling the police, the consequences to your boss of doing so should. Even if he were acquitted of criminal charges, the accusation itself imperils his job, his reputation, and the company. If convicted he faces years in prison. (Arizona recently sentenced a man to two hundred years on similar grounds.) Having no reason to believe your boss has had improper contact with children, you should not subject him to such ferocious repercussions for actions that no doubt disgust us but have done no direct harm to anyone.

Douglas A. Berman, a law professor at Ohio State University and an expert on sentencing, describes the rationale for these laws, "We punish the kind of possession many concede is not inherently harmful but which contributes to behavior which produces much harm." That is, by stopping buyers, even those who've had no contact with an actual child, we hope to stop sellers, who do exploit children. Is this effective? Tough to prove. Berman observes that the "criminalization of child-porn consumption is premised on contestable utilitarian calculations."

Why not target child-porn producers directly, much as we differentiate drug dealers from drug users? We try, Berman explains, but it's not easy. "A lot of these Web sites are offshore. And the domestic ones are good at covering their tracks." But if the intent of the law is estimable, its effect in this case would be too destructive to your boss and too ineffectual in protecting children for you to abet.

You do have duties to your employer. Because this material is on its computer, the firm risks prosecution. But short of calling the cops, your options are few. Nor would deleting the pictures eliminate all legal risk; that could be seen as destroying evidence. Your best recourse? Alas, silence.

For anyone genuinely concerned about children, there is no shortage of work to be done. Svetlana Mintcheva, of the National Coalition Against Censorship, observes "the hysteria around child pornography distracts from the more serious harm done to children both worldwide and in the United States—economic exploitation, disease, malnutrition, etc. The effort put into suppressing child porn would do so much more to protect children if it were directed into these other areas."

UPDATE: Unsurprisingly, this column provoked much disagreement, and much outrage. But I believe I got it right. It is true, as some critics argued, that child-porn consumers can be said to provide an incentive for its producers, but that connection is too tenuous to justify sending someone to jail for decades, a not unknown sentence, for looking at an illegal picture. Nor is it likely that doing so diminishes the production of child porn.

I'd considered various ways the technician might tell his boss he knew what was going on, as some readers urged. But what would be the result? If the boss were prudent, he'd merely shift his child-porn consumption from his office to his home. That might be of some benefit to the company, but dodges the larger question of how to respond to child-porn consumers.

Reporting this not to the cops but in-house, another approach some readers proposed, amounts to passing the buck, letting someone else send the boss to prison for looking at pictures. What's more, in S.M.N.'s particular case, this is a small company owned by the person who seems to have the child porn, so that further limits his options. But even if this were a larger company and there were higher-ups to whom he could report it, he should still be wary: the consequences to the boss and his family are, to reiterate, apt to be wildly disproportional to any actual harm he'd done and would have a vanishingly small chance of protecting any child. As several experts informed me, these particular images may have been recorded on another continent a decade ago.

I do agree that mine is an unsatisfying response to deeply disturbing conduct. But the unwise laws concerning child-porn consumers foreclose any better solution. It is demoralizing to do nothing in such a situation but worse still to do harm.

In addition to hearing from many civilians, I received a sharp rebuke from then Manhattan District Attorney, Robert Morgenthau:

"You could not be more wrong. Your advice perpetuates the naïve and dangerous notion that possessing child pornography is a 'victimless crime.' The children depicted in these images include preteens, toddlers, and even infants who are subjected to unimaginable horrors that include violent rape and torture. At a minimum, people who purchase and possess child pornography provide an incentive for the producers and distributors of this material to exploit the young children involved. In addition, many who collect these images engage in predatory behavior themselves. A study by the U.S. Bureau of Prisons shows that up to 85 percent of child pornography offenders admitted to molesting children.

"In your example, the employee's silence deprives the children depicted on his boss's computer of a chance to be identified by law enforcement and saved from further harm. Silence also ensures that a likely predator is at liberty to roam the community, free to become a scout leader or teacher or volunteer at a local school, secure in the knowledge that his secret is safe.

"In short, silence is not only unethical, it is dangerous."

Morgenthau misrepresents me. I did not assert that child porn is a victimless crime, only that there is no evidence that this technician's boss harmed any children. In addition, the experts I consulted refuted Morgenthau's statistics, explaining that most people who view such pictures in fact do not take any action with any actual children. Again, we must take forceful measures against those who harm children, but we must not inflict harsh punishments on those who have not.

As stern as were Morgenthau's reproaches, there was a yet more caustic rebuke from then U.S. Attorney General, Alberto R. Gonzales:

"Each image of child pornography is a crime scene, and its possession is a felony in forty-two states and under federal law. Furthermore, reproducing such images again victimizes the innocent child. The Ethicist flippantly advises silence because speaking up would be 'too ineffectual in protecting children.' But real children have been rescued by the discovery of images. Without the images, we cannot find and rescue victims or punish the predators. The Ethicist demonstrates a disappointing lack of understanding of how law enforcement works. This is unacceptable, and I urge all Americans to reject this poor advice. A child's life could hang in the balance all because a self-described 'ethicist' muses over vague excuses rather than advising immediate action."

I have responded to his arguments above and will add only that, contrary to his assertion, I was not flippant, and according to the experts I consulted, no or nearly no children have been rescued as a result of arresting solitary viewers of such appalling images (rather than, for example, targeting child-porn rings). If the images themselves can provide evidence that might eventually lead to the arrest of those who've abused children, then methods must be put in place that let a mere viewer of these images come forward without risking a decade in prison. The current system is overwhelmingly counterproductive. There are many ways to improve the lives of children. What Gonzales demands is not one of them.

**A FOOTNOTE:** To be lectured on morality by the man who misled Congress about the firing of U.S. attorneys for their politics, regarded the Geneva Conventions as "obsolete," endorsed the infamous torture memo, and defended the warrantless wiretapping of Americans, among other misdeeds that caused him to leave office in disgrace is, to say the least, a head-spinning experience.

# *Community*

WE GET AN INTERESTING SENSE OF OUR ETHICAL DUTIES TO OUR NEIGHBORS when we're apt to sneeze on them. "Wash your hands when you shake hands; cover your mouth when you cough," President Obama admonished when the swine flu epidemic struck. "I know it sounds trivial, but it makes a huge difference. If you are sick, stay home. If your child is sick, keep them out of school. If you are feeling certain flu symptoms, don't get on an airplane, don't get on a—any system of public transportation where you're confined and you could potentially spread the virus."

This modest, homespun advice is not merely good manners. It rises to the level of ethics because it concerns the effect of our actions on other people. Etiquette codifies behavior that is merely a matter of form and hence has a trivial impact on others. Whether or not to rob a guy? Ethics. Whether or not to curtsy after robbing a guy? Etiquette. Similarly, the old-school demand that a man on a bus surrender his seat to a woman—any woman, no matter how robust—is etiquette, a social convention (and a sexist one). A better approach is for a seated passenger, man or woman, to offer a seat to anyone in need, regardless of gender—a frail older man, a very pregnant woman, a weary Joe Biden (should he muster his courage and return to public transportation). This is ethics (albeit small-scale ethics): an effort to assist those in need.

And so was Obama's hand-washing recommendation, echoing the wise counsel that our parents gave us when we were children and that Ignaz Semmelweis gave to medical students in the maternity clinic at the Vienna General Hospital in 1847. It is an ethical imperative, meant to mitigate the harm we might do to others. That hand-washing also diminishes your own chance of becoming ill makes it more desirable, though it does not further elevate the moral status of the act. In ethics, intent counts; the reason *why* you wash your hands matters. That's not to deny, of course, the virtue of sparing the community the costs of your infirmity—medical care, missed work—a rationale sometimes applied to seat belt or helmet laws.

Those presidential dictates, while fundamentally ethical, are not universally applicable. Some employees, particularly low-wage workers, risk losing pay or even getting fired if they stay home from work to avoid infecting their coworkers. If we expect individuals to act ethically, we have a societal obligation to protect them when they do—for instance, by guaranteeing paid sick days to all.

Another argument for a community response, for the practice of civic virtue, even if someone displays impressive individual rectitude, he may still unknowingly infect other people with swine flu (or, if you prefer a more pork-chop–friendly designation, the H1N1 virus). Dr. Michele Barry, former dean of Global Health at Stanford University, says, "You may not be aware you are transmitting it early on." People can be contagious for as long as six days before displaying any symptoms and, she adds, "longer in kids and immunocompromised folks."

Some healthy people have taken aggressively individualistic action, asking a friend or relative who is a doctor for prescriptions for Tamiflu, an antiviral medication, to keep around the house just in case. To make such a request is unwise, to honor it unethical. In most cases, doctors "should certainly not be in the business of writing prescriptions for those they have neither examined nor taken a medical history from," says Dr. Tia Powell, director of the Montefiore-Einstein Center for Bioethics. And while it can be awkward for a doctor to turn down the aunt who will host the family's next Thanksgiving dinner, that is what medical ethics requires.

To hoard antiviral medications that are in short supply can make them unavailable to those in immediate need. Even if there were unlimited supplies of antiviral agents, Barry would caution against their prophylactic use, except by people traveling to the center of the epidemic, because using such medications improperly can breed Tamiflu-resistant strains of the virus.

Thus some individual actions, like the presidentially endorsed washing of hands, are genuinely ethical, while others, like stocking up on antiviral medications, are not. Each must be judged on its merits. What's more, universally esteemed acts do not obviate the need for community actions. And even those we deem outside the realm of ethics, that we consider to be merely etiquette, can be valuable social lubricants. Samuel Johnson was a great defender of politeness, calling it "fictitious benevolence" and asserting that "the want of it never fails to produce something disagreeable."

**UPDATE:** After this argument ran in the *Times*, some clever readers noted how counterproductive it was for schools to give awards for perfect attendance, i.e., for coming to class when you are ill and infecting other students and staff. Some other awards for profoundly antisocial behavior:

Motor Trend *magazine's SUV of the year*

*Emmy award for outstanding reality-competition program*

*Shooting Industry Academy of Excellence Awards: The 2008 handgun of the year, the Ruger LCP .380*

### PRIVATIZED FIREFIGHTERS

*Our small community of perhaps sixty homes lacks adequate fire protection. Equipment could arrive within forty-five minutes, so some feel we should purchase our own. Only fifteen homeowners have agreed to this. Should the need arise, must we provide this equipment to those that did not share in its purchase?*

*—Name withheld, Bahamas*

You must. You would accept help from people forty-five minutes away. How can you deny it to your neighbors? (I hate to use an ugly word like *hypocrite*, so picture it in a lovely floral typeface.)

Your alternatives are unappealing. If you turn your fancy new hose on a nonpaying neighbor's burning house, he is a free rider, exploiting your prudence. If you refuse, you are coldhearted. Either way, this privatized approach to mutual hazard will end in tears. That's why much of the world has abandoned it in favor of community-wide solutions.

In London after the Great Fire of 1666, insurance companies formed private fire brigades to protect the property of paid subscribers, who marked their buildings with that company's ensign. The results were predictably ghastly, and London moved toward publicly financed municipal fire brigades.

Even if you were indifferent to a neighbor's misfortune, you should recognize that his flames can threaten your roof. (And his cries of anguish can disturb your TV-watching.) If there is no political structure in place to allow a binding vote in your community, and assuming your neighbors can afford to pay their share, try this temporary fix: after extinguishing a noncontributor's conflagration, bill him—heavily—for your services. In fact, if he's around when his place bursts into flames, demand payment in advance, before you uncoil your hoses, as a civics lesson for the entire community.

### JAYWALKER

_Since I work near a museum, I often encounter parents restraining young children from crossing the street until the walk signal appears. Ordinarily, I'd freely cross against the light if no cars were coming, but I'm concerned that my doing so might undermine the parents' laudable efforts to teach their children safety. Should I refrain from setting a bad example?_

—_Theodore Hong, London_

Here in New York we—or at least I—regard crossing against the light as setting a _good_ example. It's a fine thing for our neighbors to learn that we need not totally surrender public space to private cars. I can only admire my fellow New Yorkers who risk life and limb to assert that ideal. I'm told that in your city, however, street use is organized more reasonably.

In any case, such declamatory perambulating is too dangerous for children. Thus in your circumstances, while you are not required to be a role model for the kids, you would be generous-spirited to cross at the green, not in between, reinforcing the valuable lesson those parents are striving to teach. For you to do so is worth the small inconvenience of waiting for the light to change. (But the minute those kids are a little older or around the corner . . .)

In determining right conduct, the example we set for others is not our only consideration or even our prime consideration, but it should be _a_ consideration. While we do not live our lives for other people, we must accept that we affect others by what we do, and children are especially susceptible to the influence of others. We all have an interest in kids becoming virtuous creatures—no one wants to live on that _Lord of the Flies_ island—and so we should act to encourage their upright (and safe) behavior. Most people do just that when, in the presence of children, they avoid rough language or curb the urge to tell a white lie.

If parents instead make the tolerable decision to get on with the adult business of ignoring the law, then they should remind their young charges of the distinction between what adults may do—drive, for example, or vote, or date—and what children may do. Age appropriateness is a valid consideration.

---

### REUNION RECIDIVISM

*I am thinking about organizing a thirtieth reunion for my elementary-school "graduating" class. One classmate is a registered sex offender whose presence may discourage other classmates from attending, especially with their kids. Should I invite him? Make the event adults only? Inform others of his offense? Public records show that his misdeed was committed thirteen years ago. He received probation, and there's no indication of any subsequent crime. I'd regret excluding him or violating his privacy, but I'd feel bad withholding information other classmates might want. What to do?*
*—Name withheld, Texas*

Hippocrates said, "To do nothing is sometimes a good remedy." A similar sentiment is expressed in the film *Lawrence of Arabia*, while Damascus burns.

COLONEL BRIGHTON: Look, sir, we can't just do nothing.

GENERAL ALLENBY: Why not? It's usually best.

As in medical and military affairs, so in your reunion planning. Nothing is just what you should do.

Some parents might be uneasy about this fellow, but to respond to that anxiety would be catering to prejudice not forestalling danger. There's information about my former classmates that I want—their infidelities, their plastic surgeries, their PINs—but it doesn't follow that I'm entitled to it.

If the classmate constituted a threat to anyone, you might have to act. But data from the Bureau of Justice Statistics indicate that the recidivism rate for sex offenders, contrary to widespread misconceptions, is far lower than for many other criminals. Nor need you fear that having committed one sort of crime, he is apt to commit another. The bureau reports, "Sex offenders were less likely than non-sex offenders to be rearrested for any offense."

Given these facts, your vague knowledge of his long-ago crime, the light sentence he received, and the many years he has gone apparently without being rearrested, you should leave him in peace rather than subject him to the scrutiny and scorn of his classmates. He's paid his debt to society; you ought not extract a further toll by exiling him from ordinary social interactions. (Nor should you hang him, even in Texas.)

## LIE TO A LIAR

*Recently my cell phone was stolen from my bike bag. I decided to post signs to entice the crook by offering $300 for the phone's return, a reward I have no intention of paying. Or do I have an obligation to reward the return of my own stolen property?*

*—Adam Briscoe, Houston*

You have an obligation to keep your word. There are times when it is ethical to dissemble, but this is not one of them. Were you in danger or under duress you could legitimately lie. ("Got any more cell phones?" asks the mugger with the gun. "No," says his victim, declining to mention the malodorous miniature hidden in his boot.) But, unmenaced as you are, you should employ honest methods of regaining your property. Instead of announcing a reward you've no intention of paying, call the cops.

There is also something to be said for not taking the law into your own hands. To discourage certain behavior, we restrict it to designated groups. (Those we empower to physically restrain others, for example.)

This is in part to avert the injustice likely to result from vigilantism, and it is also a matter of safety, there are risky acts no untrained civilian should attempt.

In addition, certain activities are so undesirable, their effects so malignant, that while they may occasionally be necessary, we seek to limit them severely. So it is with lying. Every lie, even those that are justifiable, diminishes the trust essential for society to function. And so, while the cops may run a sting operation (assuming they steer clear of entrapment), setting up as a fence to attract and arrest those who bring in stolen goods—certainly a form of deceit—we seek to constrain the scope of lying, to quarantine it, so as to avoid its infecting the general society.

There are other objections to your proposed deception. The person who returns the phone might be not the thief, but someone who simply found your lost property. You ought not greet altruism with mendacity. More practically, if you rendezvous with the thief, he may not see the poetic justice in your withholding the reward. And he may be one of those miscreants who respond not with an elegant argument but with a stick or a brick. To avoid both unethical behavior and an ugly head wound, you should abandon your plan.

In short—if it's not too late for that—the thief's treachery doesn't justify your own. Our conduct should reflect our own values, not those of the people with whom we happen to be dealing.

---

### THROWING CURVES

*I am in my month's trial membership at the fitness chain Curves and I love it. I must decide whether to sign up for a year, and I've learned that the owner of the company financially supports antiabortion efforts, whereas I am pro-choice. Do I have a duty to give up my Curves membership?*

*—Louise Dustrude, Friday Harbor, WA*

It depends: which do you value more, your reproductive rights or your figure? If the former, clean out your locker. You won't be alone. I've received queries from many women who are similarly conflicted. They love that Curves offers a great workout in a woman-friendly setting, and that many owner-operators of individual Curves centers are women, but they don't like seeing their payments used to support abstinence programs and what many see as pro-life organizations.

Gary Heavin, founder and CEO of Curves, is an explicit supporter of pro-life causes, having pledged more than $5 million to various groups, including some unsympathetic to the pro-choice position. The amount is ethically significant. It would be overly fastidious to shun a pizzeria whose owner annually donated $5 to the Cellphones for Parrots Foundation, for example, but Heavin's hefty contributions have hefty consequences. Similarly, your monthly gym fees add up to indirect support for a cause you disdain.

You might argue that Heavin donates as an individual, not as a corporate official. But he is the founder of Curves and the person who most profits from it, and so the ethical distinction between the man and the company barely exists. To be clear: it is Heavin's actions not his beliefs that are pertinent. You'd be wrong to avoid that pizzeria simply because its owner was a Muslim or a Jew, a liberal or a conservative. You may respond, however, to the proprietor's deeds by declining to finance them through your patronage.

Your boycotting Curves might harm a franchisee who does not endorse Heavin's actions. Her franchise fees, however, provide his income and thus implicate her in his efforts. It is incumbent on her to tell Heavin if his actions damage her business or offend her principles, and on you to let her know why you are dropping out.

Among those who also faced the Curves conundrum is the writer Anne Lamott, who e-mailed me "I quit because I couldn't get my membership to jibe with my politics." She did the right thing; there's much to be said for finding a workout routine that helps you grow physically stronger but doesn't leave you feeling morally weaker.

## BLIND FAITH

*I read for an organization that produces books and magazines on tape for the blind. Recently my assignment was to read articles from a John Birch Society magazine. As someone whose politics are somewhere to the left of left-wing Democrats, I felt uneasy, but I did my assignment, feeling that I had no right to censor what these folks had requested. Should I have refused?*

*—Martin G. Evans, Cambridge, MA*

You were right to read. Your function is akin to a librarian's—to provide requested material, not to judge those requests. The free flow of information is something those of all political persuasions can esteem. (On a personal note, I am surprised and delighted to learn that there actually are left-wing Democrats. Perhaps they're like the ivory-billed woodpecker, just when you think it's extinct, you hear its plangent cry.)

Helping to disseminate what you regard as, at best, claptrap, is a test of your commitment to the ideals of an open society and of your skills as an orator. I'm sure there were moments when it was hard to keep your performance free of scorn and incredulity. I admire your having done so. Then again, if I were your director, I might suggest—strictly as a theatrical matter—punctuating your reading with snorts of derision, the occasional outburst of laughter, and . . . no, no, no. Never mind.

While my directorial suggestions are dubious, you do face not only ethical but also rhetorical challenges. My friend Earl Howard, blind all his life, told me, "Years ago, when I was a student, I got audiobooks from Recordings for the Blind. Those readers were, to put it kindly, of varying quality. Some were pretty good; some could barely pronounce the words. If you listened to poetry, it would drive you nuts. Most blind people learned to ignore the performance and just hear the words."

Your organization could mitigate this problem if it attempted to accommodate its volunteers' preferences, aesthetic as well as ideological; some people love reading poetry aloud, some do not. But when it cannot make a perfect match, it should explain that there is civic virtue in a volunteer reading whatever he or she is assigned.

## LIBRARY COPS

*I was disturbed to see a man looking at pornography on a New York Public Library computer. When two children sat down near him, I decided to take action, but he instantly switched to an inoffensive video game. A security guard told me they were keeping an eye on a couple of people acting similarly and would catch them in the act eventually. Should I have alerted someone as soon as I became aware of this man's activities?*

*—Name withheld, New York*

A guard monitoring someone's reading? That's not my idea of how a library operates. (Or it wasn't, pre-Patriot Act.) Libraries should provide for the free exchange of ideas—not just ideas right-thinking folks like you or me find palatable, not just ideas suitable for five-year-olds. And librarians should not be forced to censor their patrons' reading, let alone eject them for looking at disturbing pictures.

Happily, even if you and the overeager guard had reported this incident, nobody would have been rousted. Caroline Oyama, manager of public relations for the New York Public Library, explains that it "does not ask adult patrons to leave, stop what they are doing, or move to another computer if another patron doesn't like the Web site he/she is viewing. Instead, we make every attempt to move the user who is offended to another computer where he/she doesn't have to see what the other person is viewing." This is a prudent policy, consistent with the library's ethos and responsive to the sensitivities of patrons of all ages.

This isn't to say that libraries should be heedless of young patrons—nor is the NYPL. It complies with the Children's Internet Protection Act, which requires it to install filtering software on its computers or lose certain federal funding. Patrons older than seventeen may have the filters turned off, but they cannot be disabled in the children's rooms. What's more, Oyama reports, "The branch libraries have polarized privacy screens on many public computers, which allow patrons to see only the screen directly in front of them." So you needn't have feared for the children sitting adjacent to your porn peruser. Feeling as you do, you'd do well to vote for greater library funding so that your local library can afford to more successfully screen its computers from the casual glances of passersby.

Incidentally, while you depict that fellow's quick shift to a video game as a cunning tactic to elude capture, a digital Moriarty foiling his e-Holmes, it might have been an act of consideration for those children who'd just arrived.

---

### ABANDONED BIKE

*A bicycle locked to a pole near my house was untouched through the fall and winter. When spring came, I balanced the lock so it would be in a different position if the bike were moved. It wasn't. Eventually I broke the lock and now ride the bike almost daily. Was it ethical to steal something that had clearly been abandoned by its owner?*

*—Kate Clifford, Philadelphia*

It's not that it was ethical to "steal" it; you didn't steal it. You claimed abandoned property, and had no reason not to.

The trick is determining if something is in fact abandoned. There are an awful lot of cars stashed by the curb with nobody near them. To your credit, you showed due diligence. You observed the bike for nearly a year and used a cunning spy-movie trick to see if it had been ridden when you weren't around. (I trust you went home now and then, at least to shower and sleep.) And all city dwellers know that bikes are sometimes leashed to poles and left to fend for themselves. What's more, you did your neighbors a service by removing what amounted to litter on wheels.

Here in New York, the police respond similarly to complaints about abandoned bikes. In some precincts, according to Noah Budnick of Transportation Alternatives, "if the bike is damaged or shows signs of obvious disuse, the police will tag it with a notice saying that the bike will be removed in two weeks if it is not moved. After two weeks, the officers return, usually with Department of Sanitation agents, and if the bike is unmoved, they clip the lock and cart the bike away." In this, they and you act ethically.

---

**LIBRARY VOLUNTEERS**

*Community members have responded to our town's tight budget by volunteering at the library, so much so that the library laid off several long-term full-time employees, people who are our friends and neighbors. Having fewer municipal employees means a slight reduction in property taxes for everyone, but it harms those left jobless. Should town residents consider that before volunteering?*

*—Name withheld, New Jersey*

Consider it? Certainly. I'm pro-thought. One thing you might think about is this sad fact, the greater the number of library volunteers, the easier it is for the town to slash its library budget. The very determination of community members to assist a cherished institution can undermine it. And yet nobody would fault a parent who volunteers as a kindergarten teacher's aide, even though by mitigating the effects of staff cuts, that parent might encourage further cuts. And so not even those unfortunate and unintended consequences you cite should automatically forestall volunteers.

Many library jobs require trained professionals, work no mere civilian can do. But for those tasks an amateur can handle, go to it. There is no shortage of work to be done by skilled municipal employees: children to be educated, accident victims to be treated, stadiums to be erected that will ultimately bankrupt the town. (Maybe not this last.) All your community needs is the will and the funds to undertake such things. My optimistic view is the money that library volunteers save will be applied to the infinite number of things that can be done only by trained professionals—or those workers who perform difficult or unpleasant jobs nobody will do without pay.

And not just at the library. Ideally, volunteers are not eliminating a job but transferring it. The money saved by a volunteer who shelves books can pay a sanitation worker to help keep you and your neighbors healthy. I suspect that few of your fellow citizens are volunteering to work the garbage trucks, that demanding and essential task.

There is a sad limitation to this analysis, a laid-off library employee is not apt to be hired to teach eleventh-grade calculus. He or she will suffer; someone else will be hired. There are winners and losers here. And it would be unfortunate if this upsurge of civic virtue resulted in only a tiny reduction in some people's property taxes, an outcome that thwarts the noble motives of those volunteers: to promote civic betterment by reallocating limited resources.

The real solution, of course, is to adequately fund—and staff—your town's library, that essential institution of democracy, of humanity. I hope that you and your neighbors will volunteer to help out with those efforts, too.

---

### SCAVENGER HUNT

*We put our paper, plastic, and other recyclables in city-issued containers in our backyard and move them to the curb for weekly pickup through our town's recycling program. A scavenger regularly removes cans and bottles, presumably to redeem for cash. I say that by depriving the city of these items, he adds to our recycling costs. I want to ask the police to apprehend the "thief." My wife says I lack compassion. You?*

*—J.M., Burlingame, CA*

It would take a colder heart than mine to call the cops on someone so needy that he survives by picking garbage. To focus your crime-busting on the poorest of the poor shows curious priorities. Are there no BP execs, no Goldman Sachs plutocrats, no producers of *Sex and the City 2*?

Thomas Hart Benton was once to give a speech denouncing John C. Calhoun, but learning that Calhoun was ill, declined to do so, declaring, "Benton will not speak today, for when God Almighty lays his hands on a man, Benton takes his off."

Benton's compassion for the physically afflicted should be extended to the economically assailed. To lead an ethical life requires us to empathize with other people and ask, "What circumstances would induce a person to behave this way? And does the most moral response to this behavior involve the police?"

You should also ask how this fellow is to live if you thwart his pilfering recyclables. Rob liquor stores? Perform liposuction? There is little social good in what amounts to criminalizing poverty. It is not that the poor have a right to steal; it is that they have no duty to starve.

I would give a different answer if this foraging were the work not of an individual struggling to survive during tough economic times, but was an organized effort involving fleets of illicit trucks staying one jump ahead of the designated recycling company. Context counts. What's more, it is not clear if your town makes a profit from recycling. If it does not, the scavenger may actually save you money by lightening the load.

**UPDATE:** While putting out the trash one night, J.M. encountered someone going through his cans right by the house. Startled and mindful of the safety of his young children, he called the police, with no discernible results. He's not phoned them again.

# *School*

WHEN I WENT TO HIGH SCHOOL, NOBODY CHEATED. OKAY, A FEW KIDS cheated, and we all knew who they were, and we treated them with contempt. Not because they were moral failures, but because they were muttonheads—they cheated because they had to. (I regret having joined in the mockery. Kids can be cruel, and I was one.)

Forty years later, when my daughter went to Stuyvesant, the best public high school in New York, she and her classmates were superior to us in every way. They worked harder, they were more sophisticated, and every single one of them without exception was a cheater. (With one exception, my daughter never cheated. She says. And I believe her.) Fine. Perhaps not every Stuy student in her era cheated, but cheating was rampant, and it was done brilliantly. Kids employed radio transmitters; they tried microprinting on water-bottle labels; they hacked into well-guarded computer systems. And this occurred despite the genuine regret of parents, teachers, administrators, and the students themselves.

If you believe that conduct is a manifestation of individual character, you must conclude several things. First, the New York City Board of Education recruited the wickedest children in the five boroughs and put them in a single school. (I'd like to meet the person who devised that satanic entrance exam.) Second, the debased nature of these evil teens should manifest itself in other areas; character must be consistent or it isn't character at all. Local stores should be plagued with shoplifting, the basketball team mired in point-shaving scandals, the debate team engaged in whatever form of cheating a debater can attempt. But none of that happened. Stuy students behaved about like any other New York teens.

If their academic misconduct was not a reflection of their character, why did Stuy students behave worse than us Mt. Penn High kids? It was not character but circumstances that shaped the conduct of both groups. Stuy students operated in and internalized the customs of a different community from mine.

Here's an example. When we had to write a term paper, we went to a physical place called a "library." (Older readers can explain to younger readers what that is.) There we consulted a reference librarian, and she—in those days it was always she—suggested promising avenues of research and noted them for us. We took this information to the card catalog, where we jotted down the names of books and authors of interest. We went to the stacks, found the books, and transcribed pertinent passages. When we got home and began to assemble this material into our papers, we'd already written out the names of the relevant books and authors, the information needed to cite our sources. Recording it was built into our methodology.

When my daughter and her classmates wrote a paper, they did their research online, cutting and pasting key passages into their documents. There was nothing inherent in this method that required recording the authors of those passages or the publications where they first appeared. This is not to excuse a failure to cite sources; plagiarism is unethical for students in both eras. Rather, it is to explain so widespread a change in behavior.

Once a culture of cheating establishes itself, it is difficult for even the most high-minded student to remain aloof from it. I didn't cheat because kids in my school didn't cheat. I did not have to wrestle with temptation or call upon my no doubt sterling personal qualities, the question never really arose.

Most of us behave much like our neighbors, in both good and bad neighborhoods. One thing that affects the habits and practices of those localities is the larger community of which it is a part, as personified by prominent people. Even if no child consciously modeled her behavior on anybody regularly seen on TV, those luminaries shape her sense of normal behavior (and abnormal lip size), if only by behaving so publicly. And so their conduct is worthy of moral scrutiny.

It took Robert Caro seven years to write *The Power Broker.* Neil Sheehan spent sixteen years on *A Bright Shining Lie.* Sarah Palin produced the 413 pages of *Going Rogue* in four months—impressively swift, particularly for a nonwriter. It is no secret that she hired someone to help her, and nothing wrong with that. But did she receive so much help as to constitute plagiarism? Or does it even matter if a public figure uses a ghostwriter?

Having an anonymous aide correct your grammar or streamline your book's structure is legitimate; these are the customary tasks of an editor. Nor is there anything discreditable about a nonwriter collaborating with a seasoned pro, as long as that arrangement is transparent. *The Yankee Years* credits Joe Torre *and* Tom Verducci. *Confessions of an*

*Heiress* employs a telltale preposition, linking Paris Hilton *with* Merle Ginsberg. The cover of *The Autobiography of Malcolm X* now proclaims, "as told to Alex Haley." Each is an honorable formulation.

Employing a ghostwriter is different and dubious. That liars have long done so—politicians, actors, athletes—does not make it right. To put your name on a book is not merely to endorse its contents; it is to claim authorship, declaring that these are your words, your sentences, your paragraphs—i.e., that you wrote the thing. To pass off someone else's writing as your own is plagiarism. We forbid students to do it for better grades; it is equally duplicitous if a putative author does it for a reported $5 million.

That Sarah Palin hired Lynn Vincent—"she turns life stories into page-turning narrative," her Web site says—to work on *Going Rogue* is incontrovertible. What Vincent actually did remains murky; she signed a confidentiality agreement. Did Vincent do enough actual writing to make Palin a plagiarist? There is cause for suspicion.

Consider the book's actual language. Palin has been mocked for being less than eloquent. Tina Fey regularly eviscerated Palin's diction simply by replicating it verbatim, no hyperbole needed. Does this passage from the book's first page seem Palinian? "I breathed in an autumn bouquet that combined everything small-town America with rugged splashes of the Last Frontier."

Setting aside the respiratory dangers of breathing in splashes, rugged or otherwise, this sort of expression does not sound like the woman unable to respond to Katie Couric's invitation to name a newspaper she reads.

People speak and write differently, of course. And a shift in style does not prove fraud. But it would raise a red flag to any savvy schoolteacher; they know how their students use language. (Teachers also consider a student's history, has he cheated in the past? The Web sites Gawker and Firedoglake have suggested that some of Palin's Facebook posts, supposedly her own, were written by others.)

Again, pols need not do their own writing, but they may not take credit for someone else's. Radical departures in rhetoric can alert us when they do. Consider the lead to a *New York Times* op-ed piece from 1995 by then Texas governor George W. Bush:

"Remember who your friends are. Always good advice in life. And now, words to keep in mind as the rhetoric of the 1996 election begins. Mexico currently wears the bright red bull's-eye in the ongoing political cross fire."

These are the aw-shucks sentence fragments and mind-numbing clichés we expect from a man famous for his verbal bumbling. Compare this to the zeugma, parallel constructions, and rhythmic cadences of the lead to his *Times* op-ed from 2002:

"The Sept. 11 attacks moved Americans to grief and horror and moved our nation to war. They revealed the cruelty of our enemies, clarified grave threats to our country, and demonstrated the character and decency of our people."

It is difficult to believe that both are from the same hand. Some scholars use statistical analysis of words and phrases to establish authorship—for example, comparing the work of Shakespeare to that of his sometime collaborator John Fletcher. It would be fascinating to see this done with both Palin's and Bush's astonishingly variable prose. I can't prove it, but I'd bet $1,000 that Bush did not write the second piece. I'd bet $500 that he didn't read it.

He'd not be the first public figure to neglect to read something published under his name. Displeased by his own autobiography, *Outrageous!*, basketball great Charles Barkley claimed that it misquoted him. But he took some responsibility: "That was my fault. I should have read it before it came out."

Barkley had the good grace to include his coauthor—that is, author—Roy S. Johnson, on the cover. Palin's name appears alone. She does thank Vincent in the acknowledgments, but she also mentions her parents, coaches, flight attendants, a Dodge dealership, and God. In this thicket of appreciation, Vincent's contribution is implicitly minimized. Thank everyone, and you credit no one.

It should be acknowledged that politicians routinely give speeches written by others, and there is no harm in it. Although no writer is credited, listeners realize that they are hearing an oratorical performance. (This can be overdone. Joe Biden got into hot water some years ago for delivering lines lifted from Neil Kinnock, former leader of Britain's Labour Party.) But books are different. The essential act in writing a book is just that: writing. To put your name on a book that abounds in sentences composed by someone else is to purvey a falsehood. That the ghostwriter consents to this deception is irrelevant. When a student buys a term paper on the Internet, the actual author is glad to take the money, but that doesn't cleanse the transaction of perfidy.

Samuel Johnson, that morally fastidious man, did much ghostwriting, sometimes for money, sometimes out of friendship—prefaces, dedications, sermons, poems, and, most ambitiously, much of a series of lectures delivered at Oxford by Robert Chambers, the immediate successor to William Blackstone as Vinerian professor of law. "Some fifty of these have been identified," says Paul Fussell in *Samuel Johnson and the Life of Writing*. Eighteenth-century ideas of originality and ownership differ from ours, as Fussell explains, but not so much as to eliminate Johnson's determination to keep these contributions sub rosa. In this, if nothing else, he and Palin might have something in common.

I don't wish to overstate the influence of celebrity "authors" on students. But if our conduct is shaped by our communities—and I believe it is—then we can't improve the former without addressing the latter.

## PUBLIC/PRIVATE

*The president of our local board of education sends her children to the public elementary schools, but when they get to high school, she moves them to private schools. Isn't it her ethical obligation either to send her children to the schools she sets policy for and espouses as so wonderful or to step down from the board?*

*—JoAnne Manse, Rutherford, NJ*

It is not. It is the obligation of board members to strive mightily to make the public schools so good that even parents with the means to opt out choose to remain. If the public schools are not yet that good, the president may honorably send her kids elsewhere; indeed, her duty as a parent compels her to. Even where a public school is excellent, parents may seek programs it does not offer—religious instruction, for example.

Enrolling her own kids at a school she administers can give a board member intimate daily insight into how her policies are working out, a real advantage in doing her job. Yet voters must select board members, not on the basis of where they send their kids, but on how well they manage the schools. And remember, some excellent educators have no kids at all.

Ultimately a board member can homeschool her kids, for all I care (as long as she doesn't do it in my home); if she's savvy, dedicated, and effective, she gets my vote.

## DEGRADING CHARITY

*At my high school, various clubs and organizations sponsor charity drives, asking students to bring in money, food, and clothing. Some teachers offer bonus points on tests and final averages as an incentive to participate. Some*

*parents believe that this sends a morally wrong message, undermining the value of charity as a selfless act. Is the exchange of donations for grades OK?*
*—Sara Lambert, New City, NY*

This is a bad policy, not because it sends the wrong message about charity, but because it sends the wrong message about math or chemistry or AP English. Grades are meant to assess a student's academic achievement, not stimulate social activism, however worthy.

This is not to condemn incentives. While some religions prize selflessness as a personal quality, ethics is less concerned with individual spiritual development than with right actions. Looked at this way, charity needn't be selfless to be worthwhile. People behave estimably and ethically for a variety of reasons—personal glory, social justice, religious obligation, love of the work itself, to prove to their jeering so-called friends that they're not the selfish jerks everyone thinks they are. It does not lessen our approbation of the National Coalition for the Homeless that staff members earn a salary. I suspect that many parents who criticize your school's policy return home from worthy paid jobs—as physicians? as firefighters? as librarians?—to shoulder altruistic tasks. Doing the former doesn't discourage them from doing the latter.

It is legitimate for a school to encourage social involvement. And rewarding participants is a way to show that society values their efforts. But the rewards must not blur the distinction between classroom and outside activities or undermine the utility of grades. Throw a party for volunteers, or arrange a trip to the beach, or hand out tiaras, but don't fiddle with their physics marks.

### PRO-LIFE CLUB

*At the public high school where I teach, a school-sponsored student club, Sharing Our Spirit, staged a "Pro-Life Day of Silent Solidarity" during school hours. Students wore armbands and did not speak. The club's faculty adviser sent an e-mail to the entire faculty, including this: "They will be standing on behalf of the one-third of their generation that have been innocent victims of abortion." Was the students' activity legitimate? The adviser's?*
*—Name withheld, Saratoga Springs, NY*

If the school rightly permits students to form clubs irrespective of ideology, from protesting the Iraq war to promoting a preemptive attack on Mars, there is no reason to bar this club. If its members do not hamper the school's educational function—and a daylong silent vigil need not—their activities ought to be allowed. The school would have a beef if, for example, a club directed students to refuse to answer questions in math class.

The teacher, too, has an ethical right to free expression, but because she is in a position of authority, she must be sure all students, regardless of their views, are welcome in her class and treated fairly. Nothing in your account suggests that this wasn't the case. And it is noteworthy that she sent her (to me, nutty) e-mail to her colleagues; she did not declaim it in class. As a legal matter, Arthur Eisenberg of the New York Civil Liberties Union cautions, "She may not turn the classroom into a soapbox for her views on matters unrelated to the curriculum."

Another lawyer I consulted noted that a public school, as a government institution, may not promote a religion. Although the club's message is expressed in secular terms, antiabortion activism is so often bound up in religious sentiment, that a religious message can be implicit. When the adviser of a school-sponsored club takes up religious advocacy, the school must intervene.

## HYPOCRITE HIGH

*I am the president of the antidrug group at my high school. All members pledged not to use drugs or they'd be kicked out, but I know that some of the most passionate and respected members have done so and laughed off their commitment to the group. Should I report them and risk destroying the group or ignore this and continue to preach a message even some of us don't believe in?*
*—Name withheld, New York*

You should kick them out of the group, but you should not report them to the cops or even to school officials. Your duty as president is not to be an auxiliary DEA agent; it is to uphold your group's rules. Members agreed that drug use would get them booted out, so you must lace up the boot.

As a less draconian alternative, you could permit transgressors to resign quietly. Public shaming is not obligatory—no pillory, no stocks, no scarlet P for pot. But go they must, even if their departure hastens the group's demise. Your failing to act would betray the trust of rule-abiding members, undermine your group's mission, and invite the mockery of the school community.

Your attitude suggests you might also rethink your own involvement in the group. Hypocrisy is an awkward position to maintain for the president of a high school club (or the former governor of a large Northeastern state).

Perhaps another lesson here is that you are not as categorically antidrug as you thought. You might be old enough to make a more nuanced distinction between truly dangerous and addictive drug usage and more benign, recreational consumption. Our society is awash in mind-altering chemicals, both legal—caffeine, alcohol, prescription drugs—and illegal. It is part of growing up to work out a safe, healthy, and pleasurable relationship to such things. You may be at a stage of life where education and reflection are more important than advocacy.

**UPDATE:** After consulting with the group's faculty adviser, this student decided that in the next school year, everyone would have to apply anew to join the group and submit to an interview.

---

## PRONOUNCED DISADVANTAGE

*My wife and I had a disagreement recently about the ethical duties of a teacher. I teach fourth graders and maintain that if a student mispronounces a word, it is my sacred duty to correct the student. It's the dictionary or the highway, as far as I'm concerned. My wife says that regional accents (i.e., Boston, Deep South, etc.) should be left uncorrected. Who's right?*
*—Michael Leavenworth, San Diego*

Whether sacred or profane, you are not Henry Higgins. You need not eradicate every flinty New England consonant or honey-toned Mississippi vowel. You should not strive to make your students speak like network news anchors. It is when a student deviates radically from the dictionary's description—*libary, eye-talian*—that you must act. In such a case, you have a professional obligation both to treat your students with respect and to teach them standard usage, something you should explain from the get-go: no knock on how kids in your neighborhood pronounce things, but here in class we must master the conventions of the larger world.

Your object is not to compel your students to assimilate into the dominant culture but to equip them with the knowledge to excel in it. While ours is a living language, in flux and rich with regional variations, some of which have connotations of race and class, were your students to use *nucular* in a job interview a decade hence, this would be regarded not as a charming colloquialism but a mark of ignorance. (Although apparently not as a bar to high office.)

But do not pester them about this on the playground. Another lesson to impart is that we use different sorts of language in different situations. Among our pals, we speak casually; we speak more formally to adults, and would speak more formally still when introducing the queen or the pope to the ghost of Miss Helen Hayes, first lady of the American theater, even in Boston or the Deep South.

---

### STRIP MAUL

*An acquaintance, an assistant professor of philosophy at a small public university, is planning to hold his bachelor party at a strip club. Should someone who represents a university, someone paid to instruct young women, participate in the commodification of the bodies of young women? Can he guarantee that he treats young women as individuals in the classroom when he pays to watch women their age strip? It is legal for him to attend strip clubs, but is it ethical?*

*—Name withheld*

Nobody should attend strip clubs, those purveyors of sexism as entertainment. Strip shows are to gender what minstrel shows are to race. But while I endorse your conclusion about these sad displays, I don't think much of the argument that gets you there. College professors do not have a particular obligation to shun them.

A professor out and about on his own time does not "represent a university"; he is only himself. To argue otherwise suggests that an employer has a broad right to limit what employees do off the job. This may be acceptable in strictly circumscribed cases involving conduct that directly and incontrovertibly imperils an employee's ability to do the job. (Some professional sports teams contractually forbid players to ride motorcycles, for example.) But to invoke more extensive prohibitions invites paternalism. It was not so long ago that employers demanded temperance or church attendance from workers. (Henry Ford was weirdly vigilant.) It would be lamentable to return to such a state.

It may be that visiting strip clubs does make this guy a worse professor, but the way to determine that is directly: evaluate his teaching. Because he cannot "guarantee" that his off-duty activities will not influence his work—how could anyone possibly do that?—the burden is on the school to confirm that its professors, all of them, do a good job, something that includes treating each student with respect.

**UPDATE**: The professor held his bachelor party out of state so as not to run into any of his students, which can be seen both as an attempt to avoid doing professional harm and a declaration that attending a strip club could do just that.

---

### CHEATING OR LEARNING?

*My college roommate calls her father, an English professor, for help on every paper she writes. This isn't just for general comments; they go over the entire paper, line by line. It seems like she has an unfair advantage over the rest of the people in her classes. On the other hand, there's no rule against getting comments, and we have a writing center where paid students help people write their papers. Is my roommate crossing the line?*

*—Name withheld, Boston*

You're overemphasizing the ethical implications of what is primarily a question of pedagogy. Your roommate's task at college is to learn. And while having this or any other help (like that available at the writing center) would give her an advantage in getting good grades, grades are above all a device to aid that educational process. If her conversations with her father hinder her education—i.e., if he's a crutch who inhibits her from doing her own work and learning to write a decent paper, or if he's a lackluster English prof with a weakness for mixed metaphors and dangling participles—then what they're doing is unwise. But if he is helping her become a better writer, that's a fine thing. If she is unsure of his efficacy, she'd do well to check with her teachers.

That said, the competition for grades—and by implication, grad-school slots, jobs, grants—is at least a part of college, and it is regulated by rules that one must obey. And so your roommate might find it useful to consult with her prof on this, too. It would be absurd if she were expected to curtail her own education to make things "fair" for other students. But she can reasonably be curbed in seeking outside help for take-home tests or other exercises meant to evaluate her skills.

There is an ethical consideration that involves not other students but your roommate herself. Her father ought not convey the implicit lesson that finagling for better grades is acceptable. A solution adopted at some New York private schools and at some colleges requires students to cite all help received on a paper, even orally, as they'd footnote other sources. This encourages students to discuss their work with friends and seek out all the help they wish, but to do so openly and honestly.

## STEEP GRADE

*I am a new university teacher. After I assigned final grades last semester, two students asked me to reconsider the Cs I gave them. One got just what his test scores indicated. The other was close to a B-minus, and while he did poorly early on, he worked hard, sought help, and improved significantly. I raised his grade to a B-minus, but did not alter the other student's. Nowhere in my course description do I state that improvement can be a factor in grading. Did I unfairly treat these students differently?*

*—Kristen Smith, Athens, GA*

You acted reasonably. A fair grading system must be consistent, applying the same criteria to all students. A determination to improve may be one of those criteria. Thus, you might legitimately give different grades to students with the same mastery of the material. What is important here is to make sure all students understand why they got the grades they did, that you are transparent about your methods, so that all students see that they are treated equitably. And if you are to treat all students equally, you'd do well to review the grades not just of those two squeaky wheels but of everyone in the class.

Feeling uneasy about our conduct often indicates that we behaved badly—the whole nagging-conscience problem. Often, but not always. And not in your case.

## OLD TESTS

*At my university, many students use tests from previous quarters to study for exams. These old tests are available to around 75 percent of the students— fraternities, sororities, and some dorms keep them on file—but not all. Every time I consider using one, I find myself in moral conflict. Is it ethical to use these tests?*

*—L.T., Michigan*

As long as you're not using the actual test you'll be taking, and as long as your professors permit this practice—i.e., as long as you're not cheating—you're free to employ these old tests as review material. But while you are meeting your ethical obligations, your professors are not. If they regard these old tests as legit study aids, then they must make them available to all (online? at the library? printed on pastries at the dining hall?). In other words, this situation demands not student abstinence but faculty action. What you might do is make sure your professors are aware of the problem and that they are resolving it.

## ADDERALL

*A friend and I will soon take the LSAT. His father, a psychiatrist, gave him Adderall to help him take the test. I asked my friend if he could share some with me, and he said that would be unethical. Is it? Isn't his dad's giving him the Adderall unethical?*

—*Name withheld, Austin, TX*

Medical ethics does forbid a psychiatrist to prescribe drugs to a close family member, but there is no druggie's code that bars his son from sharing ill-gotten pills. The more important question: is it ethical to use Adderall and the like not in response to some malady but to boost academic performance?

For you to take what some call "study drugs" may violate the law, endanger your health, and if those pills are ineffectual, waste your money, but doing so does not offend ethics, at least in some classrooms. If there were a safe, legal, and effective pill that let you learn French in a day, you'd be mad (*fou!*) to shun it. You do not forswear studying by electric light because Lincoln relied on his fireplace. You need not reject a learning aid merely because it comes in convenient chemical form. Many a student uses coffee to gain extra study hours.

Performance-enhancing drugs might give their users an unfair advantage over their unpilled peers. But academe does not exist on a level playing field. Deans, test-givers, and students themselves routinely accept greater inequities. Few who attend magnificent universities see this as an unethical edge over students at more modest colleges. Some students have parents who are lawyers, but nobody forbids those parents to help their kids learn. The equal-access problem would be solved if the Health Center handed out free Adderall to all. Until that utopia arrives, it might be heartening to realize that most students have easy, albeit illegal, access to these drugs.

Some foes of these drugs call them academic steroids, arguing that, as on the football field, those who decline to take them—and thus avoid the attendant health risks—cannot compete with those who do. Arguments supporting the use of such drugs would be more persuasive if a university were essentially a contest for grades; it is not.

Here is a more potent moral argument against these drugs: they undermine education itself and not just the drug-taker's. This was what my daughter asserted when she was a student at a small liberal arts college. These are not so much study drugs as cramming drugs. They make you more adept at amassing facts but no more able to deeply engage with, for example, art or history. Also pernicious, by relying on rote memorization, you arrive at class unable to fully participate in the discussions that are central to learning, and thus fail in your duty to your fellow students, to your professors, to the academic community you voluntarily joined.

She's right. And so I must amend my conclusion, there is no ethical barrier to taking such drugs in classes that rely on individual work—math, Latin—but you may not take them in classes where you are expected to interact with your fellow students—political science, literature. But to prep for the LSATs? Go nuts.

**UPDATE:** The letter writer acquired Adderall from someone other than her friend, but she didn't like it—"it made me nervous"—and stopped taking it long before the LSAT.

# In Transit

I HAVE, OVER THE YEARS, BECOME AN INCREASINGLY IMPLACABLE FOE OF the private car in urban life. Indeed, this predilection became such a hobbyhorse of mine that from time to time my *New York Times* editor had to remind me that there were other topics worthy of consideration.

Perhaps.

This is not a matter of incipient geriatric peevishness—well, not only—but of ethics. Two assumptions: first, ethics involves the effects of our actions on others. There can be solitary sin. You can sit alone at home and covet your neighbor's ox. But if you want to be unethical, you must get up, get dressed, go out, and steal the ox. Ethics isn't ethics until other people are involved. When you drive in Manhattan, for example, you harm those other people. A lot.

Next, ethics involves actions that are volitional. If you live in Atlanta or Phoenix or Dallas and you want to buy a newspaper or visit a friend or hold a job, you *must* drive. Here in Manhattan, you can walk to the corner for a paper, take the train to Brooklyn to visit your pals, bike to work. In Manhattan, driving is done by choice. Below are ten reasons why it is a very *bad* choice.

### #1: CARS KILL

If you introduced a transportation system by declaring "It'll only kill 30,000 people a year in the United States," it's hard to believe it would gain widespread popularity.

### #2: CARS KILL IN A WHOLE OTHER WAY: IN SLOW MOTION

Sure, running over your neighbors is a quick way to kill them, but if you're patient and work with other drivers, you can gradually kill even more people by so polluting the air that your neighbors keel over with hideous respiratory diseases. And by contributing to global warming, your auto emissions can harm future generations. It's a legacy.

### #3: ANOTHER THING ABOUT EXHAUST FUMES

They destroy the facades of buildings, through acid rain and other chemical reactions.

Remember the Elgin Marbles? The Greeks believe that Lord Elgin stole them, and they'd like them back. But there is an argument for the British keeping them. Many of the ones Lord Elgin did not steal, those still in Athens, are horribly eroded by pollution, primarily car fumes, but the ones in the British museum are in great shape. So I suppose the message is let's loot archaeological treasures. From Atlanta or Phoenix or Dallas.

### #4: CARS DISTORT OUR FOREIGN POLICY

To keep the oil flowing, we have a disconcerting tendency to invade other nations. Simply to maintain a navy to protect the shipping lanes (security guards for Exxon Mobil) is enormously expensive, soaking up money that could be spent on schools, health care, and cool refreshing glasses of pinot grigio.

### #5: CARS ABUSE PUBLIC SPACE

I don't stash my beach togs in a footlocker chained to a tree in Central Park for the winter. Why should you store your Dodge Caravan on my block? Why is your private property in our public space? Even the greenest of green cars, one that runs on hydrogen or batteries or happy thoughts, is still a car; you have to park it somewhere, and keep circling the block until you do.

### #6: CARS MARGINALIZE THE OLD AND THE YOUNG

A transit system that excludes 30 percent of the population is dubious indeed. If you are under sixteen, over eightyish, blind, or otherwise physically challenged, you probably don't drive.

This is a bit of a cheat, few babies take the subway by themselves. They're too weak to push the turnstile. But the principle remains.

### #7: CARS MAKE YOU ANGRY

When you *walk* to work, there's no "sidewalk rage," but locked in that metal box, people go nuts. If it were just your own mood, that would be between you and your therapist. But the enraged too often shoot people, and that's ethics. Or the lack of ethics.

### #8: CARS MAKE YOU FAT

. . . because you *don't* walk to work, because you drive everywhere, because you lead a sedentary life. With obesity comes diabetes and other maladies, imposing a huge cost, financial and social, on other people.

### #9: CARS MAKE YOU LONELY

Isolated in that cell on wheels, you have fewer opportunities for the chance encounters that invigorate daily life: the run-into. Who doesn't enjoy the run-into? And when you get home, the car isolates you further, because you live way out in some horrible suburb, a consequence of the sprawl caused by cars themselves. The private car is a rolling circular argument, creating the very problems it purports to solve.

### #10: CARS DESTROY WHAT DOES *NOT* EXIST

Consider the public spaces we could enjoy if Manhattan were not dominated by the private car—the imaginary city: green and welcoming, quiet, safe, and sociable. To drive damages not only what is, but robs us of what could be. And that, perhaps, is the saddest thing of all.

Our reliance on the private car was, I believe, a fatal decision, but an inadvertent one. It was barely a decision at all. There is a discredited but instructive theory that the fall of Rome can be traced to its aqueducts. The Romans used lead to seal the joints of their ceramic-tiled pipelines. As the system expanded, more and more people contracted lead poisoning, went mad, and their civilization collapsed. The private car, same deal. It will destroy us.

The alternative? Folks in Phoenix or Atlanta can't improve their ethics without improving their infrastructure. Those of us lucky enough to live in better-run cities can use public transportation. In a well-designed Jane Jacobs city, we can walk to many of our routine destinations. And there's this, from H. G. Wells, "Every time I see an adult on a bicycle, I no longer despair for the future of the human race."

What follows is a consideration of some of the ethical issues that arise from the private car as well as other modes of transportation.

## FLASHER

*A neighboring town enforces its speed limits by having police cars lie in wait for speeders. Many drivers flash their headlights to alert others to slow down and avoid a ticket. This results in the same type of driving the police are trying to enforce. So, is it OK?*

*—E.B., Massachusetts*

If headlight flashing promotes driving at the legal speed, its effects are evanescent; a moment after being flashed, a driver so inclined can blithely resume warp speed, secure that he's back in a copless zone. What's more, the intent of headlight flashing is not to encourage safe legal driving but to help speeders avoid getting caught. If you were to flash jewel thieves that the police have staked out Tiffany's—a complicated bit of headlight flashing, I grant you—this might briefly deter the burglars from robbing the place, but it hardly seems like an effective long-term anticrime stratagem. So, flashing is not okay.

Some might argue that even the presence of a police car, radar gun firing away, provides only ephemeral restraint to speeders, no better than what flashers achieve. However, if you've ever gotten a speeding ticket (or, full disclosure, several speeding tickets on a borrowed motorcycle—decades ago, when I was young and immortal) and had your license suspended, the effects linger; driving habits can be permanently altered.

There are towns that use speeding tickets not to promote safety but to generate revenue from nonresidents. If you know this to be so in your area, then flash on. You may deprive a fellow driver of the salubrious effects of a speeding ticket, but you serve the higher goal of battling that legal travesty, the speed trap. One caution: even in this situation, while flashing may be ethical, it may not be legal; some jurisdictions prohibit the practice.

## BELT WAY

*In my car, the backseats by the doors have lap belts and shoulder harnesses, but the middle seat has only a lap belt. My two children, ages three and seven, ride in the car, and occasionally we pick up another child for a playdate. Ethically, who should sit in the middle, less safe, seat—one of my children or the friend?*

*—Cheryl McCaffrey, Newtown, CT*

You should put your own kids in the shoulder belts, if their size and the law allow. It is disconcerting to acknowledge valuing your own children more than others, but while all children have a claim on your compassion and concern, your primary responsibility is to your own: particular relationships entail particular ethical obligations. (Indeed, you already provide food and clothing and probably some Nintendo-ish entertainment for them but not the neighbor kids.) Were you to give the other child one of the shoulder restraints, you'd have to place one of your kids in greater jeopardy. It's one thing to voluntarily diminish your own safety for someone else's benefit, quite another to impose such a risk on your children. (And I suppose you can't be the one to sit in back—not without teaching one of the little kids to drive, while sitting on a stack of phone books, which the highway patrol frowns on.) If you do put the friend in the more dangerous seat, you should, of course, inform his parents. If they feel uneasy with that level of safety, they can make other transportation arrangements.

There is a real-world dimension here that may obviate your need to answer this question now. Because of their vulnerability in side collisions, side seats with shoulder restraints may be no more secure than a center seat without. Leonard Evans, a research scientist and expert on traffic safety, concludes that in your situation, "it is not possible to say which is safer." So, temporarily reprieved from facing a troubling ethical dilemma—your child or a neighbor's?—you can concentrate on reminding all three kids that the U.S. Department of Transportation does not regard a lap full of gummy bears as "pretty much the same as an air bag."

## FULL STOP? FOOL STOP?

*A road on which I drive to work ends at a stop sign, where it meets another country road. I can see a quarter of a mile in every direction, and more often than not, no person or vehicle can be seen. At such times, I'd really rather not come to a complete stop, and yet . . .*
—*Alan Meyer, Newberg, OR*

A car idling obsequiously at a stop sign, at midnight, on a vast and treeless plain—the steppes of Central Asia?—when it is apparent that there are no other cars within miles, is a disheartening spectacle. There is something in the servility of this picture that chafes the spirit of a free people or a rational driver. And so I say glide on, alertly and cautiously.

It is reasonable (albeit illegal) to slow but not stop in these extreme circumstances—a rolling stop, also known as an Idaho stop. But beware of letting your car roll down the slippery slope of more ambiguous driving situations. It is risky to pick and choose among traffic laws. Furthermore, the stealth traffic cop idling nearby is unlikely to endorse my idea of ethical driving and may demonstrate his more legalistic approach by writing you a ticket.

In fairness, there is an argument for strict adherence to the traffic laws. Much of our behavior is the result of habit, not conscious decision-making, we should cultivate good ones. This is not a trivial concern but neither is it sufficiently persuasive to halt me at that stop sign at midnight in Kazakhstan.

## RIDES FREE, RATIONALIZES FREELY

*As a retired New York City police officer, I take the subway to and from work four days a week. When I show my ID and shield to station clerks, some of whom know I'm retired, they let me ride free. (Bus drivers do, too.) The public gets the added safety of having a retired police officer ride with them. I still carry a firearm and have at times aided conductors and uniformed officers. I never sit, so I do not take a seat from a paying rider. What do you think?*

*—George Kavanagh, New York*

The New York State Assembly thinks you have a point. Bill A05455 would let retired police officers ride free on MTA trains and buses. This policy may well serve the public good, but it must be ratified by law, not left to the whim of individual bus drivers, subway station clerks, and ex-cops who prefer to ride free (who doesn't?) and can devise a self-serving rationalization (who can't?). I'm convinced that my presence on the subway contributes to an atmosphere of conviviality, promoting the well-being of everyone around me. On airplanes, too. And in my apartment building. We'd all be better off if I paid for none of those. Police officers, active or retired, have sworn to uphold the laws we actually have, not the ones they wish we had.

I think both you and the Assembly are unpersuasive. If you did pay your fare, you'd be just as present and the other passengers just as protected as when you ride free. Because the subway is so swift and efficient a way to get around town, you need no extra incentive to use it; you would anyway. To challenge that assumption, you and Albany must show that letting ex-cops ride free is a cost-effective way to increase rider safety, particularly at a time when the MTA is so strapped for cash that it intends to strip children of their student MetroCards.

I do admire your argument that it's okay to cadge a free ride because you stand and hence deprive no paying customer of a seat. I'm going to use that next time I urge an usher to slip me into a Knicks game or the Metropolitan Opera or an opera about the Knicks.

---

**CARPOOL**

*Our family and another family carpool to get our kids to school. We have one child in the carpool; the other family has two, all going to the same school. What proportion of the time should each family drive?*

*—Name withheld, Connecticut*

Each family should drive half the time. You could argue, and I sense you'd like to, that driving assignments should be calculated on a per-kid basis: your family has only one-third of the kids and so should do only one-third of the driving. That would be a reasonable approach to paying the check if you were taking the kids out for snacks (two kids eat more, and hence cost more, than one) or if you were a bus company trying to divide your costs among all riders. But what's at issue here is not expense but effort, and that's what must be equitably apportioned. When you stop at that other house, it doesn't increase the workload if two kids get into the car instead of one.

It would be different if each kid went to a separate school. Then transporting the two kids from your friend's house would be more work than hauling your singleton, but that's not the case. There is a factor that would make me change my conclusion: if two additional families wanted to join the carpool, but the presence of those siblings meant there wasn't room for them. Dropping your current pool-mate and adding those two hypothetical families would mean you'd have to drive only a third—not half—the time. Assuming everybody involved lived nearby, then you'd be wise to make that change or to divvy up the driving on a per-kid basis. But as things now stand, the status quo is fine.

I can see why you'd want to remain anonymous with a hot topic like this. If this carpool thing got out, the scandal would be—actually, I'm not sure why you want to conceal your identity. But do what you like, as long as the kids buckle up.

---

### DRUNK DRIVER VS. BAD DRIVER

*I'm convinced that I'm a better driver with a couple of glasses of wine under my belt than my wife is stone sober. If we've been out to dinner and I've quaffed one or two, maybe even enough to put me over the legal limit, but my wife has abstained so as to be the designated driver, shouldn't I drive home anyway? I'd risk a ticket, but the highway would be safer for everyone.*
*—D.K., Scottsdale, AZ*

I'm convinced that I'm a better driver blindfolded than my ex-wife folded—that can't be right—or unblindfolded, but I'd hate to have to convince a traffic cop that this is so. Even if your delightfully flattering sense of your own abilities were accurate, it's beside the point. You present what traffic court judges call a "false dilemma," right before lifting your license and handing out a fat fine. You have options other than choosing between a bad driver and a drunk driver. Even in Scottsdale there must be such a thing as a taxi or a sober friend. You don't get to drive drunk because your wife isn't much good behind the wheel.

If she is such a terrible driver, why are you concerned only when you've had a few glasses of wine? Why is she ever behind the wheel? Shouldn't she head for the nearest driving school? You can even drive her there, if you stay off the sauce.

## SAFE ENOUGH

*My wife and I frequently transport our four-year-old and one-year-old by bicycle. They wear helmets and ride in a trailer or bike-mounted seats. People sometimes challenge us, asking if this is safe. The chances of our being hit by a car are low, but the consequences could be catastrophic. Is it OK to take the kids by bike when our admittedly safer, albeit not risk-free, car is available?*

*—Derek Pelletier, Portland, ME*

Your parental duty requires you to find not the safest conceivable mode of travel, but only one sufficiently safe. If you made the former your standard, even the car would be too dicey and you would have to haul your kids to school in the M1A1 Abrams Main Battle Tank—ripping up the asphalt, sucking down petroleum, frightening the neighborhood cats. Guided by the latter formulation, many parents, including me, sometimes transport their kids by bike. Or I did when my daughter was younger. At twenty-three, she's reluctant to squeeze into the little trailer.

Different parents tolerate different levels of risk for their children. Some allow their kids to go rock climbing while on fire; others forbid them to leave the house unless they're swaddled in Bubble Wrap. Hypothetically. I've never actually met anyone like that. But the general observation holds, there is no universal and immutable scale for your ethical obligation here. But there is a better way to describe your duty, seek prudent not utopian transportation.

There are other ways this choice affects your kids and your community. If you forswear the bike and travel with them only by car, you teach them to do likewise, promoting the sedentary lifestyle that contributes to obesity and other health problems, and you express acceptance of the environmental damage cars inflict even on non-drivers—two disheartening lessons.

As significant as what vehicle you deem suitable is how you use it. You are right to put your kids in properly constructed carriers and to make sure that they wear helmets. I hope that you bike safely, choosing routes with the fewest cars and, even better, those with protected bike lanes. In the longer term, you might actively promote the construction of safe biking and walking infrastructure in your community. And remember—in a car or on the bike—no cell phones, no texting, no bourbon, no blindfolds.

---

**CAR TALK**

*When my 15-year-old daughter and I are in the car, we vie for control of the radio. My solution has been to divide the time 50-50; however, my daughter insists that this is not fair, as I have control over the radio when she is not in the car. Hence, I owe her more time. What's the ethical way to share the radio?*

*—Félix Alfonso Peña, Reading, PA*

Yours is one of several equitable solutions. In the tiny democracy of the car interior, all travelers are citizens with equal radio rights. If there are two people, each controls the audio environment half the time. Your daughter's argument is predicated on the fallacy that the car is the only place she can listen to music. And that what happens in there when she's at school is germane. The question isn't how to apportion all automotive radio authority just how to divvy it up when you two are riding together.

One benefit of your approach is that it prevents a majority from tyrannizing a minority. Imagine three people in the car, two parents and a child, and a system of strict majority rule. The parents could form a potent geezer voting block, filling the car with the tedious doo-wop of their youth and never letting the lone child pick a tune: democracy in action. Making radio dominion proportional to population lets the riders hear music they like (if also music they don't). And it provides a potent incentive for family planning—parents with fifteen kids are in for a lot of Raffi followed by years of Britney or the current Britney-equivalent.

This last danger can be thwarted by handing out headphones and music players, creating autonomous music regimes (a sort of in-car federalism) that increase each passenger's freedom of choice (and the driver's freedom from hip-hop) but also, sadly, diminish the sociability of travel.

I prefer a consensus approach. You and your daughter seek songs that you both enjoy, with each of you possessing the power to veto anything deemed truly headache-inducing, a power to be exercised sparingly. Peace will reign, and you'll each be exposed to music you've never before heard and might just enjoy.

Neither your system nor mine is universally embraced. When my daughter rides with her mother, the latter claims radio-rule as a driver's perquisite, indeed as an essential of auto safety. (Apparently a few seconds of Kanye West could make the car burst into flames.) But this is less an expression of justice than an exercise of power. I do, however, agree that only the driver should control the brake pedal. Even wheeled democracy has its limits.

---

## CAR PHONE

*There is a speakerphone built into my car, the legal way to talk while driving in my city. When I get a call and family members are in the car with me,*

*I immediately inform the caller. I think it's common courtesy. My husband thinks I have no obligation to let a caller know that he is listening. How do you think this should be handled?*

—*L.M., Washington, DC*

This should be handled by never using the phone while driving. To do so increases your chance of an accident fourfold, akin to driving drunk. And there is no significant difference between speaking on a handheld or hands-free device: the increased danger is a cognitive not a mechanical problem. (That many states, including New York, bar drivers only from using handheld phones is an act of breathtaking cynicism or dazzling ignorance. They might as well ban only gray cell phones but allow beige ones.)

If you imperiled only yourself, you could be as thrill-seeking as you wished, but by talking on the phone while driving, you endanger other people on the road, and that's unethical, albeit not illegal. To ponder the social niceties ancillary to your misconduct is quibbling. You might as well ask, when swinging a baseball bat in a crowded room, if you should curtsy and say, "Excuse me."

But, sure, fine, alert your caller that he or she is on speakerphone. You'd do that in the office or at home, locales where, like the car, a caller is apt to assume that only you can hear him. To withhold the information that your husband is present is to abet eavesdropping. Although it would be poetic justice if the unknowing caller voiced a few choice remarks about your husband who'd have to suffer in silence, lest he blow his cover. Alternatively, you could wait until you get into a car crash and let EMS alert your caller.

IMAGINARY UPDATE: L.M. ignores my advice and heeds her husband. Talking on the phone while driving with him in the car, she gets into an accident. Fortunately, nobody's hurt. But the caller, an eccentric philanthropist, hears the shrieks of fear, realizes that the husband is in the car, and changes his mind about giving the couple a million bucks. It's like Aesop's fables. With flaming wreckage.

---

## THE OLD RACIST LADY

*On the commuter train my wife and I take to work, most passengers are African American. An older white woman who is a frequent rider walks with a cane and seems uncomfortable standing, but if she can't find a seat beside a white person, she stands. This is so well known that some passengers refer to her as "the old racist lady." Ordinarily I would surrender my seat to an older person, particularly someone partially disabled, but I do not for her when other seats are available. My wife agrees she is a racist, but offers her a seat, putting her next to me. (We're white.) Who's right, me or my wife?*

*—T.H., Boston*

You are. You need not—should not—surrender your seat to this woman. Why would you? There are empty seats available, but she declines to take one. To give her yours would be to abet and, in effect, endorse her racism.

The bigotry of someone elderly and powerless might seem more quaint than threatening to your fellow passengers, and yet I'm impressed by their forbearance. Rather than give her a tolerant sigh and a comical nickname, I'd be tempted to give her a kick in the pants. No, no. Of course not. Just gently push her out the door at the next stop in a revenge dream late one night.

# *Love & Sex*

TAXONOMY IS NOT A SCIENCE. OKAY, IT IS A SCIENCE, PARTICULARLY WHEN it involves botany or zoology. But there is not a single way of assigning things to categories. A short discussion of David Letterman's much-publicized affair might precede a chapter on work. It's not that his erotic exploits were particularly arduous—I've no knowledge of that—but that they involved employer-employee relations. I suppose this episode might also be examined under the rubric of technology, as I learned about it on one of those terrific high-def flat-screen televisions. Money? Well, of course; many moral decisions have financial implications. But I will consider it here as related to love and sex, as dense a moral thicket as any. In doing so, I focus primarily on one aspect of this episode—there are others—not adultery per se, but adultery on the job.

I wrote for *Late Night with David Letterman*, the 12:30 A.M. NBC version of his show, for seven years, so when the sex scandal—extortion plot? ratings boost?—broke, I took a personal interest, as did some of my former coworkers. The e-mail flew. Our rough consensus was that Dave's actions were no doubt deeply wounding to his wife and others close to him, but that he did not victimize his paramours. He was Bill Clinton, not Roman Polanski. But in reaching that initial conclusion, we overlooked some unfortunate consequences of such behavior on a work environment.

In thinking about this, I drew on my undependable memory of office gossip, which, even when fresh, was no more reliable at our office than any other. But if not infallible, gossip can be instructive when it concerns ongoing behavior. Almost from my first days at the show, early in 1984, there was talk about Dave catting around with employees, interns and assistants and NBC pages, and that these women were willing— eager—partners. None felt coerced. None felt harassed. All seemed delighted to be involved with a man they found charming, attractive, amusing. And while the concept of consent gets fuzzy when there are gross imbalances of power—it's hard to see how there can be meaningful consent between a corporal and a colonel, a prisoner and a guard—it is noteworthy that over twenty-five years, we know of no former girlfriend who has taken legal action against this wealthy public figure. (I don't want to overemphasize this; silence can also indicate fear of retribution or a discreet payoff.)

But even if Dave did no harm to his girlfriends, he injured the rest of the staff by creating a sense that favoritism prevailed. To grant a subordinate access, opportunities, and influence for extraprofessional reasons, particularly with a boss as aloof as Dave, can demoralize all who work for him. When, for example, Dave puts his declared paramour Stephanie Birkitt on camera, he gives her a professional opportunity other staffers crave. And, as a former colleague remarked, since CBS ultimately finances the show and hence paid for Birkitt's appearances, in a way it subsidized Dave's love life. The nicest gift I ever got from a network was a jacket with the show's name on the back.

(Few of the former colleagues I spoke to—okay, feverishly gossiped with—wanted to be quoted by name. Unlike me, they still have television careers. And a sense of dignity.)

There is a sort of defense, albeit morally ambiguous, of Dave's putting Birkitt on camera. He is more or less funny—that is, more or less good at his job—depending on whom he's talking to. When we writers worked on a "remote," a segment videotaped away from the studio— Dave visits the toy fair; Dave gets his photo taken at the DMV—an essential task was to find people he would hit it off with. He's better with some than with others. We did something similar when we prepared a studio piece that had Dave interacting with audience members. Before the show, we spoke to people in the ticket-holders line and selected those apt to have a rapport with Dave. It may be that he found Stephanie Birkitt so delightful, so effervescent, that he'd be particularly amusing bantering with her. But even if this explains his putting her on air, it does not excuse it.

The suspicion of favoritism is pernicious for anyone whose work is judged subjectively, but comedy writers are particularly vulnerable. No response is possible to that dismal three-word verdict: "it's not funny." If your piece is not put into production, or you're not used as a performer, or you're simply not hired, how can you be sure you've failed on your merits? How can Dave himself be sure?

This is worse still for the strikingly small number of women writers ever employed on the show. (One of them e-mailed me "The show's track record makes you want to shout, 'Bring back tokenism!'") During my tenure, there was only one woman writer on a staff that included about ten men. (Merrill Markoe, who helped create the show, had a more senior position.) Seeing other women employees benefit from sexual favoritism disheartens those rare women writers on the show and can discourage others from applying.

The U.S. Equal Employment Opportunity Commission finds that Title VII of the Civil Rights Act of 1964 "does not prohibit isolated instances of preferential treatment based upon consensual romantic relationships," but is less sanguine when such treatment permeates an office.

"If favoritism based upon the granting of sexual favors is widespread in a workplace, both male and female colleagues who do not welcome this conduct can establish a hostile work environment in violation of Title VII regardless of whether any objectionable conduct is directed at them and regardless of whether those who were granted favorable treatment willingly bestowed the sexual favors. In these circumstances, a message is implicitly conveyed that the managers view women as 'sexual playthings,' thereby creating an atmosphere that is demeaning to women."

I do not believe that such conduct was widespread at the show, at least during my time, but it can be invidious even if limited to the boss when that boss is so central to the enterprise. A talk show isn't structured like General Mills or General Motors or any of the generals. To a large extent, Dave *is* the show. The writing is meant to manifest his sensibility. It is he who decides what pieces make it to air. He has ultimate authority over hiring and promotion. If Dave does something, it in effect becomes pervasive.

It's not just current employees who can be injured by such behavior. Merrill Markoe, far and away the best writer the show ever had— *The Late Show* still does pieces she devised decades ago, Stupid Pet Tricks among them—was involved in a long-term romance with Dave that began before he got his own show. (Full disclosure, Merrill is my friend.) She must find it unnerving to be in any way associated with a parade of undistinguished paramours. At the height of the scandal, she e-mailed me, "I had a *NY Post* reporter in my driveway. I didn't say anything to her or anyone else who called. (Though I did give her a sugar-free Popsicle.) I did put one sentence up on my Web site: 'This is a very emotional time for me because as you may know Dave promised me many, many times that I would be the only woman he cheated on.'"

To some of us veterans of the show, Dave seems chastened, but will he alter his behavior? Another former writer e-mailed "And the #1 Sign David Letterman is changing his ways: 'Mr. Letterman's office. Lloyd speaking.'"

Many people praised Dave's forthright and rueful on-air acknowledgment(s) of his misbehavior, in contrast to the sandbagging and circumlocution of various Sanfords and Ensigns. I join in the admiration but with this caveat, the ability to apologize eloquently does not mean that the regretted conduct never occurred, nor does it place that conduct beyond discussion. And it must be noted that Dave's genuinely impressive candor was exhibited only after he got caught.

## ONLINE LIE

*I'm a thirty-six-year-old woman but look closer to thirty. In online dating, men my age often filter out women over thirty. I'm considering posting a profile listing me as thirty-four so men will at least see my picture and profile, where I'd immediately clarify my actual age, so as not to mislead anyone or waste anyone's time. Is it OK to slightly—and briefly—game the system to bypass an arbitrary filter?*

*—K.B., New York*

If we reconstitute your question into its crystalline form—may I lie if the duration of my deceit is brief?—then you don't look so good. But ethics demands a consideration of social context, and given yours, this lie is benign. Paradoxically, it is only by engaging in this evanescent deception that you have a chance to present a faithful self-portrait.

Those doing online dating will routinely screen by age, at least initially. (JDate.com, for example, allows a "quick search" using only location and age as criteria.) Your tactic lets you thwart this filter to present yourself to someone who, if he knew more about you, might want to meet. As long as you clarify your age in your profile, potential dates will almost immediately know your true age. The worst they can complain of is being slightly inconvenienced. Their compensation: a chance to consider someone they may well enjoy. This approach is imperfect and is inapt for nearly all other aspects of life, but in these particular circumstances it is at worst a slight misdemeanor, not a felony.

I draw a rough practical line where folks are actually dragged out of the house and down to the bar on false pretenses, and so I would not allow this tactic beyond what can be swiftly gleaned online. Men have been known to lie about their height, thinking that if they have a chance to turn on the charm in person, their date will overlook their being only three feet tall. And bald. And one jump ahead of the law. Perhaps. But the way to convey that is by writing a profile so charming it compensates for scant height, scant hair, and abundant years of waiting for parole.

## SHOWER SHOW

*As a gay teen who only recently came out, I wonder about showering at the gym with other men. For obvious reasons, men and women shower separately, and while I don't suggest segregated gay showers, is it right for me to be surrounded by naked men who have no idea that I may see some of them in a sexual way?*

*—Name withheld, New York*

As you outgrow your teens, you'll find that naked strangers can be other than erotic, as a visit to a family nude beach will demonstrate, but for now, enjoy your shower. While you should not act toward others in ways that discomfit them—e.g., no making an unwanted aquapass at a stranger—you may give your imagination free rein. There are no thought-crimes. Indeed, like most people, I've sometimes enjoyed a steamy reverie about a stranger seen on the street (and that fabulous Charlotte Rampling, whom, alas, I never see in the shower), and no harm done. It is actions, not imagination, that ethics seeks to guide.

There is a genre of teen sex comedy that features an adolescent boy who becomes invisible, tiptoes into the girls' locker room, and ogles naked cheerleaders. You might argue that his behavior is unethical because he deceives the cheerleaders; they don't know he's there. (You might also argue that the script is sophomoric, but I can't imagine who'd argue against you.) However, each man in your shower room knows that other men are present, and those with any knowledge of life know that some of those present may be gay. What your shower mates do not know are your thoughts, nor are they entitled to. In any case, the radical alternative to your behavior, skipping your post-gym shower altogether, is too noisome for even the most intolerant among us to advocate.

## CLOTHES MAKE THE . . .

*A gentleman of my acquaintance has expressed a desire to take me shopping. He likes the idea of going to dinner with me in an outfit he purchased. I've accepted birthday and Christmas gifts from men, but I've never been "taken shopping" by a man to whom I was not at least engaged. It feels somehow wrong. Is it?*

*—Name withheld, Las Vegas*

You're right to be guided by your uneasy sense that this is somehow wrong. In these vague circumstances, anxiety is a girl's best friend (as the song says, or should). The giving and receiving of presents is an exchange rich with meaning, and sometimes with ambiguity. You correctly infer that particular gifts suggest particular relationships, and that bestowing something as intimate as clothing is reserved for those with whom we actually are intimate. One guideline: if your would-be benefactor has not seen the part of the body the garment will cover, you should be cautious about accepting it. Lingerie can be impertinent. Woolly caps are innocuous.

Such gifts can signal a shift in a relationship, acceptance endorses that transformation. In your case, that is, your gentleman is offering greater intimacy and you must decide if you wish it. If not, decline the gift. To accept the gift while rejecting its meaning is to tell a kind of lie.

There's another side to this. His wanting to clothe you and take you out tiptoes toward the perverse, toward possession, toward games of dominance and submission. It is for you to accept or reject this invitation. In intimate matters, two consenting adults may do as they wish, as long as they understand one another, are honest with one another, and harm no one.

Incidentally, I'm impressed that you've been taken shopping only by men to whom you have been engaged; it sounds like quite a list.

---

### SENIOR SEX

*My wife of thirty years and I are in our sixties. A few years ago, she asked that we no longer engage in sex. "It's not such a big deal anymore," she said. She would not see a doctor or consider other help. I began an affair with a widow. Recently my wife found out and went ballistic. If she can casually renounce sex, can't I seek it elsewhere?*

*—Name withheld, Massachusetts*

Your greater transgression is not adultery; it is dishonesty.

If your sex life with your wife is indeed ended, you may honorably consider other alternatives. A fulfilling erotic life is an important part of marriage, indeed of human happiness. Many religions enumerate conjugal duties. (Doesn't it sound joyful put that way?) Some states make the failure to fulfill them grounds for divorce. And although your wife has not broached your seeking an erotic life outside the marriage, surely she has considered that you might do other than go quietly sexless to the grave. That's something the two of you must talk about.

You and she might decide that, because she no longer wants sex, you may seek it elsewhere—discreetly, tactfully, striving not to cause her embarrassment. Or she might find this modus vivendi intolerable and, if forced to choose, would decide to live apart from you. But you gave her no chance to decide anything. She may not compel you to join her in forsaking sex, but she may demand your honesty, regard, and consideration. Your desire is worthy of respect; your deceit is not.

What your wife wants is not merely fidelity, of course, but the repudiation of what for many people is a profound and exultant part of life. So be it. People change, even about something so fundamental, even when they pledged, at least implicitly, through their conduct, to live in a particular way. Your wife may wish to live differently at sixty than she did at thirty. (If we were bound by every promise we made many decades ago, I'd be having cupcakes for dinner, washed down with orange soda.) But she may not unilaterally impose on you the abnegation of erotic happiness. As Sir Toby Belch chaffs Malvolio in *Twelfth Night*, "Dost thou think, because thou art virtuous, there shall be no more cakes and ale?"

I doubt that she regards her waning sexual desire as a casual matter. This warrants further discussion with each other and with experts on sexuality and aging, who might have ideas neither of you considered.

**UPDATE:** The couple has settled into an uneasy routine of don't ask, don't tell.

---

### ETHICAL FLIRTING

*A friend was flattered by the flirtatious attention of a handsome, bare-chested bartender at a gay nightclub. He later found out that the bartender is straight but flirts with the customers to increase his tips. My friend feels it is dishonest of the bartender to pretend to be gay. I feel a gay man should expect no more sincerity from a bare-chested bartender than a straight man would from a waitress in a formfitting T-shirt. What are the ethical boundaries for flirting with customers?*

*—S.C., New York*

Flirting is not seduction; it is social play. The essential guideline for all forms of play is this: try not to injure the other players. Nothing in your story indicates that this bartender acted hurtfully. Indeed, as long as he stays behind the bar, his flirtatiousness is fine. If he were to ask people on dates to weasel them out of their life savings, then he'd err. The same rule applies to the waitress who flirts with a customer in whom she has no off-the-job interest. As long as she and the customer understand their interaction, it's entirely benign. Better than that, her playfulness makes the bacon and eggs go down easy. Gay and straight don't really come into it.

Your friend might reconsider the idea that bartenders all over town are falling at his feet. Modesty and social savvy are called for whether you do your drinking at a gay bar or at Hooters. (Of course, if you had social savvy, you wouldn't be drinking someplace with a comical name.) He should remember that he and the bartender have a business relationship, and for tapsters, amiability is virtually a job requirement—nobody likes (or tips) a dyspeptic bartender.

Both you and your friend might also reexamine your assumption that a man who spends eight hours a night flirting with other men is unwaveringly straight. Such categories may be more amorphously defined than you suggest. Thus, your friend might someday be cheered to discover that he wasn't rejected for his sexual orientation, but on his merits.

---

**JDATE**

*Some friends and I use a Jewish Internet dating service. When I mentioned an ad placed by a Hispanic woman who likes to date Jewish men, a female friend of mine remarked that "they should stay away from our stuff." I argued that the Hispanic woman was up front about her ancestry and so did nothing wrong. Please shed some light.*

—D. G., Long Beach, NY

You can, of course, be Hispanic and Jewish—Jews in Barcelona do it every day—and if that's the case here, problem solved. But even if the controversial Hispanic woman is a gentile, I still see no problem. She has been open about her background and her desires. However, she may want to examine the feelings that draw her to a group rather than to a particular individual. A benign stereotype is still a stereotype, like the persistent typecasting of Jewish men as good fathers, intelligent, compassionate, and great lovers. (We are, of course, but that's a separate issue.)

If another participant in the dating service finds her appealing, then the two of them can rendezvous. It's not for some third party to veto that decision. This service should for people who wish to date Jews, perhaps primarily, but not exclusively their coreligionists; it ought not be a segregated Semite preserve. Maybe it should be subtitled: for Jews and those who love them, or want to.

Needless to say, a whites-only dating service would be repugnant, trading on racism, on superficial characteristics over which people have no control. Furthermore, it would be essentially exclusionary. By contrast, a Jewish dating service defines people by their behavior and beliefs, by something volitional, and is open to all who share those values. In theory, anyone can choose to embrace Jewish customs and search for a like-minded spouse with whom to establish a Jewish household and live according to Jewish precepts. That is, members of a minority culture, eager to preserve and practice a way of life, may honorably seek each other out online or in person. But you may not impose Jewish beliefs on someone else, so let the Hispanic woman and her Jewish suitors dance the night away. Err on the side of inclusion.

Incidentally, if by "our stuff" your woman friend is alluding to me or any portion of me, she is a bit presumptuous. (I could hypothetically become her stuff, but she'd have to take me to dinner first. At least.) Even if she's only talking about my stereo or my Rollerblades, she's making me nervous.

## FEMALE FRIENDS

*I am a man engaged to a woman from another state who will move here and likely adopt my friends as her own. The issue is I have slept with all my female friends. Do I have a moral obligation to tell my fiancée? I don't want her to be uncomfortable around them, but I want to be open and honest.*

*—B.J.M., New York*

"All" is a very large number indeed. Unless you have few friends. But you seem like a friendly sort of fellow. Alarmingly so.

Yes, you must tell your fiancée for the reason you note, so she doesn't feel uncomfortable (although I'm skeptical that full disclosure will produce the serenity you crave). Her well-being is important to you. You should not let her blunder unknowingly into a roomful of people, each of whom knows something significant that she does not. She has a right to know what she's getting into, less for what it reveals about your past than for what it might imply about her future.

This is a delicate matter. You might broach it this way. Gather your female friends and your fiancée, and say to the latter, "These women have something in common. Can you guess what?" She'll venture various wrong answers—a love of the ballet? careers in physics? allergies to cats?—after which you'll chuckle benignly and reveal the truth. Beyond the good-natured acceptance that will no doubt greet this revelation—

all your exes will surely be pleased to find themselves members of a sort of club. They'll probably start getting together once a month. With snacks.

You may have a more tactful alternative. Different people want different amounts of information. Some want to know everything about a partner's past, some prefer to leave it shrouded in mystery. Gently sound out your fiancée; if she's the sleeping-dogs sort, you're off the hook.

One final thought, don't throw away the receipt for the engagement ring.

---

## CYBER-CYRANO

*I persuaded a shy male friend to try Internet dating. He posted his profile and photo but never actually wrote to anyone. So I got him to let me take over. Now I am courting three women over e-mail, in the guise of a thirty-five-year-old man. I am a woman (but, it turns out, I have a way with the ladies). This now feels a little less innocent, but if it gets my shy friend together with a nice woman, is it wrong?*

*—Name withheld, New York*

This isn't an ethics question, it's the premise for a romantic comedy. In the hipster art-house version, you discover erotic possibilities you'd never before considered. In the square airplane version, the most alluring of your e-mail correspondents turns out to be—surprise—a man writing as a woman to help a friend, and you two fall truly and deeply in love. In the modern violence version, your shy friend feels humiliated by the whole episode and goes on a killin' spree, with you as his final victim.

Okay, it is an ethics question, and one that illustrates the perils of overreaching. You did well to help your friend look for love, but erred when you engaged in impersonation. Now it is your turn of phrase his intended inamoratas are drawn to, your flirtatiousness and allure. You'll succeed only in bewitching a woman who expects your friend to be someone else, a dubious basis for romance. That's why I don't have the ghost of Shakespeare compose my love poetry for me. Such bait-and-switch is associated more with disreputable electronics dealers than honest wooers. When the truth comes out, the women you deceived will feel hurt and embarrassed, a good guide to the impropriety of your deception.

As you know, literature offers a cautionary tale about such tactics, things didn't work out well for Cyrano or Roxane or Christian. And so as a matter of efficacy as well as ethics, you must abandon your imposture. At a minimum, your friend must immediately replace you at the keyboard. Ideally, he'll fess up to everyone and hope, the malfeasance being well intentioned and evanescent, that his dates are more charmed than wounded by this brief and tender treachery.

---

### BETRAYAL?

*I struck up a close friendship with a man. We take longs walks or simply talk for hours. I trust that our relationship will remain platonic but somewhat intense, because he is married and I am in a committed long-term relationship. Yet this feels like a nonsexual affair, because we haven't told our partners about it, an omission that feels like a sort of betrayal. May we continue to see each other in this way?*

*—Name withheld*

That you feel you are betraying your partner is sufficient reason to make a change, although doing so will be dicey now that this "somewhat intense" connection is established. What is unsettling is not that you've done anything discreditably lurid but that you are keeping a significant secret from your partner, what sterner folks could call "sneaking around." (And by "sterner folks," I mean me.) Your partner assumes you are candid about things that are important to you, but you are not.

It is your own language that is disturbing—"affair . . . betrayal." As you imply, it is possible to have a dangerous liaison even with your clothes on and despite your intentions for the future. This is not to demand emotional (or even physical) monogamy. Different couples have different rules. Some people reserve a lot of privacy for themselves; others reveal all. Rather, you ought to be kind to your partner and true to yourself, heeding the dictates of your conscience and honoring the implicit agreements of your relationship. And that means either coming clean to your old partner or breaking it off with your new friend.

**UPDATE:** She (as it happens) spoke to her partner and says, "While he does not attribute any good or neutral intentions to the other man, he has expressed his trust in me and my decision whether or not to continue meeting my 'friend.'" She has not severed that connection.

---

**DEAD LETTER**

_I work for a charity selling donated goods. An acquaintance brought in items of his late father's. Slipped inside a book of poetry was a letter from a lover ending what was clearly an extramarital affair. My instinct is to destroy it, but the father did save it for years and left it where he must have known his children would find it. The mother is dead, so it can't hurt her. And perhaps the son is aware of the affair. Should I give the children the letter?_

_—Name withheld, New Jersey_

Would your acquaintance want to know about the affair? Some children crave a deep understanding of their late parents; some cling to an idealized version. If your acquaintance is among the former, give him the letter. If not, or if you are simply unsure, consign it to the flames. Or frame it on your bedroom wall as a reminder of the labyrinthine recesses of the human heart.

It was the father's prerogative to make—or not make—such a deathbed disclosure. I do not agree that he "must have known" his children would discover the letter. After all, they didn't. What's more, people misplace things all the time. (I still can't find some eleventh-grade calculus homework that I swear I completed.) You've no idea of the father's intentions, conscious or unconscious, but you know this, if he had wanted to reveal his infidelity, he could have announced it in his will, or written a tell-all memoir, or put this letter where it would have been more reliably discovered, posting it on his refrigerator door with little magnets. Indeed, he might already have told his son, as you mention.

This is not to advocate a policy of laundering a late parent's past—the dead have few claims to privacy—but to assert that this unsettling information cannot prompt the son to take any significant action, neither of his parents is living. And so it is reasonable to weigh the effect of this revelation on the hearts of the children. There are times when you must divulge even disturbing information about the dead. If, for example, the father were a personage—a surprisingly long-lived Abraham Lincoln perhaps—then the claims of historic truth would be compelling. But here you may let the disloyal dead sleep undisturbed.

# *Religion*

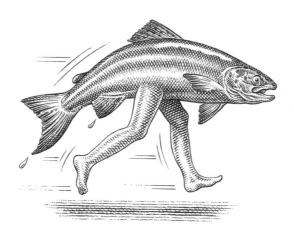

WE AMERICANS ARE A RELIGIOUS PEOPLE. DEPENDING UPON WHICH study you find convincing, more than 90 percent of us believe in God or something godlike. More than half of us pray at least once a day (or tell pollsters we do). Belief in the devil has increased in recent decades, from about 50 percent in 1990 to more than 70 percent currently. About three-quarters believe there is a heaven, and the same percentage believes that angels exist. Hell? A CNN poll conducted just after the killing of Bin Laden showed that 60 percent of us believe that he's there.

And so it is not surprising that among the columns that consistently provoked the most—and most passionate—response are those that dealt with a clash between religious and civic values. Etiquette holds that religion, especially another person's religion, should be treated with deference or, better still, silence by nonbelievers. Hence the familiar dinner-party injunction: don't discuss religion or politics. Even at a tableful of coreligionists, feelings can run high, and there is a reluctance to combine digestion with discord (particularly when knives are nearby). To the observant, a nonbeliever's comments on church doctrine can feel less like a discussion of theology than a personal attack.

Yet despite the risk of provoking the ire of believers, we should discuss the actions of religious institutions as we would those of any other—courteously and energetically. This is a mark of respect, an indication that we take such ideas seriously. To slip on the kid gloves is condescending, akin to the way one treats children or the frail or cats.

My political beliefs, my ideas about social justice, are as deeply held as anybody's religious beliefs, but I don't ask believers to treat me with reverence, only civility. They should not expect me to walk on tiptoe. It is not as if religious institutions occupy a precarious perch in American life. It is not the proclaimed Christian but the nonbeliever who is unelectable to high office in this era when politicians of every party and denomination make a public display of their faith. The newly elected President Obama barely had a chance to shower and shave after his inaugural balls before establishing the White House Office of Faith-based and Neighborhood Partnerships. And he's supposed to be the humanist, the policy wonk, the rationalist. (Angels? Really?)

Some of my most indignant detractors declared religious practice a matter of free association, what people do voluntarily among themselves is nobody else's business. But children raised in a particular faith did not choose it. And sometimes one spouse is pushed into a pew by the other. Even when membership is truly volitional, once a group reaches a certain size and acquires power and influence in the larger community, to treat it like four people getting together in someone's rec room to play bridge is disingenuous. Its actions are still subject to moral scrutiny, whether the group is the Boy Scouts or NASCAR or the Roman Catholic Church.

Other of my critics aver that actions undertaken as a religious duty occupy a privileged place. But merely designating something "religious" does not exempt it from commentary. The roster of historic enormities justified by religious doctrine is too long and too familiar to bear repeating. (Okay, just a few: the Crusades, the Inquisition, colonialism, slavery, Pat Robertson.)

We do accord special status to religious groups, even writing it into our Constitution. Some actions that are generally forbidden are permitted if undertaken as a religious obligation. For instance, Sikh transit workers in New York may wear turbans. Jewish prison inmates may wear beards if doing so is a religious duty. But not everything goes. Polygamy is outlawed. Nor would we allow human sacrifice, even if requested by a deeply observant Inca. That is, we do not regard these things uncritically. And remember, it is not just religious practice but free expression that the Constitution protects. To muffle a discussion of religiously motivated acts is to dilute the discourse that is essential to democracy.

And so it was dispiriting if unsurprising, a few years ago, that the editorial pages of our most important newspapers did not castigate the Vatican when it invited Anglicans who were, as the *New York Times* demurely put it, "uncomfortable with female priests and openly gay bishops" to reunite with the Catholic Church. If a secular institution, Walmart or Microsoft, for example, made a similar offer—Tired of leadership positions being open to women and gay employees? Join us!—it would be slammed for appealing to misogyny and homophobia. And while some disapproval was directed at the Roman Catholic Church, it was muted.

A few blogs spoke more forcefully. Daily Kos headlined its coverage, "Vatican Welcomes Bigoted Anglicans." But the tone set by, say, network news was diffident. That's not courtesy; it's cowardice. Perhaps the networks fear being charged with anti-Catholic bias, not an unreasonable concern, as I was reminded whenever I responded to questions about the intersection of religious and secular life. But to condemn a particular Vatican action need not be anti-Catholic bigotry. Criticism is not contempt.

One group did provide a lively critique of that pronouncement—the religious press. Some of the sharpest writing came from those critical of their own church—Father George Rutler, for example, a convert from Anglicanism, wrote "It is a dramatic slap-down of liberal Anglicanism and a total repudiation of the ordination of women, homosexual marriage, and the general neglect of doctrine in Anglicanism." Incidentally, Father Rutler does not think the secular media is timid but thickheaded: "The press, uninformed and always tabloid in matters of religion, will zoom in on the permission for married priests."

He may have something. Perhaps both the mainstream media and the secular public are less fearful of being branded as bigots than of being revealed as doofuses. Nevertheless, we should stop talking about religious affairs only in timorous whispers, and the observant should stop expecting us to.

Some readers responded to this argument by insisting that religion be treated differently from other forms of discourse because it is based on faith and hence is not amenable to rational analysis. I don't agree. Once religious beliefs are mustered in consideration of public policy, as they are routinely in regard to, for example, reproductive rights or marriage, then debate must be conducted rationally. You have to make your case. Even when a believer's action affects only coreligionists, it is still subject to moral scrutiny. What's more, such namby-pamby pleas give short shrift to the intellectual rigor (and courtesy) that can be found among religious thinkers.

Some readers defended Catholicism's ban on women priests by arguing that women have a different but important role in the church. This is the separate-but-equal argument that, in another context, the Supreme Court repudiated in *Brown* v. *Board of Education*, concluding that separate is inherently unequal. That's as true in religious life as it is in the secular realm.

Many people objected to my use of "bigotry" to describe the restrictions that adherents of several religions impose on women and homosexuals. But surely that is the correct term for denying some people full participation in an institution not for their individual qualities but for their membership in a particular group. That's what bigotry is, even when buttressed by canon law.

## CHORISTERS

*I sing in a full-time all-professional church choir. Like most of my colleagues, I am not of the same faith as the church. During services we sing sacred texts, but few of us recite the spoken prayers, feeling that doing so would go against our own beliefs. Recently the clergy mandated that we recite the prayers along with the congregation. Is that ethical?*

*—A.R., New York*

To sing and to speak do feel different. (To confirm this for yourself, try declaiming Ray Charles' immortal "What'd I Say.") And yet, while your boss would have done better to tell you from the start what the job entailed, this new demand is reasonable.

By singing those sacred songs, you already engage in religious expression. To participate in spoken prayer is not so different, a sort of hymn-singing without music. Indeed, you may have been asked to do so because of the strength and beauty of your voices. Dr. Martin Tel, director of music at the Princeton Theological Seminary, says, "The spoken prayers and responses are but an extension of the sung prayers and also draw on the musical skills of the chorister."

The clergy would be wrong to insist that your church's electrician put down his wire cutters and enter the sanctuary to pray with the congregation. The electrician's professional function is unrelated to enacting religious rites. Yours, however, is to lift your well-trained voice in prayer, sometimes melodically, sometimes not.

Think of your task as akin to that of a hired mourner at a funeral in Europe in the Middle Ages or in ancient Greece—as a performance, the honorable work of a skilled professional, not a manifestation of personal faith. There's no hypocrisy in it, even for choristers whose beliefs differ from those of the church.

## SUNDAY SCHOOL

*I volunteer as a Sunday-school teacher at my Catholic church. While I consider myself Catholic and understand Catholic beliefs, I do not agree with all that the church teaches. When a student asks me about a topic on which the church and I differ, may I reply with my own beliefs in addition to the official doctrine?*

—*B.J., Washington, DC*

Your church asked you to teach a class in Catholic doctrine not one in B.J.'s Views of Catholic Doctrine, a reasonable, if inhibiting, request. But to give students an understanding of both this doctrine and the state of the modern church, you may—you should--provide some context. It is a matter of fact, and not a trivial one, that many Catholics differ with their church on all sorts of things. (For example, American Catholics practice contraception at about the same rate as non-Catholics, church policy notwithstanding.) To point out that opinions differ within your religious community would be to convey something objectively true, pertinent to the discussion, and informative for the students. You would not be offering your personal views, which are beside the point in this setting. Indeed, a Jew or a Muslim, a Hindu or an atheist could honorably teach this class using these guidelines, giving the students a rich understanding of the subject but not broaching the teacher's personal beliefs.

**UPDATE:** B.J. presents church doctrine "their way," then tells his students that some Catholics feel differently and discusses how. He urges his students to think about these things and talk them over with their parents.

## FALSE VISA

*We hoped to attend a symposium, "The Middle East in the 21st Century," on a ship that would dock in Saudi Arabia, Bahrain, Oman, and Kuwait. Because we are Jewish, we wondered if we would be welcome. Our tour director said everyone would be identified on visa applications as Christian. We felt uneasy with this and withdrew. Should the sponsoring organizations hold events in countries that bar Jews? Shouldn't they have told us unprompted that they'd file false visa information?*

*—Lillian Cartwright and Alan Skolnikoff, San Francisco*

There is no ethical obligation to comply with flagrantly unjust laws. Here in the United States in 1950, for example, there was no moral imperative to cooperate with segregation. (Indeed, there was a duty to resist it.) Honorable people might debate the legitimacy of some laws, but travel restrictions based on religion are clearly deplorable. The United Nations' Universal Declaration of Human Rights bars religious discrimination. Had you acquiesced in deceit on a visa application in the face of such laws, you'd have committed at worst a minor moral transgression (albeit one that, like all lies, exacts a social toll). In any case, while some of the countries you mention restrict some Jewish activities within their borders, none forbid Jews to enter. So is lying necessary?

Even if circumstances inclined you to submit falsified documents, the sponsors may not make that decision for you and should have alerted you in advance to their plans. Nobody enjoys a surprise party at a border post, let alone a stretch in a Saudi jail.

There is nothing inherently wrong with traveling to a nation that engages in dismal practices. To enter a country is not to endorse its every policy (or few Western Europeans, given prevailing opinions, would come to the States). Such visits can even do some good by promoting an exchange of ideas and increasing mutual understanding.

## PSYCH!

*I am a psychiatrist who happens to be an atheist. Occasionally a patient asks me what religion I follow and, displeased by my answer, seeks another psychiatrist. I am a physician not a priest. Religious beliefs seem as relevant to my profession as they are to an accountant's. Nevertheless, candor sometimes costs me a patient. May I claim a belief in God to avoid damage to my credibility and business?*

*—Vaidyanath Iyer, The Woodlands, TX*

To rephrase your question just slightly: may you lie to a patient to initiate a relationship of trust? Okay, I've rephrased it totally and unflatteringly, but the answer—no—is provided by the American Psychiatric Association's "Principles of Medical Ethics," which requires you to "be honest in all professional interactions." And rightly so.

What you may do is decline to answer such questions. Dr. Glen O. Gabbard, a professor of psychiatry at Baylor College of Medicine, told me in an e-mail that "it is not dishonest to use restraint in responding to questions of a personal nature." He added, "One can also inquire about the reasons for the question." The patient's reply might offer insights useful in treatment.

The patient's question need not reflect mere prejudice but express a desire for a psychiatrist whose experience will yield a deeper understanding of the patient. Some women seek a female psychiatrist, some homosexuals a homosexual. You need not be a Presbyterian to effectively treat a Presbyterian. Even a gay female Presbyterian.

And so you should respond courteously to such queries, answering those about your training and technique, but not those you deem irrelevant to the work: Are you Jewish? A Republican? An opera buff? This demurral could cost you a patient or two, but so be it. A patient's determination to make an unwise decision does not justify a doctor's deceit.

## HOMILETIC DISTRESS

*We recently discovered that the senior pastor at our large congregation has never written his own sermons, a requirement of his job. He has been taking them from Web sites and preaching them word for word. He then has them printed up and handed out under his name. Is this man to be trusted with a congregation? What is your opinion of this?*

*—Ruth Klarner, Mableton, GA*

Such Web sites abound, and they bear a striking (and, from my secular perspective, amusing) resemblance to sites proffering term papers to students. There is SermonCentral.com. ("Find Free Sermons Online: Browse 120,000 Christian Sermons, Bible Sermons, and Sermon Outlines.") Or a canny pastor can avoid not only the asperity of writing but the tedium of reading, at SermonAudio.com. ("Enjoy our library of 424,079 free sermons from conservative churches worldwide.")

It is certainly unethical for your pastor to recite someone else's sermon without citing its author. Unlike a politician or actor or host of a late-night talk show, he is assumed to speak his own words. Indeed, in most denominations it is a job requirement. To print those sermons under his name is yet more discreditable, descending from the passive deceit of uncredited oration to the active mendacity of falsely claiming authorship.

Such malfeasance is something of a trend. Clergymen have recently been suspended and even fired for similar offenses in Michigan, Missouri, and California. This recurrence does not justify the deed, of course, but it might lead us to reconsider our assumptions about clerical duties.

Perhaps pastors should not have to write sermons. Leading a congregation demands an impressive assortment of abilities. One must be an administrator, a fund-raiser, a psychologist to the congregants, a biblical scholar, an inspiring speaker. Must one also be a gifted writer?

This is not to condone your pastor's transgressions, but to note that it is a rare person who excels at all that the job requires. (Similarly, few barbers today are really good surgeons, once a requisite of that position.) If an otherwise excellent pastor is clumsy with his pen, wouldn't his congregation be better served by hearing him deliver the profound and stirring words of a more talented author?

As a matter of rhetoric, yes; as a matter of faith, probably not. For some denominations, writing a sermon is not in essence a literary but a religious act—a spiritual discipline, a way of communing with God. The aesthetic value of the resulting homily is beside the point. If that is an article of your pastor's faith, then his transgressions are multiplied; not only plagiarism but sin.

He now faces the formidable challenge of regaining your trust and—unless his job is redefined—composing his own sermons. However, he is in the business of sin, repentance, and redemption, and so is surely entitled to be a beneficiary of the doctrine he proclaims. And to his credit, he has done some good, giving small-minded people like me the entertaining spectacle of a teacher of morality caught in an immoral act, hypocrisy as spectator sport, a joy my friends eagerly anticipate as they eye me for missteps.

### LOST FAITH

*I am a member of the clergy and I no longer believe in the tenets of my faith; indeed, I am an atheist. I am praised for my services, counseling, teaching, etc., and I receive glowing reports in staff reviews, but it is a futile, empty performance. On the one hand, my congregation is happy with me, but on the other, I feel like a fraud. Must I disclose my doubts to my congregation, knowing it would cost me my job?*

*—Name withheld*

Your unnamed denomination is the key to your professional obligations. We don't demand that most workers be true believers, only that they do their jobs well. A librarian may detest the Library of Congress filing system and yearn for the forsaken Dewey Decimal. Even in a house of worship, we don't question the spirituality of the guy who repairs the synagogue's boiler or the woman who does its books. But the clergy may be different. In some religions their essential task is to be a teacher and leader; in others faith is the sine qua non.

The Rev. Dr. Alida Ward of the Greenfield Hill Congregational Church in Fairfield, Connecticut, takes the latter view. "If, as is clearly the case here, the preacher can no longer hold on to his or her faith, then, yes, the most fundamental and necessary qualification for this 'job' has disappeared." She adds, "It simply isn't fair to a congregation not to believe what you're telling them to believe."

From this Christian perspective, you must come clean. (Ward suggests you consider teaching in a seminary.) To do otherwise would make you a spiritual snake-oil salesman, like a stereo dealer who pushes a CD player he knows works poorly and is likely to burst into flames. Hellish flames. But from one Jewish point of view, this is the wrong metaphor.

Steven Nadler, a professor of philosophy and Jewish studies at the University of Wisconsin-Madison, says, "I'm not convinced that, with the possible exception of Orthodox Judaism, it is a rabbi's job to promote a specific set of theological ideas. His job is to explain what the demands of Judaism are and to lead people in study and prayer. He is a teacher, not a salesman, and outside of the sciences it is not the job of a good teacher to tell you what to believe, but only to show you how to go about figuring out for yourself what you should believe."

This interpretation imposes no obligation either to step down or to discuss your inner life with your congregation. Your doubts may actually be an asset, suggests Rabbi Jonathan Gerard of the Temple

Covenant of Peace in Easton, Pennsylvania, "My suspicion is that your writer has merely lost faith in an older and unacceptable notion of God. He or she should continue to serve his or her congregation for out of this will come new spiritual insights. We all feel inauthentic at times."

Ward adds that your experience is widespread for civilians as well as your coprofessionals, "Most people of faith, if they are honest with themselves—clergy included—will admit to passing through periods of doubt and spiritual confusion." But unlike Gerard, Ward permits only transitory doubts in the clergy.

Because people of various religious traditions differ about this matter, my conclusion is that you must adhere to the doctrines of yours. If your denomination demands faith, you must reveal your doubts and, if called to—not an inevitability—step down. But if your religion does not impose such a demand, then you've no ethical obligation to resign, although your own desire for authenticity may lead you to. There's little contentment to be found by persisting in work for which you have no heart.

---

### YOUNG EARTH

*I'm a history professor—my period is 1500 to 1800—with an MA student who wants to pursue a doctorate. While she is smart and capable, she is very religious, subscribing to the "young earth" theory that the world is only six thousand years old. I am to work with her for a year, then recommend her to PhD programs. Must I do so if I find her views incongruent with those of historians?*

*—Name withheld, California*

Unless your student's religious beliefs mar her work—and you don't suggest they do—they are irrelevant. Judge her on her scholarship not her spiritual life, however nutty. If she were studying the Sumerians, she might have a hard time working out how they accomplished so much so soon after the earth was formed, what with all those dinosaurs running around trampling the pottery. But this young-earth nonsense need not blot her understanding of, say, Oliver Cromwell or, indeed, much else in your period.

We all harbor irreconcilable ideas. (People are no damn good, but I'm a fine fellow. Being overweight is a grave threat to my health; please pass the doughnuts. Life is short; let's watch TV.) Yet most of us get along pretty well. (Except for those fat guys stuffing themselves in front of *Deal or No Deal*. They're no damn good.) What's more, people have an impressive ability to compartmentalize. If your student can indulge her religious notions in church on Sunday and do great work in the library on Monday, more power to her.

You might regard your year together as a chance to teach a promising scholar to sharpen her critical reasoning, that vital tool of the trade, and thus to reconsider this young-earth applesauce.

## SHABBAT

*I am a hospital physician. My department schedules us to work a few weekends a year. Like other doctors, I'm occasionally assigned to split a pair of weekends with someone who practices religious observance on Saturdays, so he can work two Sundays, landing me with two weekends of obligation. Is it ethical to make me accommodate someone else's religious practices?*

*—Name withheld*

It is vexing to draw an unwanted weekend shift, even when this is, as you note, a rare occurrence. But unappealing is not a synonym for unethical; your department does no wrong. Indeed, the law requires it to act as it has. Judith Conti, a lawyer with the Washington, DC, Employment Justice Center, explains, "Arrangements like this are very common, very commonsense, and very respectful. There is a legal obligation for an employer to take reasonable steps to accommodate religious observation."

An employer may require employees to take such time as a personal day or a sick day or the like, or to swap shifts with an amenable colleague. And it is okay for your department to dragoon you to fill in while a colleague prays. Someone has to work the vacated shift. Some hospitals wisely seek volunteers. But if too few come forward, press-gangs may drag physicians off the golf course (or out of the lab or library). This is routinely done to staff some unpopular shifts—nights, for example, or Sundays. Your hospital simply adds another day for religious observance. Scheduling should be equitable, transparent, and responsive to employee wishes, but it need not—cannot—always give everyone his ideal shift.

The problem is not that your department and the law go too far but that they don't go far enough. Why grant religious observance greater consideration than secular pursuits? Is my time spent reading Aristotle (by which I mean watching basketball on TV) less worthy than yours spent contemplating the Eternal (by which I mean dozing through the sermon of a less-than-eloquent preacher)? Employers should not make judgments about how employees use their time off; instead they should provide flexible scheduling and leave it to the employees themselves to decide how to use their free time.

---

## PRAY TELL?

*My two teenage sons and I were pallbearers at the funeral of my wife's father, a practicing Catholic. I am a lapsed Catholic. We have reared our*

*sons as atheists like us, so when it came to reciting prayers, genuflecting,*
*and crossing myself, I elected not to, concerned that I might give the false*
*impression that I was a believer and confuse my sons. Was I obligated*
*to perform or not perform these parts of the ceremony?*

*—M.H., Connecticut*

Your participation in the service was not hypocrisy; it was an act of compassion and affection for your family. To join in some parts of the service does not require you to join in every part. As long as you did not leap to your feet and denounce the beliefs of others or violate the strictures of the congregation—you could not, for example, have taken Communion—surely at such a moment you may follow the dictates of your conscience.

Had you joined in the prayers, that needn't have been a betrayal of your principles; it could have been a genuine expression of sympathy with those assembled, or nostalgic contact with your youth, or a desire to comfort your wife—all honorable motives. And whatever course you chose could have been made understandable to your sons simply by discussing it with them.

Incidentally, your conduct is not as idiosyncratic as you imply. As any clergyman can tell you, congregants display a range of spiritual engagement, from rapt devotion to mechanical recitation to audible snoring.

## UNTOUCHABLE

*The courteous and competent real estate agent I'd just hired to rent my house*
*shocked and offended me when, after we signed our contract, he refused*
*to shake my hand, saying that as an Orthodox Jew he did not touch women.*
*As a feminist, I oppose gender discrimination of all sorts. However, I also*

*support freedom of religious expression. How do I balance these conflicting values? Should I tear up our contract?*

*—J.L., New York*

This culture clash may not allow you to reconcile the values you esteem. Though the real estate agent dealt you only a petty slight, without ill intent, you're entitled to work with someone who treats you with the dignity and respect he shows his male clients. If this involved only his own person—adherence to laws concerning diet or dress, for example—you should of course be tolerant. But his actions directly affect you. Sexism is sexism, even when motivated by religious convictions. I believe you should tear up your contract.

Had he declined to shake hands with everyone, there'd be no problem. What he may not do, however, is render a class of people untouchable. Were he, say, an airline ticket clerk who refused to touch Asian Americans, he would find himself in hot water and properly so. Bias on the basis of sex is equally discreditable.

## UNTOUCHABLE: THE RESPONSE

When a column generated particularly vigorous disagreement, I generally received a few hundred e-mails. The handshake column shattered the previous record by an order of magnitude. I stopped counting when the angry e-mail hit four thousand. Sermons were preached against me in several synagogues. I was editorialized against. In Jerusalem.

It wasn't just Jews who condemned me. Many Christians felt I'd trampled on religious freedom. But it was my own community that was most ferocious. The phrase *self-hating Jew* was bandied about. I might have hated someone at that point, but it wasn't myself.

Responding to this mail gave me a chance to think further about my reply, and doing so deepened my conviction that I'd gotten this one right.

I'd understood—and felt that my readers knew without being reminded—that Orthodox Judaism's ban on touching those of the opposite sex who are not close family members derives from sexual modesty (among other reasons). But so do many of the proscriptions in sexually segregated societies, from the chador to allowing only men to vote. Even in secular life, a wide range of policies—forbidding women to take certain jobs (to protect them from harsh conditions); devising separate rules for women's basketball (in deference to their presumed delicacy)—were defended as being for these women's own good. That the intent of such strictures is ostensibly benign makes them no less sexist and no less contrary to the values of an egalitarian society.

It would be possible, I suppose, to envision a sexually conservative yet egalitarian culture—weren't the Shakers a bit like that?—but Orthodox Judaism is something else. For one thing, the origins of this custom are bound up in the menstrual taboo, the notion that women could be unclean, impure. (Since men can't know when a woman is menstruating, it is safer to avoid all physical contact rather than risk being tainted.) Or consider not counting women in a minyan—hardly egalitarian. Against that background, my view of the conflict seems reasonable. When an esteemed Orthodox woman rabbi can offer a nonsexist defense of the rebuffed handshake, I'll be happy to reconsider my position.

I agree, as would the woman in my column, that this was a small matter and one she might choose to overlook, but she's not obliged to. She asks only to be extended the same courtesy, including a deal-sealing handshake, that this fellow offers his male clients. And while a handshake was not absolutely essential in their circumstances, most forms of civility transcend stark necessity.

None of us would accept an appeal to religious freedom made by a white person who refused to touch an African American. Something akin to this defense was used at Bob Jones University when it barred black and white students from dancing with one another: the school's notion of Christianity forbade it. If we reject such arguments when applied to race, surely we should accord the same respect to gender.

Some readers were too literal and too legalistic in their reading of the client's question and my reply, asserting the sanctity of contracts. But I took her to be asking if she need subjugate her feminist principles to her devotion to religious tolerance, expressed in the shorthand: tear up the contract.

And yes, if the genders had been reversed or another religion substituted for Judaism—questions raised by some of my antagonists—the principle and my position would be unchanged.

Nor does the fact that the prohibition against touching is practiced by both men and women make it less sexist. The miscegenation laws in the Jim Crow South embodied this same pseudosymmetry, restricting both blacks and whites, but they were clearly antiblack in intent. (And, incidentally, sometimes justified by appeals to Christian doctrine, as was slavery.) Similarly, one purpose of this Orthodoxy, at least in its origins, is to insulate men from the putatively irresistible sexual provocation women present merely by existing.

As to the "separate restroom" argument, raised by some readers and once trotted out to oppose the ERA, that some behaviors reasonably include gender distinctions does not suggest that all such distinctions are reasonable. Certainly, the woman who posed this question does not find this reasonable. (And, it should be added, many restaurants in New York get along just fine with restrooms labeled neither "men" nor "women" but "restroom.")

Less logical and more hurtful were the overheated charges of anti-Semitism, an ad hominem attack I utterly reject. To criticize an aspect of Orthodox Jewish practice is not to deprecate Judaism, any more than to suggest a reform in American life is to be anti-American. In fact, one feature of both the Conservative and Reform movements is the integration and equality of both sexes in Jewish life. That is, most Jews share my rejection of sexually segregated societies.

Interestingly, a less confrontational solution to this contretemps was suggested by several Orthodox rabbis, who noted that while Orthodox Judaism does bar such physical contact, it also discourages giving offense or causing embarrassment to another person. These rabbis harmonized those two goals in their own conduct by declining to initiate a handshake with a woman, but if a woman extended her hand, to take it.

### UNTOUCHABLE: THE AFTERMATH

I am resolutely secular in my work and in my life. Raised in a Reform Jewish household, I was bar mitzvahed and confirmed, but since then I've not been in a synagogue except for other people's commemorations—bat mitzvahs, weddings, sadder occasions. And yet, looking over a decade's worth of columns, the positions I took are not so different from the values I grew up with. Seldom did I write a column with which my mother strongly disagreed.

As the column became better known, I began receiving speaking invitations—from universities, corporations, civic and professional associations. (I once addressed the American Arborists Association: ethics and trees. I learned some frightening things about poplars.) Jewish groups were well represented—synagogues, Jewish Community Centers, Hillels, and Hadassahs. My *mishpocha*. My family. I came to see that my core constituency was Hadassah, highly educated and deeply engaged Jewish women of a certain age. They lived in a moral universe; they asked tough questions; they got all the jokes. A room full of my mother. I had, I suppose, imagined a younger and hipper core constituency, but I am enormously grateful to have one at all, and I suppose I should face the fact that I myself am neither young nor hip. I am, for all practical purposes, an educated Jewish woman in her sixties. Okay, for only some practical purposes.

And so it was, I suppose, all but inevitable that the most ferocious condemnation of any of the columns came from my Jewish readers. You always hurt the one you love? Perhaps. Or you're always hurt by the one you love. Either way. Who else has the insight, the intimate knowledge to do the bloody deed so effectively.

All e-mail responding to the column was negative. Nearly all. And unsurprisingly. How many fan letters do any of us write in a typical week? That e-mail was often astute and engaging. The column dealt in complex questions that I had to answer in 680 words, two questions at a time. I necessarily omitted many aspects of a conundrum; I oversimplified for a living. Many times the readers discussed a facet of a question that I'd neglected. I didn't mind when readers attacked my argument. I had my say; they get theirs. I did mind when they attacked my character, or my fashion sense, or my nose. It turns out, being called an idiot even by a total stranger is disconcerting. I learned to toughen up.

Happily, such vituperative screeds were the exception. Most of this correspondence was courteous and generous spirited, written with a sense that we were in this together, collaborating to sort out challenging and pertinent problems. Posting my e-mail address at the bottom of the column shifted the writer-reader relationship to something more egalitarian, more democratic, more conversational.

As the mail taking issue with the handshake column flooded in, the Orthodox Union, the largest organization of Orthodox congregations and individuals, called the *Times* and demanded a meeting, and the paper agreed to arrange one. I've disdained nearly every word David Brooks has written for the paper, but nobody got the two of us together for lunch.

Adam Moss, then the editor of the magazine, phoned to say that he couldn't force me to attend this gathering, but he "strongly advised" me to. When your boss strongly advises, it is prudent to comply.

I worked at home and was seldom at the *Times* building. Heading for the meeting was vaguely infantilizing; I was a kid again, summoned to the principal's office. It concentrates the mind wonderfully. I thought, only slightly self-dramatizing, that I could lose my job over this, and I loved my job.

I was waiting in Adam's office when the OU delegation was announced. I'd expected one or two people, but we opened the door to a roiling mob. Or so it seemed. There were two lobbyists, two lawyers, and one rabbi. Nobody looked happy. I shook hands with each as we were introduced. Then they sprang their cunning trap: one of the delegates was a woman. Shake her hand? Don't shake her hand? My best option seemed to be to simply swoon away. Instead I decided to be guided by her. I'd not give offense by offering my hand, but if she extended hers, I'd take it. She did not.

The room was crackling with hostility as the delegates took turns excoriating me. The lawyers argued that I made a mockery of the First Amendment. The lobbyists asserted that I was Bad For The Jews, that by wielding the authority of the *New York Times*, I was calling down oppression on my people. The very title of the column exacerbated my offense: The Ethicist! It might not be so bad if we'd change the name to something that reflected the triviality of my mind, the paucity of my education. If memory serves—and it doesn't; it mocks—they suggested "Ask Randy, That Big Dope." The erudite rabbi said something Talmudic that I didn't quite grasp.

It went on and on. It is considered rude to glance at your watch while someone is denouncing you, but I estimated that we were in there for forty days and forty nights. My estimate was exaggerated, but not by much. The demolition continued for about two hours, a long time to hear yourself reviled. But over those hours, something happened.

Nobody's opinion changed, but the mood in the room softened. The discourse grew less heated, more courteous. And when the delegates departed, the good-byes were, if not affectionate, at least civil.

I think that's why Adam was eager for me to attend this meeting, to learn that people can be impressively accepting of disagreement if they feel that they are heard, that their concerns are taken seriously, that they are treated with respect.

It is a lesson I tried to apply as I continued to write the column. Tone is all. Readers will endure—will welcome—views unlike their own if those ideas are expressed without contempt. I tried to make the column a place where people could argue amiably, could disagree without discourtesy.

After the delegation left, I remained behind to debrief with Adam. Okay, to preen just a bit about how well the meeting had gone, to thank him for conducting it so skillfully.

A little later, when I got down to the lobby, the OU delegates were still there. I'd utterly misjudged their feelings. Their fury had not abated. They were waiting to give me a merciless beating. I've no wish to be beaten up by anyone, but there are some people I particularly want not to be beaten up by, and venerable rabbinical sages are among that group. It would be just too embarrassing.

But the delegation was not angry. Quite the contrary. They greeted me like an old friend. In part, it was like an encounter of adversaries after a schoolyard fight; the air has been cleared, we can be pals. Also significant was where we were running into one another, the lobby of the *New York Times*, as Jewish a locale as Masada. We were at the center of a certain kind of Jewish universe—cultural, intellectual, even moral—and proud to be there. The very air promoted concord. We spoke almost tenderly to one another, and then I headed out the door for the subway.

On the platform, waiting for the 3 train, I realized with some humility that it wasn't just what I wrote that so outraged the OU; it was where I wrote it. I'm not insanely coy; I hope people were engaged by the writing itself. But if I'd written the same column elsewhere, it would not have been regarded the same way, or perhaps regarded at all. It is the *New York Times* that has the awesome power to command interest, to convey authority. I am not a philosopher. I have no PhD. I have no credentials to validate my moral reasoning. But the *Times* is potent enough to pluck me from obscurity and put real power in my hands. That afternoon I saw that the *Times* could pick any old dog on the street, crown him the Ethics Dog, and people would ask the dog's advice. I was that dog. I was the cocker spaniel of the Jews, and happy to be. It was a wonderful job.

# *Epilogue*

NOW AND THEN, AN EXASPERATED READER DENOUNCED THE ETHICIST AS nothing more than Ann Landers—a fancy-pants Ann Landers, a pretentious Ann Landers. Just Ann Landers.

I wish.

Few writers become as popular as Eppie Lederer, and few popular writers are as innovative. In 1955, when she took over the Ask Ann Landers column, agony aunts, as such writers were known, practiced a kind of faux-Victorian gentility. The job and its discontents are disturbingly portrayed in Nathanael West's 1933 short novel, *Miss Lonelyhearts*. The queries from advice-seekers are mawkish and sentimental, "stamped from the dough of suffering with a heart-shaped cookie knife." The replies from Miss Lonelyhearts are melodramatic and false: "Life, for most of us, seems a terrible struggle of pain and heartbreak, without hope or joy. Oh, my dear readers, it only seems so."

Overwhelmed by the work, Miss Lonelyhearts languishes in speak-easies, gets into brawls, has tawdry affairs. He—for Miss Lonelyhearts is a young man—even beats up a woman who had written to his column and is eventually shot by her husband.

I don't believe that Lederer ever beat up anyone who sought her advice; instead, she transformed the genre. Her column was cheerful and direct; its prose colloquial; its tone straight from the shoulder; its advice that of an amiable neighbor, a trusted friend. In the biopic, at least the 1950s version, she would be played by the wise and wisecracking Eve Arden.

I admired Lederer's jaunty self-assurance, but I understand Miss Lonelyhearts' crisis. To write an advice column requires you to declare yourself unambiguously on matters about which honorable people may differ—and they do, vociferously. The captious mail flows freely. Lederer seemed to handle such criticism gracefully, but it took me some getting used to. Being called a jerk, even by strangers, even when you know you are right, is not pleasant. Such letters tend to begin, "Dear Sir, I am appalled"—no you're not; you are, at most, annoyed—and to end, "you should be ashamed." It hurts my feelings. I had to toughen up. No wonder Miss Lonelyhearts fell apart. But how did Eppie stay so affable?

Historians of the future will read her columns not as advice but as anthropology, a compendium of the conventional wisdom of mid-century America: Tip the pizza guy. Quit smoking. Pay your taxes. "It is unfair to denigrate all teenagers because of a few rotten apples." "A business degree is no substitute for common sense." "In my opinion, the majority of folks are honest." "A sense of humor can salvage almost any situation."

But if the sort of advice she provided can be criticized as commonplace, as conventional wisdom, she must nonetheless have been the most liberal voice in many of the 1,200 papers that carried her column, a proponent of ideas that would have seemed radical had they appeared on the editorial page. She was a staunch supporter of gun control, a defender of reproductive rights, a foe of the Vietnam War. By presenting her views in the form of an innocuous advice column, not as politics but as common sense, she operated as a sort of stealth progressive.

This is not an easy thing to do. Shortly after my own column began, it was denounced in several right-wing periodicals, in one case under the headline "'The Ethicist' Better Termed 'The Marxist.'" And when my tenure ended at the *Times*, I was particularly gratified to read "'Ethicist' Columnist Randy Cohen Departs, Leaving Leftist Legacy Behind." I may have suggested, in passing, that "corporations donate to charity to buff their images" or "clean air—why not?" or endorsed the idea of public school. Apparently ideology-detecting radar has become more acute since Ann Landers began or perhaps, with the country veering so far to the right, qualifications for Marxism have been lowered substantially, like some sort of ideological grade inflation.

Lederer's primary concern was not policy but practicality. "This is my mission—to help those who ask for it." Her antecedents are not only Miss Lonelyhearts but also *A Bintel Brief* (a bundle of letters), the advice column that began in the *Jewish Daily Forward* in 1906 to help Eastern European immigrants cope with American life. How do I find a job? Should there be hostility between Polish Jews and Russian Jews? Can intermarriage work?

Ann Landers was a modern *Bintel Brief*, explaining America to Americans, assisting its readers with the exigencies of living. And in later years, the aid Lederer propounded with disconcerting frequency was "I urge you to seek professional help at once." This was not a euphemism for "You're nuts!" (although some of her petitioners no doubt were), but evidence of a shift, not just in her column but in the country, to the professionalizing of comfort.

Traditionally, advice givers, whether columnist or clergyman or grandmother, were valued for their personal opinions, the distillation of their experience and insight. What Lederer increasingly offered was not the guidance of a sagacious amateur but a referral to a trained professional.

"We direct thousands of people to physicians, lawyers, psychiatrists," she wrote. "We have a complete file of service agencies for every city in which this column appears. We send readers to Legal Aid, the Family Service Association, homes for unwed mothers, mental health clinics, Alcoholics Anonymous, the YMCA—the list is a long one."

There was something dispiriting about this shift from the cozy comforts of homespun philosophy to the impersonal efficacy of social services. But perhaps in an age of bureaucracy, of being put on hold for hours, of being shunted from one unresponsive office to another, Ann Landers was just what we needed. Her readers certainly thought so. Their continued devotion demonstrates how unambiguously she achieved her goal, to be useful. If I performed a similar service both in the *Times* column and in this book, I would be proud.

## *ACKNOWLEDGMENTS*

SOME OF THE MATERIAL IN THIS BOOK FIRST APPEARED IN THE *NEW YORK Times* magazine when its editor was Adam Moss and later Gerry Marzorati. I am grateful for the opportunity they gave me and for the work of Dean Robinson, my editor at the magazine for most of the time I wrote "The Ethicist."

I'd also like to express my appreciation to my agent, Lydia Wills, and the folks at Chronicle, including my splendid editor, Leigh Haber, as well as the excellent Jennifer Tolo Pierce, Liza Algar, Doug Ogan, and Lisa Tauber.

I crowd-sourced this book's title, reaching out to readers of the column. It was Jessica Poundstone who devised "the ethics of everything." "Be Good" had long been on my list of potential titles, but I want to salute Elissa Moses, Jessie Jackson, and Nina Lombardo who also suggested it. Thanks to you all.